MADE IN CHINA YEARBOOK 2016
DISTURBANCES IN HEAVEN

Edited by
Ivan Franceschini,
Kevin Lin, and Nicholas Loubere

AUSTRALIAN CENTRE ON
CHINA IN THE WORLD

mismatched shards of China

PRESS

PRESS

© **The Australian National University**
(as represented by the the Australian Centre on China in the World)

First published February 2017 by ANU Press
The Australian National University
Acton ACT 2601, Australia
Email: anupress@anu.edu.au
This title is also available online at press.anu.edu.au

National Library of Australia Cataloguing-in-Publication entry
Title: Disturbances in heaven / edited by Ivan Franceschini, Kevin Lin, Nicholas Loubere.
ISBN: 9781760461072 (paperback) 9781760461089 (ebook)
Series: Made in China Yearbook 2016.
Subjects: Labor policy--China. Civil society--China. China--Politics and government.
Other Creators/Contributors: Franceschini, Ivan, editor. Lin, Kevin, editor. Loubere, Nicholas, editor.

All rights reserved. No part of this publication may be reproduced, stored in a retrieval system or transmitted in any form or by any means, electronic, mechanical, photocopying or otherwise, without the prior permission of the publisher.

This publication is made available as an Open Educational Resource through licensing under a Creative Commons Attribution Non-Commercial Share Alike 3.0 Australia Licence: https://creativecommons.org/licenses/by-nc-sa/3.0/au/

Note on Visual Material
All images in this publication have been fully accredited. As this is a non-commercial publication, certain images have been used under a Creative Commons licence. These images have been sourced from Flickr, Wikipedia Commons and the copyright owner of each original picture is acknowledged and indicated in the source information.

Design Concept by Tommaso Facchin; Illustrations by Marc Verdugo.
Typesetting by Sharon Strange.

The Australian Centre on China in the World is an initiative of the Commonwealth Government of Australia and The Australian National University.

This project has been produced with the financial assistance of the Australian Centre on China in the World (CIW), Australian National University, and the European Union Horizon 2020 research and innovation programme under the Marie Skłodowska-Curie grant agreement No 654852. The views expressed are those of the individual authors and do not represent the views of the European Union, CIW, or the institutions to which the authors are affiliated.

TABLE OF CONTENTS

INTRODUCTION (PP. 6-9)
DISTURBANCES IN HEAVEN (P. 6)
Ivan Franceschini

BRIEFS (PP. 10-13)
JANUARY-MARCH 2016

STEER YOUR WAY (PP. 14-39)
THE CHINESE WORKING CLASS: MADE, UNMADE, IN ITSELF, FOR ITSELF, OR NONE OF THE ABOVE? (P. 16)
William Hurst

REMOULDING THE STATE SECTOR: BACK TO THE 1990s? (P. 20)
Kevin Lin

LAYING OFF RESPONSIBILITY: MICROCREDIT, ENTREPRENEURSHIP, AND CHINA'S INDUSTRIAL RETRENCHMENT (P. 24)
Nicholas Loubere

MIGRANT LABOUR AND THE SUSTAINABILITY OF CHINA'S WELFARE SYSTEM (P. 28)
Beatriz Carrillo

FORUM: INTERPRETING CHINESE LABOUR: INFORMALISATION OR EMPOWERMENT? (P. 32)
Anita Chan, Kaxton Siu, Sarah Swider

BRIEFS (PP. 40-43)
APRIL-JUNE 2016

HAMMER TO FALL (PP. 44-73)
REVISITING CHINESE LABOUR NGOs: SOME GROUNDS FOR HOPE? (P. 46)
Ivan Franceschini

THE RESISTANCE OF WALMART WORKERS IN CHINA: A MISSED OPPORTUNITY (P. 50)
Anita Chan

WHAT DOES WUKAN HAVE TO DO WITH DEMOCRACY? (P. 56)
Luigi Tomba

THE FOREIGN NGOs MANAGEMENT LAW: A COMPENDIUM (P. 60)
Ivan Franceschini, Elisa Nesossi

FORUM: A CIVIL SOCIETY UNDER ASSAULT (P. 68)
Ellen David Friedman, Kevin Slaten, May Wong

BRIEFS (PP. 74-77)
JULY-SEPTEMBER 2016

EYE IN THE SKY (PP. 78–105)
THE NEGLECTED SIDE OF THE COIN: LEGAL HEGEMONY, CLASS CONSCIOUSNESS, AND LABOUR POLITICS IN CHINA (P. 80)
Elaine Sio-ieng Hui

CHINESE WORKERS AND THE LAW: MISPLACED TRUST? (P. 84)
Ivan Franceschini

CHINESE WORKERS AND THE LEGAL SYSTEM: BRIDGING THE GAP IN REPRESENTATION (P. 88)
Aaron Halegua

CHINA'S RELIGION LAW AND THE PERILS OF COUNTING CONSCIOUSNESS (P. 92)
Thomas David DuBois

FORUM: INTERPETING THE RULE OF LAW IN XI JINPING'S CHINA (P. 98)
Joshua Rosenzweig, Ewan Smith, Susan Trevaskes

BRIEFS (PP. 106–109)
OCTOBER–DECEMBER 2016

HEART OF DARKNESS? (PP. 110–125)
FIGHTING THE RACE TO THE BOTTOM: REGULATING CHINESE INVESTMENT IN ZAMBIAN MINES (P. 112)
Mukete Beyongo Dynamic

THERE AND BACK AGAIN: CONCEPTUALISING THE CHINESE GOLD RUSH IN GHANA (P. 116)
Nicholas Loubere, Gordon Crawford

A CHINESE EMPIRE IN THE MAKING? QUESTIONING MYTHS FROM THE AGRI-FOOD SECTOR IN GHANA (P. 122)
Jixia Lu

SOUL SACRIFICE (PP. 126–141)
PARADISE UNDER CONSTRUCTION (P. 128)
Christian Sorace

THE COW AND THE GOAT DESCEND THE MOUNTAIN: FIGHTING MODERNITY WITH POEMS (P. 132)
Ivan Franceschini

CHINESE DREAMS OF HAPPINESS: WHAT ARE THE CHANCES? (P. 136)
Gerda Wielander

BIBLIOGRAPHY (P. 142)

DISTURBANCES IN HEAVEN

'There was a rock that since the creation of the world had been worked upon by the pure essences of Heaven and the fine savours of Earth, the vigour of sunshine and the grace of moonlight, till it one day split open, giving birth to a stone egg, about as big as a playing ball which then turned into a stone monkey.'

These words, translated by Arthur Waley, open the classic sixteenth-century novel *Journey to the West*, a masterpiece of Chinese literature. This is the story of the monk Xuanzang's pilgrimage to India to collect Buddhist sutras for the court of the Tang emperors. One of his escorts is the Monkey King—Sun Wukong, 'Aware-of-Vacuity'—a mischievous and ambitious character born out of a primordial stone. At the beginning of the journey, Sun Wukong is nothing but a failed rebel. Having taken offence at not being assigned an office high enough in the heavenly hierarchy, he had dared to challenge the supreme divinity of the Chinese pantheon, the Jade Emperor, creating disturbances in his celestial palace. For this reason, he had been imprisoned under a mountain for five hundred years, until Buddha had decided to give him a chance at redemption: he was to accompany and protect Xuanzang in his travels. Even then, the Monkey King proves unruly and the only way to control him is to trick him into wearing a magic metal headband that causes him terrible pain whenever he does not obey the orders of his master.

According to the traditional Chinese zodiac, 2016 was the year of the fire monkey. What better character than Sun Wukong to inspire this inaugural volume of the *Made in China Yearbook*? In this past year, Chinese workers and rights activists from all walks of life have struggled under heightened repression by the Chinese party-state, but showed remarkable endurance even under these dire circumstances. With their fights, however small or short-lived, they repeatedly challenged the message of 'harmony' of the Chinese authorities, creating 'disturbances' in the imaginary heaven engineered by the party-state. All of this is nothing else but proof of the survival of the monkey spirit in Chinese society. Even when trapped under a mountain of repression, or in terrible pain due to the curse of the magic headband of state control, the monkey still manages to briefly wriggle free, reminding us that not all is well and not everything is predictable.

However, what happened in 2016 leaves little room for optimism concerning the future of the labour and rights movements in China. Although the Chinese government has never been reluctant to repress dissent, in this past year we have witnessed an authoritarian drift that only a few years ago would have been unthinkable. Not only have labour activists fallen victim to more regular and severe forms of intimidation by the party-state, but new laws and regulations have also been passed in order to curtail civil society space by, among other things, restricting international sources of funding for labour and rights NGOs while at the same time limiting their abilities to register as social organisations or charities and raise funds domestically. This happened in concomitance with an economic slowdown, prompting local governments to erode labour protection by freezing minimum wages and lowering the rate of social security contributions shouldered by companies in order to prevent capital flight. However, Chinese workers have continued to be restless, as they see their very livelihoods threatened by these new developments, but in absence of any meaningful representation they have been largely unable to resist these trends.

This Yearbook aims at tracking the changes that have been taking place in the realm of labour and civil society in China in the past year. All chapters have already appeared during 2016 either in the open-access journal *Made in China: A Quarterly on Chinese Labour, Civil Society, and Rights,* or in the Essays section of the website *Chinoiresie.info*, but they have been updated to reflect recent developments and references have been included. The whole project—journal, website, and book—stems from a belief in the need to bridge the gap between academic research and the general public. We also believe that recent developments in China call for more serious analysis from both scholars and practitioners, as well as for critical engagement with a broader international audience interested in forging international solidarity. More pragmatically, we were compelled to re-edit this material and compile this volume because we think that such a book will be a useful reference for a wide audience—especially scholars, activists, unionists, policy-makers, and students—with an interest in Chinese labour and civil society.

Besides a series of 'briefs', in which we summarise some of the most important events that took place in China over the past year*, we have regrouped the chapters into five general sections. The first section, 'Steer Your Way', focuses on the relationship between the party-state and workers, offering some perspectives on how the Chinese authorities have navigated the uncharted waters of labour politics in a time of global economic uncertainty. It opens with three chapters that deal with the reform of the state industry and its impact on the Chinese working class. In the first, William Hurst invites readers to consider the fractured and segmented history of the Chinese working class, as well as its rapidly homogenising present, and emphasises the need to refrain from too-facile comparisons with other foreign experiences; in the second, Kevin Lin looks into the new wave of mass layoffs announced in the state coal and steel sector and outlines similarities and differences with the previous massive restructuring of the state economy in the late 1990s; in the third, Nicholas Loubere, offers an analysis of the political and ideological implications of resorting to microcredit to promote entrepreneurial activity among laid-off workers. The section also includes an article by Beatriz Carrillo, in which she describes the trajectory of China's welfare system towards the inclusion of migrant labour and highlights the challenges posed by the economic slowdown, and a forum in which labour scholars Anita Chan, Kaxton Siu, and Sarah Swider discuss how precarisation has impacted the Chinese workforce in key sectors of the economy.

In the second section, 'Hammer to Fall', we focus on grassroots organising by Chinese workers, activists, and farmers, describing some instances of resistance in front of increasing repression. In it, Ivan Franceschini describes how Chinese labour NGOs have evolved in recent years and argues that the latest crackdown by the party-state might also open some small window of political opportunity; Anita Chan highlights the historical importance of the recent struggle of Walmart workers in China and dissects the factors that led to its ultimate failure in spite of much initial optimism; and Luigi Tomba analyses the protests that recently took place in Wukan village, challenging some widely-held assumptions about the political nature of such land-related social movements in the Chinese countryside. To conclude the section, we publish a compendium of the highly controversial Law on the Management of Foreign NGOs' Activities within Mainland China that came into force in January 2017 edited by Ivan Franceschini and Elisa Nesossi, and a forum in which international labour activists Ellen David Friedman, Kevin Slaten, and May Wong discuss the implications of the new legislation for labour NGOs in China.

In the third section, 'Eye in the Sky', we look into the ambiguous role of the law as a tool of social control. The section opens with three chapters related to the labour law. First, Elaine Sio-ieng Hui reflects on the role of labour law in China as a vital vehicle through which the Chinese party-state has constructed capitalist hegemony with regard to state-capital-labour relations in the country; Ivan Franceschini then discusses the 'rights awakening' of Chinese workers, challenging some widely held assumptions regarding the rights awareness and legal knowledge of the Chinese workforce; finally Aaron Halegua delves into the challenges that Chinese workers face when they seek to enforce their rights through the legal system. We also included a chapter by Thomas DuBois in which he analyses the new Religion Law in China within the context of the debate on 'universal values' and offers his take on the relationship between academia and activism; and a forum, edited by Elisa Nesossi, in which legal scholars Joshua Rosenzweig, Ewan Smith, and Sue Trevaskes put the concept of the rule of law in China into a wider historical and political perspective, deconstructing its multiple dimensions and specificities.

In the fourth section, 'Heart of Darkness?', we look into Chinese labour and investment in Africa, offering a series of thought-provoking perspectives with a focus on two countries—Zambia and Ghana—where conflicts related to Chinese capital and labour inflows have recently emerged. Mukete Beyongo Dynamic examines the claim that Chinese investments in Zambian copper mines have led to a 'race to the bottom' in labour standards, criticising this view as overly simplistic in that it doesn't take into account the agency of local actors. Regarding Ghana, Nicholas Loubere and Gordon Crawford investigate the media discourse and popular depiction of Chinese miners in Ghana as stealing resources from marginal sectors of local society, revealing that in fact we still do not know much about who these people actually are, or the labour relations that exist between the miners themselves. Finally, Jixia Lu draws from her fieldwork in Ghana's agricultural sector to challenge both the western narrative that frames China's expanding presence in African countries as a project in empire building, and the narrative of the Chinese authorities depicting engagement as a form of South-South cooperation that is beneficial to the local populations.

Finally, in the fifth section entitled 'Soul Sacrifice', we do some soul-searching through a series of essays in which the authors review artistic works or intellectual trends that offer insights into the impact of modernity on the inner life of the Chinese people. First, Christian Sorace reviews Zhao Liang's *Behemoth*, a recent documentary on the environmental and social tragedy behind China's economic miracle. Ivan Franceschini then discusses *The Cow and the Goat Descend the Mountain*, an album of ancient Chinese poems set to music by folk singer Zhou Yunpeng, taking an opportunity to reflect on the role of poetry as a form of resistance. Finally, in the face of much loneliness and pressure experienced by Chinese citizens today, not least migrant workers, Gerda Wielander considers the role of happiness in the 'Chinese dream' and looks at the different options from the field of psychology and psychotherapy available to Chinese citizens for achieving happiness, as well as at the role of the state in choosing between these.

All of these chapters have been written with the aim of reaching as wide an audience as possible. For this reason, in them you will not find the theorising typical of much academic literature on labour and civil society. Similarly, we have tried to go beyond parochial divisions by including writings by contributors coming from different backgrounds and disciplines, such as labour scholars, legal scholars, activists, and lawyers. We have also welcomed essays by writers who hold generally optimistic views about the future of the Chinese labour movement, and others who remain definitively sceptical. In such difficult times, it is only through such a dialogue that we can take the discussion forward, not only gaining a better understanding of the challenges that Chinese workers and citizens are facing today, but also giving credit to the Chinese authorities wherever this is deserved. Such understanding is a necessary precondition to build those bridges of international solidarity and mutual comprehension so important in the period of global turmoil that we all now face, as the whole world seems to be descending into provincialism, xenophobia, and worse. It is in times like these that we need more than ever to keep alive the monkey spirit that resides inside each and every one of us.

Ivan Franceschini
Canberra, 11 January 2017

---

* The content of the briefs is based on news that has been widely reported by various media outlets and on social media. Below each brief we list some of the outlets that have published about the story and in the electronic version of the volume we provide links to some of the articles.

Ju Xiaolin, new Vice-Chairman of the ACFTU.
PC: SOUTH CHINA MORNING POST

JAN/MAR 2016

China Arrests Labour Activists amid Crackdown on Human Rights Defenders

In early January, five Chinese labour activists detained since early December 2015 were formally arrested in Guangdong province. China's slowing economy has led to a surge in labour disputes and made organised labour a particularly sensitive issue and a target of state repression. Zeng Feiyang, Director of the Panyu Migrant Workers Centre in Guangzhou and a prominent labour activist, was charged with 'disrupting social order'. Three other activists of the same organisation, Meng Han, Tang Huanxing, and Zhu Xiaomei, were arrested on the same charge, with Zhu subsequently released on bail. He Xiaobo, Director of Nanfeiyan, a labour group based in the neighbouring Foshan, was arrested on a charge of embezzlement. Among the arrested activists, Zeng Feiyang was the target of a concerted smear campaign in the Chinese official media. The official *Xinhua News Agency* and the *China Central Television* accused Zeng of embezzling funding, of promoting himself as a 'star of the labour movement' without regard for workers' interests, and of sexual misconduct. Nanfeiyan and the Panyu Migrant Workers Center both sued the *Xinhua* journalist for libel over his report.

(Sources: **Radio Free Asia, Reuters, Xinhua**)

Ningxia Officials Address Migrant Workers' Back Pay After Bus Attack

On 5 January, Ma Yongping, a migrant construction worker angry about unpaid wages, set a public bus on fire, killing seventeen people in Yinchuan, the capital of the northwestern province of Ningxia. Ma had complained on social media about non-payment of his wages, but his grievances had been ignored by local officials. A government report revealed that in the first ten months of 2015, the capital city of Ningxia, Yinchuan, recorded more than five hundred cases of unpaid wages, 22.3 percent more than in the same period of the previous year, involving about ten thousand migrant workers who were owed 1.48 billion yuan. In response, the Ningxia provincial government identified twenty-seven construction companies that had delayed the payment of salaries, subjected them to criminal punishments allowed by the recently amended Chinese Criminal Law (fines and jail terms of up to seven years), and forbade them to bid on future government projects. It also launched a campaign to ensure that companies pay migrant workers on time before the Chinese New Year. On 19 January, the State Council released a strongly worded new opinion on the non-payment of wages for migrant workers, aiming to establish a regulatory regime that 'keeps the problem of unpaid wages for migrant workers fundamentally in check' by 2020.

(Sources: **Caixin**, **State Council**, **Wall Street Journal**)

Remains of a public bus set on fire by a migrant construction worker in Yinchuan, Ningxia

Grassroots Worker Elected to Top Trade Union Leadership

Ju Xiaolin, a technician and former migrant worker from Shaanxi province, was appointed Vice Chair of the official All-China Federation of Trade Unions (ACFTU). Ju is the first migrant worker to hold such a high post within the ACFTU. A technician with only a high school diploma, Ju has worked for China CREC Railway Electrification Bureau Group since 1987 and in 2014 was elected to the National People's Congress as a deputy. After the appointment, official media featured several stories on Ju actively promoting migrant workers' interests by submitting policy proposals during the National People's Congress held in March. This move reflects the central government's attempt to make the ACFTU more appealing in the eyes of the rank-and-file workers, especially migrants like Ju himself. However, Lu Hui, an Associate Professor in sociology at Peking University, cautioned that 'institutional reform is needed at the lower level of trade unions to attract and retain more experienced migrant workers.' It is unlikely that a migrant Vice-Chair will affect such institutional changes, as trade union reforms are stalling.

(Source: **China News, Xinhua 1, Xinhua 2**)

Ju Xiaolin, new Vice-Chair of the ACFTU.

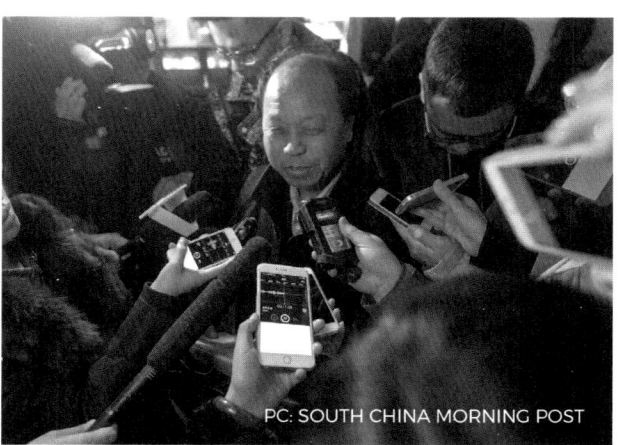

Chinese Blogger Demands Answers over Funding to Help 'Left-Behind Children'

Zhou Xiaoyun, a well-known blogger, took legal action against the governments of Bijie city and Guizhou province, demanding that they reveal what happened to a one hundred and eighty million yuan provincial fund established to help 'left-behind children' (liushou ertong), a term that generally refers to children currently living in the Chinese countryside without the daily care of their parents, who have migrated to other areas for work. The government of Bijie established the fund in 2012, after the death of five boys who had tried to shelter form the cold in a trash container had sparked a public debate over whether the local authorities were doing enough to help these disadvantaged children. The fund should have been used toward improving the living conditions and medical care of left-behind children. However, when four more Bijie children killed themselves in June 2015 by drinking pesticide, blogger Zhou Xiaoyun decided to file a request to the local government to disclose details about how the fund had been used. After being told that such information did not exist, Zhou filed another request and again the government only provided general figures. Zhou's additional demand that the Guizhou provincial government intervene to ask the Bijie government to publish documents about the fund was similarly dismissed. Finally, in late December 2015, Zhou filed an administrative lawsuit against the two governments at the Guiyang Intermediate People's Court. The lawsuit was accepted and the case was heard in court in June 2016, but Zhou's request was denied. In mid-February, the State Council released a guideline on the protection of left-behind children, requiring local governments and village committees to pay close attention to the situation of these children and ensure they are properly taken care of.

(Sources: **Guiyang Wang, Sina.com, South China Morning Post, Xinhua**)

Labour Contract Law Under Attack for Harming Flexibility

On 7 March, during the National People's Congress, Minister of Finance Lou Jiwei criticised China's Labour Contract Law for harming the flexibility of the labour market, constraining productivity, and harming workers by reducing job opportunities. Lou stated that the Labour Contract Law restricts the ability of companies to fire their employees and is thus discriminatory towards people entering the workforce. Earlier, on 29 February, Minister of Human Resources and Social Security Yin Weimin had announced that the Ministry is investigating the possibility of revising the Labour Contract Law to tackle the inflexibility of the labour market and high labour costs. With the slowing economy, the Chinese government is also trying to rein in wage increases, favouring business interests at the expense of increasingly discontented workers. China's Ministry of Human Resources and Social Security recently urged 'steady and cautious control' over minimum wages and proposed a formula change that would slow wage increases. Meanwhile, in March, Guangdong province, one of China's main manufacturing hubs, announced a two-year freeze on minimum wages.

(Sources: **Caijing, Caixin, Daily Mail, Wall Street Journal, Zhongguo Xinwen Wang**)

(Left) Lou Jiwei, China's Minister of Finance. (Right) Yin Weimin, Minister for Human Resources and Social Security.

Mass Layoffs Announced in the Coal and Steel Industries

According to Yin Weimin, Minister for Human Resources and Social Security, 1.8 million workers in the coal and steel industries will be laid off as part of the government's efforts to curb industrial overcapacity and pollution. However, other sources say as many as five to six million workers could lose their jobs. The so-called 'zombie' state firms will be the main target of the restructuring, with the Chinese government attempting to cut capacity gluts in as many as seven sectors, including cement, glassmaking, and shipbuilding. This is likely to become China's most significant industrial retrenchment since the restructuring of state-owned enterprises and mass layoff of state-sector workers in the late 1990s. The Chinese government will spend one hundred and fifty billion yuan to deal with the social and economic consequences of this latest wave of layoffs in the next few years.

(Sources: **Quartz, Reuters, Sina**)

Charity Law Passed by the National People's Congress

On 16 March, the National People's Congress passed a landmark Charity Law. While the new Law will make it easier for Chinese nonprofit groups to obtain a legal registration and raise funding, it also includes strict regulations to prevent fraud and impose tighter supervision. The legislators introduce tax incentives to encourage enterprises and wealthy people to donate to charities, a move aimed at boosting an ailing internal donation market. The new Law mandates that charities should be recognised by authorities before they solicit public donations, with organisations raising funds from the public without a license risking fines of up to twenty thousand yuan. According to official data, at the end of June 2016, in China there were about six hundred and seventy thousand registered social organisations, including more than five thousand foundations.

(Sources: **China Daily, NGOs in China, The Wall Street Journal, Xinhua**)

STEER YOUR WAY

The Chinese Working Class:
Made, Unmade, in Itself, for Itself, or None of the Above?

William Hurst

China's working class has undergone several rounds of momentous and wrenching change over the past hundred years. But what has this all meant for interest intermediation or political representation for labour in China? In order to address these questions, we must accept and understand the fractured and segmented history of the Chinese working class, as well as its rapidly homogenising present. We must also refrain from too-facile comparisons with European or other post-socialist or developing countries.

China's working class dwarfs those of all other countries. It has undergone several rounds of momentous and wrenching change over the past hundred years—from early industrialisation and urban growth, through the Japanese invasion and the Second World War, to the 1949 Chinese Communist Party (CCP) takeover and Maoist Era mobilisation, the advent of reform and 1980s growth, globalisation since the mid-1990s, and adjusting to a 'new normal' in the aftermath of the world financial crisis of 2008. But what has this all meant for interest intermediation or political representation for labour in China?

In order to address these questions, we must accept and understand the fractured and segmented history of the Chinese working class, as well as its rapidly homogenising present. We must also refrain from too-facile comparisons with European or other post-socialist or developing countries, if we are to make the most accurate possible predictions about what might emerge in terms of class compromise or incorporation, and how far and in what directions any such model might travel.

Zhao Jiancheng, *Mining Brightness: The Real Story of Migrant Workers.*

From Segmentation to Homogenisation

Conventional wisdom has always held the Chinese working class to be among the most profoundly and multiply segmented in the world. Divided in the pre-1949 period by cleavages of native place, skill level, and urban versus rural status—as well as region—the proletariat began life as a kind of compound organism. During the Maoist Era, the cellular boundaries of the work unit (*danwei*) system and the relatively impregnable ramparts dividing city and countryside that the household registration (*hukou*) system provided, helped reify and intensify this segmentation. With more than a touch of irony, the world's largest workers' state managed to eviscerate its working class as a unified political and social actor. Following the advent of reform, changes have been more complex.

During the 1980s, workers began to stream into cities from rural China, at first on temporary assignments, but gradually as longer-term migrants and residents. At the same time, new industrial sectors sprung up, notably in small-scale manufacturing and services, as well as newly resurgent rural enterprises. By the mid-1990s, when monetary reform opened the Chinese economy in earnest to globalisation, there were at least three distinct and important sectors employing significant numbers of workers outside rural areas (where local enterprises had already begun to wane): old-line state-owned enterprises (SOEs), export-oriented manufacturers (both domestic and foreign-owned) employing mainly rural migrants, and smaller self-proprietorships and local firms concentrated in services and some smaller manufactures. Each of these sectors was to experience its own form of crisis in turn.

As early as the 1980s, but especially in the years after 1997, the state sector lost roughly half of its workforce to attrition, early retirements, lay-offs, and firm bankruptcy (Hurst 2009). Just as SOEs were beginning to stabilise and new and improved social welfare and assistance programmes for the unemployed were being rolled out in a meaningful way, the 2008 world financial crisis hit, causing Chinese exports to plunge sharply. Export processing manufacturers laid off as many as thirty million migrant workers in a little over six months, precipitating massive social and economic disruption across the countryside. Much of this sector has yet to fully recover as of late 2016. Other countries in South or Southeast Asia or in Africa are proving cheaper destinations for off-shoring from advanced industrial economies, or even from China itself. Labour-intensive manufacturing on the scale that appeared so ascendant in the late 1990s and early 2000s may never revive. Throughout, depressed incomes and lack of job security have precluded the rising consumption necessary to boost services to a higher level.

As I have outlined elsewhere (Hurst 2015), what had long been one of the world's most fragmented working classes—in terms of how it came into being, the conditions of work, forms of incorporation into the polity, etc.—has since 2008 become increasingly homogenised. While SOE workers enjoyed rising fortunes from the government's massive injection of capital aimed at forestalling recession, migrants' prospects declined. As state sector employment has become much less secure and benefits have continued to erode, basic social protections and job security for those in the private sector (including migrants) have improved markedly.

Though their historical origins and 'conditions of proletarianisation' may remain strikingly different, the various segments of China's working class have come to share rhythms of working life, similar places on the social ladder, precarious economic livelihoods, and political mobilisation in the face of repression to a remarkable degree. On the one hand, we may see this change as a decline for a once-vaunted leading element in Chinese society. But, on the other, we must recognise recent shifts as having produced a far more unified and potentially assertive Chinese proletariat than has existed for at least the last several decades.

Quo Vadis, Chinese Proletariat?

A simplistic knee-jerk answer to this question might be, 'to be crucified again'. But such an answer would assume that China's continuing economic development and social change must rely upon maintenance of working classes repression if the CCP is to achieve political stability. It also assumes that the fragmentation and quiescence that has characterised much of the Chinese working class in recent years will endure. Recent structural shifts undermine both assumptions, and suggest that the road ahead may well be paved with greater mobilisation and potentially even seismic changes in the forms and functions of workers' interest representation across the Chinese economy.

Indeed, it may well be that the only way to cement the sort of changes Xi Jinping and the rest of the Chinese political leadership have called for—especially a bold move into higher value-added industries and toward a greater reliance on consumption, as opposed to exports, for boosting GDP—would be for China finally to break out of its 'insurgency trap' in labour relations (Friedman 2014). As Eli Friedman has explained, the lack of genuine representation by independent unions or other vehicles for workers' interest intermediation has left China vulnerable to an incomplete double-movement (Polanyi 1944). Unable to provide institutionalisation and genuine political incorporation to workers left socially dislocated by the advance of the market, the CCP and the Chinese state are forced to contend with workers' ongoing mobilisation and increasingly radical activism. In such a context, progress up the product cycle or toward a more consumption-based economy appears unlikely.

This places Chinese workers in a potentially powerful yet uncertain position and leaves the state with unpalatable and risky response options. Workers can choose to continue with disunited activism in hopes of at least maintaining stasis or perhaps advancing some new social protections. They can work proactively with the state and Party to forge a new role for official unions or, more likely, develop some new template for institutionalisation of class compromise and incorporation of workers into the polity. Or they can press forward with bold unified mobilisation in support of independent unions or other vehicles of representation. The state and Party, in turn, can choose to promote independent unions (which appears incompatible with basic CCP principles and thus ideologically anathema), to remain trapped in a cycle of repression and accommodation in response to workers' fragmented mobilisation (which risks the rise of a united and destabilising labour movement, repression of which could prove unwieldy at best), or develop a proactive strategy for some alternative form of working class incorporation.

At present, I am optimistic that workers and their state interlocutors can avoid protracted or broad-based class conflict that could result from unified activism or too ham-fisted generalised repression. I even see some reason to hope for an innovative long-term solution, from which a new formula of institutionalisation and incorporation may yet emerge. But I fear that the short term is likely to see continuing confrontation on the shop floor and persistent stalemate at the macro-level. Such an unhappy equilibrium of slow-burn conflict may well take hold even more deeply than it already has, if no way out can be found within the next several years.

Implications for Other Aspects of Chinese Politics and for Workers Elsewhere

What happens in China has obvious and direct effects on workers the world over. China is also, on its own terms, a critical case, worthy of study as representative of a number of types, in addition to its intrinsic importance. Yet, few have examined the implications of Chinese labour politics or potential class compromise for the rest of the world or even outlined how their unique contours might be seen in a comparative light. To do this well, we must first dispense with any assumption that in China one might be able to discern any reflection of Europe's past.

Indeed, traditional comparative analysis of labour politics has tended to accept axiomatically certain truisms—notably that the experiences of working class formation, mobilisation, and incorporation throughout the world have been broadly similar to those of Western European countries between roughly 1848 and 1945, even if they have diverged in important respects. If we, however, allow for a sort of Lobachevskian geometry of comparison, suppositions of similarity in the absence of strict congruence fall away for the analysis of labour politics as surely and quickly as they do for the study of triangles. China's future may thus not resemble anything Polanyi could have predicted or that might be read from the annals of European history. It may also provide new insights that could travel further afield, but not necessarily to the countries that may seem obvious comparators.

Specifically, if a genuinely new and innovative method of institutionalisation or accommodation of working class mobilisation can be found that does not involve the creation of independent unions or mechanisms of interest intermediation, this would be innovation indeed. It would represent not just a true form of 'responsive authoritarianism', but a fundamentally different kind of corporatism or class compromise than has been seen anywhere before. Like those other modes of incorporation that sprang forth during the first half of the twentieth century, it may also provide an exemplar for other countries well beyond the set of large developing or post-socialist countries we might be tempted to think of. A first step in making good guesses about how such a new bargain might be struck or how far beyond China it might travel would be nailing down much more specifically the proper universe of comparison for Chinese labour politics (something well beyond the scope of this essay). When we know what mirrors to hold up to China, we will be much better able to analyse its changing face and gauge how far and in what directions its reflection might radiate or refract.

William Hurst

William Hurst is an Associate Professor at the Department of Political Science at Northwestern University, Chicago. He works on labour politics, contentious politics, political economy, and the politics of law and legal institutions, principally in China and Indonesia.

A miner in Jin Hua Gong Mine, Shanxi 1999
PC: P. Van Den Bossche

Remoulding the State Sector: Back to the 1990s?

Kevin Lin

Recent protests by state workers are once again raising concerns about an increase in labour unrest in the state sector in China. The current surge is reminiscent in many ways of the tumultuous protests that took place at the turn of the century, when the Chinese authorities carried out a drastic restructuring of the economy. The similarity is striking, and the eerily familiar images of protesting state workers only add to the sense of déjà vu. But is history really repeating itself?

In the first quarter of 2016, a week-long strike at an ailing state-owned steel factory in Guangzhou (Denyer 2016a), a street protest by miners in Heilongjiang denouncing the governor for a misleading remark about their wages (Buckley 2016), and a symbolically powerful convergence of coal miners in the once revolutionary area of Anyuan in Jiangxi (Denyer 2016b), have raised concerns that a new wave of protests is likely to take place in the state sector in China.

It has been more than a decade since the last major wave of protests by state workers subsided. Between 1997 and 2003, the state sector shut down and privatised a large number of state factories, leaving between twenty-five and forty million workers temporarily or permanently unemployed, decimating entire working-class communities, and prompting tens of thousands of workers to take to the street (Hurst 2009).

However, right around the time when China's rural migrant workers in the export-oriented manufacturing sector started to grow restless and more organized in the early 2000s, the resistance of state industrial workers to the marketization of state-owned enterprises (SOEs) suffered a historical defeat (Philion 2009). This was due to a combination of outright suppression, selective compensation, and the gradual winding down of the marketization process.

The current upsurge in many ways evokes memories of the tumultuous wave of protests in the state sector at the turn of the century. The similarity is striking: in the face of falling profitability and a bloated labour force, state workers once again demanded to be paid their proper wages or an adequate severance in the case of layoff. The eerily familiar images of protesting state industrial workers only add to the sense of déjà vu. But is history really repeating itself?

In many respects, the state sector today has been deeply transformed (Hsieh and Song 2015). Decades of reform have converted China's command economy into a modest but strategically significant state sector. The very process that led to the shutting down and sale of factories also brought about a radical restructuring of labour relations and the production process, creating the conditions for a decade of rapid recovery and expansion. This, in turn, has remade SOEs into some of the largest conglomerates in their respective industries, ensuring a decade of relative industrial peace.

After the Global Financial Crisis

However, early signs of stress appeared soon after the global financial crisis. For a few years, the decline in the growth rate of profits in the state sector was non-threatening. Still, an ideological battle was fought around the idea that further reforms were necessary and desirable (Lin 2013). International financial institutions, mainstream economists, and foreign chambers of commerce, amplified by the media, harshly criticised the inefficiency and corruption of the SOEs and repeatedly advocated for the withdrawal of state subsidies and a further downsizing of the state sector. For a period in late 2015, state sector reforms seemed to be back on the agenda (Bland 2015). However, to the disappointment of critics, the aim of the reforms was to strengthen the sector rather than further privatisation (Wei 2015).

Recently, China's economic predicament has begun to precipitate a widely anticipated crisis of industrial overcapacity (The Economist 2016). Profit margins in the steel industry are surprisingly low, and workers' wages and conditions are very poor at what has been described as zombie economy (Wildau 2016). Steel factories and coal mines are reported to have not been paying wages for months and many workers have already been laid off. When I visited a steel plant in the southern city of Kunming in 2012, I found a factory that was barely surviving on a meagre profit and where workers worked long shifts and earned just above the minimum wage.

Miners at Lao Ye Temple Mine, Datong, Shanxi
PC: P. Van Den Bossche

In the last couple of years, there have already been several cases of protests in the state sector (Wong 2015). But it is only now that we are seeing the full extent of the industrial overcapacity and declining profitability in the steel and coal sectors, and the toll that these conditions are taking on the workers. It is, therefore, no wonder that workers are taking collective action. Yet, is this likely to become a repeat of the wave of protests of the late 1990s?

In terms of the scale of the layoffs, whereas in the late 1990s the Chinese authorities targeted SOEs across the board, the current layoffs seem to affect mostly two sectors: steel factories and coal mines (Buckley and Hernandez 2016). There is no evidence that the party-state is interested in an overhaul of the entire state sector like it did two decades ago. The projected layoffs range from 1.8 million workers (about ten percent of the steel workforce and twenty percent of the coal miners) to five or six million (Lim et al. 2016), which are in themselves devastating figures but still pale in comparison to the twenty-five to forty million workers who lost their jobs during the previous wave of reforms. In fact, today the entire state sector—excluding public services such as schools and hospitals—employs less than forty million workers.

Another Social Volcano in the Making?

In any event, 1.8 million workers will still be a considerable source of social instability. Moreover, by its very nature the protests in the state sector pose a more direct challenge to the party-state than those in the private sector. To deal with this threat, the Chinese authorities seem to have learned their lessons from the past. They have pre-emptively allocated one hundred billion yuan (about fifteen billion US dollars) to resettle and help laid-off workers find alternative employment.

Yet, although these funds have already been earmarked to compensate laid-off workers, if the recent protests are any indication, managerial irresponsibility and recklessness are a more likely scenario than peaceful settlement. Conflicts at the factory level may still be unavoidable.

Will the layoffs spread to other sectors as a consequence of the deepening economic crisis? This cannot be ruled out. The steel and coal sectors are not the only industries with overcapacity, and there is a chance that the Chinese economy may sharply contract. But thanks to state subsidies, access to state-bank credits, and industrial protection, China's SOEs today are much better equipped than two decades ago to absorb shocks and losses (Zhang 2013). Furthermore, the Chinese state is likely to the fiscal resources to support the state sector and to contain the layoffs to only the designated sectors.

But the protests of state workers are also happening at a particularly fraught time, when tens of thousands of migrant workers in the export sector have been mobilising (Tang 2015), a factor that was much less significant in the late 1990s. This surely has the potential to render the situation more explosive. However, the location of the state sector protests may not significantly overlap with that of the struggles in the export sector. While a recent strike of steel workers did take place in Guangzhou, coal mines and large steel plants tend to be concentrated in inland, northern and north-eastern China instead of the southern coastal regions, a rustbelt/sunbelt distinction that has remained unchanged for the last two decades (Lee 2007).

Perhaps one of the biggest uncertainties is the disposition of state workers. Who are they? How do they differ from the Maoist state workers? Are they more likely to protest? Over the last two decades, the generations who had any memory of and sentimental attachment to Maoism and who witnessed the wave of layoffs in the 1990s have been largely replaced by a younger labour force. As a result of this generational break, state workers may no longer use the Maoist discourse, which was a pivotal part of the protest repertoire for state workers in the earlier waves of unrest.

But state workers today are confronting their own challenges. Two decades of labour intensification, lengthening working hours, and a rising salary gap between workers and management has bred resentment and deep dissatisfaction. As a consequence of the labour reforms, blue-collar state workers may begin to identify themselves with colleagues in the private sector than their predecessors. Perhaps this will become a basis for state workers to begin connecting with their counterparts in non-state sectors, thereby developing a class-consciousness and bridging the labour divide between state and private sector (Hurst 2015; see also the chapter by William Hurst on pp. 16-19 in the present book).

New Challenges, but also Opportunities

Whether history will repeat itself remains unpredictable. The actions of the Chinese government both at the national and provincial levels will play a fundamental role in shaping the response of the workers. Recent developments such as the attempts to freeze minimum wages and roll back social insurance at the discretion of the provinces and municipalities, as well as the possibility of a watering down of the 'overly protective' Labour Contract Law (see the brief on p. 13 in the present book), will most likely accentuate the damaging effects of the restructuring on workers and possibly ignite more and angrier protests.

For the reasons discussed, this time we are likely to see dynamics at play that are very different from those that characterised the last wave of labour unrest. This should be seen as a positive development. For all of the courage and determination of the state workers involved in these earlier rebellions, it is important to recognise the limitations of these mobilisations. It is undeniable that this will be another difficult time for China's state workers, but the new challenges are also infused with opportunities for the development of a stronger and unified labour movement.

Kevin Lin

Kevin Lin researches labour politics and civil society in China. His writings are focused on the labour and employment relations in the state-sector, and the development of China's emergent labor movement and its intersection with a nascent civil society.

A rural credit cooperative in a township where the author conducted fieldwork.

Laying Off Responsibility:
Microcredit, Entrepreneurship, and China's Industrial Retrenchment

Nicholas Loubere

In early 2016, the Chinese government announced that state-owned steel and coal companies would be restructured, resulting in the loss of 1.8 to six million jobs. In April, seven government agencies jointly release a set of guidelines outlining a strategy for mitigating the fallout from this latest round of mass layoffs. One of the key elements of this strategy is the encouragement of entrepreneurial activity through tax relief and subsidised 'microcredit' for laid-off workers. Does the promotion of entrepreneurship and self-employment have the potential to meet the needs of the newly unemployed? Or is this strategy actually part of a wider ideological project aimed at individualising responsibility for social welfare and fragmenting labour?

When the news broke earlier this year that Chinese state-owned steel and coal companies would be laying off anywhere between 1.8 to 6 million workers over the next two to three years, the government quickly moved to provide assurances that the socioeconomic fallout would be mitigated through one hundred and fifty million yuan in assistance for the newly unemployed (see the chapter by Kevin Lin on pp. 20-23 in the present book). On 15 April 2016, the Ministry of Human Resources and Social Security, along with six other national government agencies, jointly issued guidelines broadly outlining the ways in which the laid-off workers will be supported (Ministry of Human Resources and Social Security 2016). While the guidelines do not provide details of how much funding will be allocated to the different types of assistance, or which agencies will be responsible for their implementation, the document does specify four key measures aimed at reducing the negative outcomes of the restructuring: career counselling and retraining for laid-off workers; the facilitation of early retirement for eligible individuals; information sharing across regions to facilitate the movement of workers to areas where they are needed; and support for laid-off workers who wish to engage in self-employment through entrepreneurial pursuits.

The government's strategy, therefore, can be seen as having two distinct objectives. The first seeks to streamline the current system of government employment through redistribution and retirement. The second is aimed at redefining what constitutes 'normal' employment in China through a re-orientation towards entrepreneurship and self-employment. The guidelines state that this second objective will be achieved through tax relief for new enterprises, and subsidised loans for the laid-off workers who initiate them. This column critically examines some of the implications that arise from replacing large-scale wage employment with credit to promote entrepreneurial activity. In particular, it shows that the promotion of micro-entrepreneurship as a 'solution' for mass layoffs shifts responsibility for livelihoods and welfare from the state to marginal individuals and groups, while, at the same time, reducing the capacity for collective action by organised labour (Bateman 2010). The column also questions—at a fundamental level—the ability of individual entrepreneurship to fill the gaping hole (in the economy and society) left by mass layoff events.

An Entrepreneurial Solution

This is not the first time that targeted credit for micro-entrepreneurship has been identified as a means of dealing with socioeconomic problems in contemporary China. In the 1980s and 1990s, various government ministries established or supported microcredit programs targeting poverty and 'underdevelopment' in rural areas. In the wake of the large-scale restructuring of state-owned enterprises (SOEs) in the late 1990s and early 2000s—which, according to some estimates, resulted in twenty-five to forty million workers being made redundant (Hurst 2009)—the government established the 'Employment Microcredit Program' (*xiagang shiye zaijiuye xiao'e danbao daikuan*) in urban areas most affected by the retrenchment. The program provides small loans at zero percent interest in an effort to allow the newly unemployed to unleash their 'natural' entrepreneurial abilities and spark 'bottom up' employment opportunities (People's Bank of China 2002).

After being piloted for a few years, the Chinese government considered the Employment Microcredit Program to be a policy success and it was scaled up nationwide. Initially, microcredit was only available in cities to those who could provide formal documentation proving their laid-off worker status. This formal documentation was not always forthcoming, however, as navigating the bureaucracy often took certain types of knowledge and connections, and many SOEs did not even establish re-employment centres. In 2006, the program was extended to rural areas, with the target group being expanded to include migrant workers laid off from urban enterprises who wished to return to their rural origins to start businesses. Currently, the Ministry of Human Resources and Social Security administers the program. It recommends borrowers to local branches of state-owned banks and organises for the Ministry of Finance to pay the interest on the loans. In most localities loans of one hundred thousand yuan are provided to individuals for up to one year. Borrowers do not need collateral, but should instead have a 'trustworthy' guarantor.

Shifting Responsibility for Livelihoods and Welfare

The Employment Microcredit Program is conceived of as reducing the negative impacts of retrenchment by creating an alternative to large-scale wage employment. This fundamental reshaping of how livelihoods are produced is one of the ideological goals of the microcredit movement. In the words of Muhammad Yunus, the founder of the Grameen Bank in Bangladesh and the most prominent advocate of microcredit globally: 'One of the significant social impacts of the microcredit movement has been the realization that the key to alleviating poverty is often *not* the creation of 'jobs'—that is, salaried work for large corporate employers—but rather the encouragement of self-employment for all individuals...' (Yunus and Jolis 2001, 85). In other words, the microcredit movement considers self-employment as a valid (and even superior) alternative to large-scale wage employment, and sees entrepreneurship as being a universal human quality that, if nurtured, has the potential to allow individuals to provide for themselves.

Therefore, the promotion of microcredit as a response to layoffs should be understood as involving a transfer of responsibility for livelihoods and social welfare from the state to households and individuals. Indeed, for the majority of workers laid off in the 1990s and early 2000s, microcredit was offered as a replacement for the 'iron rice bowl' (*tiefanwan*)—i.e. stable life-long employment in a state 'work unit' (*danwei*) that included a salary and benefits. While most workers that will be affected by the impending retrenchment no longer enjoy 'iron rice bowl'-style employment, they will, nevertheless, be saddled with the burden of seeking out entrepreneurial ways of earning a sufficient income for survival (and repaying their loans). And failure to successfully take on these new responsibilities comes with dire consequences. This rewriting of the social contract is not only significant because it represents an individualisation of responsibility, but also—and more crucially—because this responsibility is being devolved to individuals who are relatively marginal and lacking in resources, such as low-level SOE employees and migrant workers living from pay-check to pay-check.

Labour Relations in a Society of Entrepreneurs

What does this rewriting of the social contract entail for labour relations in China? In addition to devolving responsibility from the state to individuals, the provision of microcredit in an attempt to foster entrepreneurship implicitly necessitates the fragmentation and atomisation of labour. While Ivan Franceschini's chapter in this volume (see pp. 84–87) highlights the fact that many Chinese workers do not have a clear conception of what 'collective rights' or 'collective action' actually entail, the goal of microcredit to redefine 'the household as a production unit and self employment as a natural way for people to make a living' (Yunus and Jolis 2001, 54) effectively renders these concepts meaningless. The industrial proletariat—with all their collective ambitions and grievances—are replaced by marginal (and indebted) micro-entrepreneurs struggling in competition with each other for their very survival.

Ultimately, therefore, the provision of microcredit to laid-off workers is about more than simply unleashing pent-up entrepreneurial spirit and allowing people to provide for themselves. Rather, it is a key element in a wider project engaged in systemically transforming labour relations in China. After all, there is no solidarity between competing micro-entrepreneurs. Nor is any labour negotiation possible, as it is the intangible 'invisible hand' of the market that determines working conditions and remuneration for the self-employed entrepreneur. In this way, the shift from large-scale wage employment to a society of atomised micro-entrepreneurs is part of a strategy to deal with the spectre of organised labour unrest, which is one of the Chinese government's major preoccupations (see the chapter by Ivan Franceschini on pp. 46–49 in the present book).

An Answer to Unemployment?

There are also other critical questions that need to be raised with regard to the fundamental ability of individual entrepreneurship (financed through microcredit) to fill the employment gap left by industrial retrenchment. For one, this strategy neglects the fact that, even in the best of cases, many entrepreneurial endeavours fail. In the case of the most recent round of layoffs, most of the newly unemployed micro-entrepreneurs will be from just two industries: steel and coal. Moreover, if past rounds of retrenchment are any indication, they will be comparatively less educated/skilled, approaching middle age, and predominantly female with a substantially higher load of family responsibilities. They will, therefore, primarily have the same skill sets and will probably engage in the same types of entrepreneurial activity. This suggests a sudden influx of certain kinds of business in a highly competitive and unforgiving market—i.e. a 'race to the bottom' undertaken by a new, and increasingly desperate, 'micro-entrepreneurial class' composed of the newly unemployed. While some will undoubtedly be successful, many others will fail and, as such, will be pushed further to the margins as they default on their debt and have no access to the livelihood resources previously provided by their employers.

It is also important to point out an implicit paradox in how microcredit is envisaged as assisting the unemployed. On the one hand, microcredit programs are conceived of as promoting a type of 'grassroots' or 'bottom-up' development that is separate and autonomous from the wider structural contradictions in the economy that produced the unemployment in the first place. However, in order to achieve this development, the would-be entrepreneurial beneficiaries of microcredit must become incorporated into the 'modern' socioeconomic system through integration into the market where they will sell their wares or services. In other words, there is really no escape from the socioeconomic processes that put these microcredit borrowers out of work. Their entrepreneurial pursuits do not exist in some alternate dimension; instead, they are intricately linked to the dominant market-oriented system operating in contemporary China that has created the conditions requiring mass layoffs. For example, in one of the townships were I conducted fieldwork the local economy appeared to be thriving, with 122 small and medium businesses operating in the township centre. However, over thirty-one percent of these businesses were directly related to the housing construction industry, which relies on the sustained flow of remittances from migrant workers in urban areas back to the township to build new houses for their 'left-behind' family members.

In short, this was no 'grassroots' economy, but was instead an economy fully dependent on the system of domestic migrant work—often through employment in the large urban SOEs now engaged in mass layoffs—for its continued existence.

Conclusions

Ultimately, the issues raised in this short piece suggest that microcredit and the promotion of entrepreneurship for laid-off workers should be seen as an ideological re-orientation, rather than a 'solution' to the social and economic problems resulting from a sudden increase in unemployment. Restructuring SOEs and encouraging laid-off workers to become entrepreneurs through the provision of subsidised credit shifts responsibility for livelihoods and welfare from the employer (in this case the state) to the individual, while fragmenting labour relations and collective identity. Microcredit is also an objectively flawed response to retrenchment, as it is not possible for individual entrepreneurship to sufficiently meet the need for employment created by the mass layoffs. Instead, microcredit for entrepreneurship is a smokescreen that serves to temporarily obscure the fact that China is (and has been) undergoing a sustained social, cultural, and economic transformation that is fundamentally rewriting the social contract in order to devolve responsibility to the individual, while simultaneously eroding the possibility for individuals to contest these developments through solidarity and collective action.

Nicholas Loubere

Nicholas Loubere is an Associate Senior Lecturer in the Study of Modern China at the Centre for East and South-East Asian Studies, Lund University.

Migrant Labour and the Sustainability of China's Welfare System

Beatriz Carrillo

Social welfare in China has emerged as a major cause of migrant workers' discontent. Reforms of the social welfare system in China since 2002 have expanded coverage and protection of vulnerable populations, but structural problems remain for migrant workers to access and receive the full benefits of the social safety net. How has the social welfare system evolved, and what are the challenges facing migrant workers? How can the system be made more sustainable?

Social welfare in China has emerged in recent years as a major cause of migrant workers' discontent and collective action. Reforms of the social welfare system in China since 2002 have expanded coverage and protection of vulnerable populations, but structural problems remain for migrant workers to access and receive the full benefits of the social safety net. How has the social welfare system evolved, and what are the challenges facing migrant workers? How can the system be made more sustainable?

Social welfare—understood broadly as encompassing public services, social insurance, and social relief—has long been primarily the privilege of the urban population. From the inception of the People's Republic in 1949, urban citizenship—defined by people's household registration (hukou) status—provided urban residents with access to employment, housing, education, and social insurance not available to rural hukou holders. China's rural-urban divide has, thus, in many ways been defined by this gap in welfare provision.

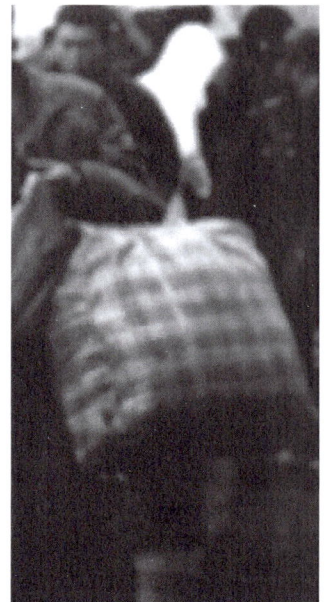
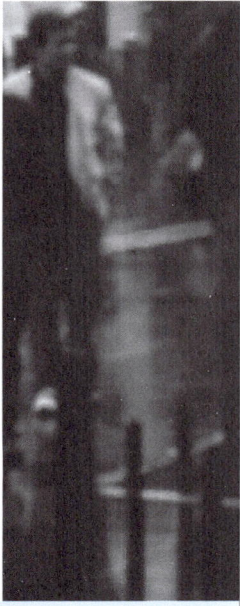

Migrant Workers in Shanghai
PC: Peijin Chen

The traditional 'iron rice bowl' (*tiefanwan*) system, based on work units (*danwei*), provided urban workers with 'cradle to grave' employment, services, and security, but—perhaps more importantly—it also gave these workers an identity and a sense of entitlement. This perception of having a right to state provisions was not developed among China's vast rural population, since they received very limited or no state funding for welfare provision. With the start of the reform era, workers' identity and sense of entitlement had implications for the demands for provision they made on the state, but also with regard to whose benefits the state decides to maintain or cut.

By the late 1990s, for example, China's previously privileged old working class was laid-off in the millions from state-owned enterprises—the majority left without welfare benefits (see also the chapter by Kevin Lin on pp. 20-23 in the present book). In the meantime, up until 2015, civil servants had largely retained their superior social insurance benefits, funded in their entirety by the state. In contrast, having had limited or no experience of state support, most rural-to-urban migrant workers had not had a sense of entitlement to urban goods and welfare, not least because in most cases their rural *hukou* continues to deny them membership in the cities. And yet, among the second generation of rural migrants—born after 1980 and with weaker links to the countryside— that has begun to change (Pun and Lu 2010). These workers are demanding better pay and working conditions. Their reaction to, and demand for, social insurance entitlements, however, has been less enthusiastic. This is in part due to the shortcomings and limitations of the social insurance system itself.

A Fragmented System

China's social insurance system is highly fragmented. While *hukou* differentiation may be the more obvious element of that fragmentation, other factors related to the way in which these insurance programmes are funded, managed, and implemented have perhaps had more serious implications for their provision. Like economic policy, social policy implementation in China is highly decentralised, and thus dependent upon local state capacity, particularly financial well-being. The more developed and wealthy provinces of the east coast have thus been better able to meet policy mandates from the central government around the delivery of public goods, social insurance, and welfare benefits, and have often even surpassed the level of benefits established by the centre. In contrast, having no revenue to match their welfare responsibilities, many local governments in the central and western parts of China offer, at best, very patchy provision. A longitudinal study on the social determinants of health, for example, found region (where a person lives) to have the strongest effect on an individual's health status (gender and age being the other two most important determinants) (Baeten et al. 2012).

This decentralisation, including the fact that funds for social insurance are pooled locally, has meant that funds accrued in individual worker accounts have not been transferable between jurisdictions. This lack of transferability is one of the biggest disincentives for migrant workers to enrol into the social security system, even when special insurance programmes for migrant workers have been created, as has been the case in Shenzhen and in other cities (Mou et al. 2009; Watson 2009). Furthermore, these social insurance programmes for migrants usually provide lower benefits than those covering formal urban employees, and there have been various well-publicised cases of employers not paying their contributions into those schemes (China Labour Bulletin 2016). Rural migrant workers are thus—understandably—reluctant to join a system that will result in less cash-in-hand and limited benefits only available in situ.

Attempts at Harmonisation

In order to allow for the transferability of funds accumulated in individual workers' social insurance accounts, since 2008 the central government has promoted the 'harmonisation' of rural and urban social insurance programmes, with the aim of creating a unified national social security system (Cai 2011; Shi 2012). In practice, however, this rural-urban harmonisation has thus far tended to result in local welfare protectionism, whereby the more prosperous provinces are unwilling to share their larger fund pools with workers from outside their jurisdiction. Chongqing's municipal government, for example, has successfully unified its rural and urban social insurance programmes for those with a local *hukou*, but those from outside the municipality remain left out (Shi 2012). Given that rural migrant workers are now more likely to be working outside their home province, in the short to medium term the rural-urban harmonisation process is likely to only benefit a minority of migrant workers.

The policy and rhetoric coming from the centre, however, has continued to promote the inclusion of rural migrant workers into the urban social security system, as evidenced by the latest iteration of the Social Insurance Law, passed in 2011, which made the enrolment of migrant workers into the urban social insurance programmes compulsory. Local governments have nonetheless not been too keen to police the implementation of this law, for fear of upsetting local businesses and industry. Employers in China have indeed faced some of the highest employee insurance contribution rates in the world, with rates of up to forty percent of employees' wages (KPMG 2016). In some provinces and municipalities, contributions into the old age social insurance alone have stood at more than twenty percent of the payroll (CCTV 2016). This serves to explain the prevalence of casual and informal employment without benefits, in which the majority of rural migrant workers are involved.

Economic Slowdown as the Latest Challenge

China's economic slowdown is likely to result in yet fewer employers willing to enrol migrant workers into the social insurance schemes mandated by law. In response to this, earlier this year the central government reduced employer contribution rates for pension and unemployment insurance, and for the housing provident fund (Ministry of Finance 2016). Nevertheless, the central government is likely to continue to put pressure on sub-national governments to enrol rural migrant workers into the social insurance system, because it now realises that the financial sustainability of the system will depend on bringing in more contributions from the working-age population. As a cohort, rural migrant workers are, on average, younger than their urban counterparts; these younger worker's social insurance contributions are hence necessary to sustain the needs of China's ageing population and the sustainability of the pension system (Frazier and Li 2017).

The first generation of rural migrant workers is also ageing and has begun to demand access to medical insurance and to a pension. More generally, the needs and demands of rural migrant workers for public services and social security are also changing. For example, the number of migrants travelling with their families has increased substantially over the last couple of decades (Wen and Hanley 2016). These migrant families have different housing needs, their children need access to local child care facilities and schools, play areas, medical services, and so on.

While workers' movements, strikes, and demonstrations have, in several instances, won rural migrantst workers better working conditions and pay, the expansion of social insurance and welfare programmes has largely been a top-down affair. More recent demands by migrant workers over social insurance payments, such as in the case of the 2014 strike at Yue Yuen—a shoe manufacturer and Adidas and Nike supplier—have also served to influence the government's decision to expand rural migrant workers' social insurance rights (Schmalz et al. 2016).

Again, the concern over a reduced worker/pensioner ratio and the burden that this will place on China's social security system is likely to maintain the commitment of the centre to expand coverage to include rural migrant workers. Some provincial governments, as stated earlier, are likely to continue to delay that process. Apart from financial considerations, Mark Frazier has also argued that it would be unwise for the Chinese government to retreat from the politics of inclusion and access to social policies introduced as part of Hu Jintao's campaign to build a 'Harmonious Society' (*hexie shehui*) and continued under Xi Jinping's 'Chinese Dream' (*zhongguo meng*) (Frazier 2014). Rather, what economic slowdown might bring about is a reduction in the level of benefits that employees receive, as signalled by the recent cutback to mandated employer contributions into social insurance programmes (Ministry of Finance 2016). Universal coverage may well soon be achieved, but at a very basic level of coverage. Whether this will constitute a real safety net for all remains to be seen.

Beatriz Carrillo

Beatriz Carrillo is an Associate Professor at Xi'an Jiaotong Liverpool University in Suzhou, China. Her research focuses on social exclusion and inclusion of rural migrant workers, welfare policy, social determinants of health, and philanthropy in contemporary China.

FORUM

Edited by Ivan Franceschini and Kevin Lin

Anita Chan

Anita is Visiting Fellow at the Political and Social Change Department, The Australian National University. Prior to that, she was Research Professor at the University of Technology Sydney. Her current research focuses on Chinese labour issues. She has published widely on Chinese workers' conditions, the Chinese trade union, and labour rights issues.

Kaxton Siu

Kaxton is an Assistant Professor in the Department of Applied Social Sciences at Hong Kong Polytechnic University. His research concentrates on globalisation, labour, youth, social movements, and the political economy of development in East and Southeast Asia, particularly China, Vietnam, and Hong Kong.

Sarah Swider

Sarah is an Associate Professor of Sociology at Wayne State University. Her research focuses on informal and precarious workers. She examines the employment relations that define informal and precarious work, how they organise and protest, and examines how these workers are reshaping workplaces and urban spaces.

Interpreting Chinese Labour: Informalisation or Empowerment?

Edited by Ivan Franceschini and Kevin Lin

The struggle and activism of Chinese workers has been a topic of primary interest since the beginning of the reform era. Still, expectations have never been higher than in the past few years, with an unending stream of media articles and academic papers hailing the new-found rights awareness of Chinese workers—especially the so-called second generation of migrant workers—as a critical development with the potential to disrupt the very foundations of the Chinese industrial and political system. This narrative describes a boom in strikes, sees social media as a revolutionary mobilisation tool, and portrays younger workers as eager to fight for their rights. Amid the euphoria, is such optimism warranted?

In fact, significant literature in both Chinese and English has argued that the discontinuity between the old and new generation of migrant workers has been exaggerated. However, these voices have been subsumed under the catchier narrative. In a recent article, Ching Kwan Lee has critiqued the work of fellow labour scholars for adopting an excessively optimistic view of labour activism in China (Lee 2016). In particular, Lee has identified and challenged four claims advanced by the supporters of what she calls the 'empowerment thesis': the idea that Chinese workers are increasingly active and motivated to mobilise; the assertion that the new generation of migrant workers is more class and rights conscious than the first; the alleged maturation and radicalisation of labour activism, with workers' demands changing from defensive to offensive; and the claim that consistent increases in wages in China should be considered as evidence of workers' effectiveness and empowerment.

Arguing that such claims have scarce factual basis and that they overlook structures of inequality and power imbalances that lead to precarity, she launched an appeal to her peers: 'In this day and age of global precarisation, it has become ever more important that labour scholars, of China or elsewhere, resist the temptation of subjectivism and voluntarism, and recall Gramsci's famous motto: pessimism of the intellect and optimism of the will'. Heeding this advice—and in order to gain a better understanding of precarity and its effects on the Chinese workforce—we have invited three labour scholars who have researched precarious labour in its various manifestations in the Chinese labour market to offer some insights based on their experience in the field.

What form has precarity and informal labour taken in the industries that you have researched, and what effects has it produced in the labour force?

Kaxton Siu: Over the past decade, I have been researching Chinese workers in toy, garments, electronics, and sanitary industries. Some of them work inside factories, while others, like street cleaners, work out in the open. The forms of precarity and informality, as well as their impact, differ from one industry to another. For workers in factories, major forms of precarity are still in the domain of working conditions, such as excessively long working hours, unpaid overtime, low wages, wage arrears, and occupational hazards. As for workers in the service industry such as street cleaners, most of them do not have stable jobs. Many of them just engage in irregular casual work, become part-timers, do not have regular working schedules, and receive very low wages, etc.

Sarah Swider: My research has mostly focussed on the construction industry, which is characterised by a bifurcated workforce. Most professional, managerial, and administrative jobs are full-time, stable, include benefits, and are filled by urban workers. In contrast, field positions, which are on jobsites, are mostly informal jobs filled by peasant workers from the rural areas who face precarity in their work and lives in the cities. They work under several different kinds of employment configurations, which shapes their precarity and vulnerabilities. I have documented three prominent employment configurations in this industry: *mediated*, *embedded*, and *individualised*. Many peasant-workers toil under *mediated employment*, named this way because their employment relationship is mediated by middlemen; usually large contractors who bring them into the city, house them, feed them, and pay them only at the end of year-long (informal) contracts. Others work in *embedded employment*, using social networks to find work, which embeds their work into these social networks, and in turn regulates the employment relationship. Finally, some workers toil in *individualised employment*. These jobs are found through street markets, and employment relations are highly despotic as unrestrained employers use violence, or the threat of violence, to deal with workers. These varied arrangements of precarious and informal work capture the increased fragmentation that makes it difficult to build solidarity. However, as informal workers, they tend to engage in struggles for recognition as workers and/or as citizens rather than struggles for increases in wages, benefits, and traditional worker/union demands. In general, formal precarious workers engage in struggles to increase wages; informal precarious workers engage in struggles to get paid at all. Formal precarious workers struggle for better benefits and representation; informal workers must struggle to be recognised as workers, and therefore, to be deserving of benefits.

Anita Chan: Many scholars have focussed their attention on industrial relations in the labour-intensive export sector in South China, but there have been few studies of capital-intensive industries such as the automotive industry. Back in 2011, I carried out a questionnaire survey with several hundred workers from five auto-assembly plants—note, not auto-supplier plants—all joint ventures with German, American, and Japanese partners. To my surprise, I found that the disparity between regular workers and agency workers is not big; in fact, it is remarkably small. For instance, not only the difference in length of contracts between the two groups tended to be small, but also the gap in their take-home wage was relatively little, with agency workers receiving on average 80.8 percent of the salary of their regular peers. The gap was further mitigated through annual bonuses. There was also no significant difference in work hours—both categories worked around nine and a half hours a day—and, even more importantly, all of them maintained almost the same neutral to positive attitudes towards management. The only significant difference concerned union membership: while sixty-eight percent of the regular workers were members of the company union, only 28.4 percent of the agency workers declared themselves as being union members. The reason behind this is that, from a managerial perspective, satisfying workers' material needs and keeping a stable and motivated workforce are of paramount importance in this industry. For this reason, agency workers have to be made to feel that they are having a fair if not equal deal compared to regular workers. And, let's be honest, companies can easily afford this!

Alongside reports of precarious labour conditions, in the past decade a notable shift in the narrative of Chinese labour has occurred. While in the past Chinese workers were often described as being 'under assault' by their employers and the forces of globalisation, now there is much emphasis on their so-called 'rights awakening', especially among the youngest generation of migrants. Looking at the sectors you research from a long-term perspective, do you think that workers' consciousness has changed significantly? And, does workers' consciousness and agency play a measurable role in shaping their labour conditions today?

Kaxton Siu: In recent years, much research has been done on the collective actions of Chinese workers and the impact of such mobilisations on workplace labour conditions, as well as on the responses of the Chinese state (for instance, experiments of types of collective consultation). However, from a long-term perspective, it seems that the discourses about the younger generation of migrant workers and Chinese workers' 'rights awakening' have been overstated.

On the one hand, it has been seen that the sudden rise of Chinese workers, witnessed for instance during the famous Honda strike of the summer of 2010, could not be sustained and turned into a significant political force influencing the labour policy of the Chinese government. On the other, various initiatives of the Chinese state, such as various 'collective consultation' experiments in different localities, diverged in their outcomes. Particularly, in some industries—such as the sanitary industry—where workers are more informal and precarious in terms of their working conditions and workplace bargaining power vis-à-vis employers, these official initiatives still cannot improve the livelihoods of vulnerable workers. As for workers' consciousness, despite what I mentioned above, from a long-term perspective, we indeed have witnessed some development of working-class consciousness among Chinese workers over the past twenty years. As many studies and factory ethnographies have documented, in the early 1990s, not only did Chinese migrant workers lack any sense of class consciousness; they also had a very fatalistic outlook. Their migrant worker identity, especially for young female migrant workers (*dagongmei*), was primarily constructed as an outcome of particular socio-economic and institutional structures, namely: the Chinese household registration system, the Chinese patriarchal structure, and the managerial domination by foreign capital inside factory workplaces. However, since the mid 2000s, we have seen some strike cases that demonstrate significant development in workers' consciousness. Not only have workers started to demand wages above the legal minimum, but workers have also started to organise themselves with fighting spirit and solidarity in the face of massive police suppression and violence. That being said, the majority of present-day Chinese migrant workers are still waging isolated uncoordinated rights-based protests and strikes. Only a few have gone beyond rights-based demands to an interest-based level in requesting more than what is stipulated in current Chinese labour law. Only very few Chinese migrant workers are conscious enough to ask for setting up or re-electing workplace trade unions, or to organise strikes beyond individual factories at regional and country-wide levels.

Sarah Swider: This narrative of Chinese labour has been largely based on the experience of manufacturing workers. The number of factory workers who are still working under secure 'iron-rice bowl' conditions established under state socialism is dwindling. At the same time, there is an increasing number of peasants that have left the fields, but kept their land, and entered the factory to become 'peasant-workers'. These two groups have very different social positions within society, different relationships to land and capital, and both are changing. As such, for each group a different worker consciousness emerges under marketisation. This is coupled with a generational shift characterised by younger workers who only have experience with state-led capitalism. However, construction workers are quite different. The construction industry has always relied heavily on peasant workers. These peasants were disadvantaged under the state-socialist system of the past, excluded from partaking in the 'iron rice bowl'. Today, under marketisation, they play an important role in urbanisation, but they are still disadvantaged, excluded from the benefits of urbanity and modernity. In other words, there has been no shift in their social position or their relations to land and capital. However, their changing environment does have an affect on them, and this is leading to a shift in worker subjectivity. Despite their continued connection to the land, many of these migrants are now spending most of their lives in the cities, which in many cases exposes them to other workers and protests. Thus, the paths that they imagine are possible, the number of potential avenues of protest, and the targets and the goals of the protests have grown and changed over time. Protests among construction workers, especially those focussed on wage arrears, are likely to be 'public drama protests' in which workers use drama to gain attention from the public, local and state officials, and other employers in the contracting chain to apply pressure so that they get their wages paid (Chun 2005). These protests are usually collective actions, they are dramatic and creative so as to draw attention, and while they may publicly blame the contractors, they often indirectly target the state-owned enterprises (SOEs) or the companies further up the contracting chain, depending on the money flows. These protests are often successful because: a) they are sporadic so the government cannot predict or prevent these actions; b) they gain attention from the public and media that increases the costs of squashing the protests; and c) they garner symbolic power rather than power from disruption, which is more likely to gain support from different groups.

Anita Chan: Some scholars believe that agency workers and student interns in the automotive industry in China are second-class industrial citizens who harbour deep grievances due to this discrimination. In their opinion, this engenders labour activism. Personally, I think that this is an overstatement. Through my research, I found that the treatment these agency workers receive and their attitudes and aspirations are not decidedly different from regular workers, and certainly do not provoke a sense of injustice and anger. After all, for a whole decade since the mid-2000s there has been no big protest in China's auto assembly plants. My survey points to an overwhelming unwillingness to seek collective representation, less still to take militant action. For instance, when I asked the workers how would they solve a grievance, 44.9 percent of agency workers and 49.2 percent of regular workers said that they would go to their supervisor; 24.7 of agency workers and 21.3 percent of regular workers said that they would not ask anyone; and 13.6 of agency workers and 13.3 percent of regular workers said that they would just look for another job. Only 4.4 percent expressed a choice that entailed publicising their grievances beyond the workplace and soliciting external help, with as little as 0.4 percent of the respondents willing to go on strike. On the contrary, I found that both groups of workers were quite responsive to the paternalism of the company, with seventy percent of the agency workers and a slightly higher percentage of regular workers feeling let down if they did not receive festive gifts or money through the union or management. We also have to take into account the fact that compensation in the automotive industry is relatively high—in the companies in my survey the average basic wage was about double the local legal minimum wage and the take-home pay for both types of workers ranged from two to four times that of the local minimum wage.

Since the early 1990s the Chinese authorities have been adopting an increasingly complex body of labour laws and regulations, much of it quite favourable to workers. Is this turn to the law a sign of a genuine commitment by the authorities to protect worker rights against precarity? Have the Chinese labour laws limited or fostered precarisation?

Kaxton Siu: The 1994 Labour Law was the first comprehensive labour legislation passed in China since the founding of the People's Republic. The passage of the law stirred up a debate among government bureaucracies. At that time, the All-China Federation of Trade Unions (ACFTU) fought to ensure that the spirit of the law was advantageous to workers. However, the law did induce a change in workers' awareness, and migrant workers in the Guangdong region gradually began to use the law as an instrument to 'protect rights' (*weiquan*). Note that these rights refer to *legal* rights and not to inalienable human rights. The social discourse on 'rights protection' entails acceptance of prevailing laws as the standard by which work conditions and wages should be set. With the passage of the 1994 Labour Law, many Hong Kong labour NGOs, usually staffed by a few people, began setting up offices across the border, mostly in Shenzhen. These organisations played a significant role in popularising the idea of 'rights protection' among Chinese migrant workers in the area. Their programme focused on raising awareness among migrant workers of the details of the Labour Law and other regulations related to workplace health and safety. They taught migrant workers how to read their pay slips and pointed out where the payment and work hours fell short of legal requirements. They helped injured workers to seek compensation, which requires an expert understanding of how to assess grades of injuries and litigation procedures. Their persistence paid off within the space of a decade. Most migrant workers today in this part of China know about the legal maximum overtime, about the region's official minimum wage, and about industrial injuries compensation. Taking bosses to court for underpaying, going to the authorities to lodge legal claims for back pay, and suing for compensation for workplace accidents have become commonplace. Litigation is a legitimate form of protest. From a historical perspective, the passage of various labour regulations by the Chinese government has had positive impacts in protecting workers against further precarisation. However, we should note that the 1994 Labour Law was passed not because workers had been collectively making demands on the government, but because there was a consensus within the political elite that social stability had to be maintained by having a law to regulate industrial relations.

Sarah Swider: The law is contradictory in nature. In the process of defining 'workers', it leaves many out of the category (Huang 2013); in the process of carving out protections, it creates unprotected activities and spaces (Xu 2008-2009); in defining some actions and activities as legal, it makes others illegal (Portes et al. 1989). Furthermore, the law is often intentionally ambiguous, leaving it to local and national leaders to interpret. Finally, laws and interpretations are only as good as the enforcement (Gallagher et al. 2015), which requires a different set of institutions and resources than those required to make laws (Gallagher and Dong 2011). Thus, laws are not an adequate tool for limiting precarisation or limiting worker vulnerability, and this holds true across different national contexts. However, the multitude of complex labour laws that have been instituted in China still matters for workers. In some instances, the laws have become another tool in a worker's arsenal to deal with industrial conflict, and in other cases, the laws hold symbolic power, sending a message to local-level government and international capital to pull back on exploitation (Lee 2002). In sum, laws make a difference but sometimes in unexpected and/or complex ways.

Anita Chan: There is indeed a problem of implementation, as the law has substantially failed to control the growing number of agency workers and abusive work practices. While not all auto assembly plants use agency workers—for instance BYD and Hyundai in Beijing do not—the five joint ventures in my sample do, even for up to half of their workforce. But the length of contracts of the two types of workers are both short. The average length of contracts for regular workers was about three years, whereas for agency workers it was about two years. There is a chance for agency workers to become regular workers, and regular workers having signed two short contracts can get a permanent contract, but this is quite rare. In this sense, even regular workers' employment is quite precarious. They are aware that in times of recession, they may be laid off as well. If we consider that these companies are all joint ventures in which one of the partners is an SOE at the provincial or city-level, it may appear paradoxical. But in reality the SOEs are the ones that employ the largest number of agency workers. There is a historical legacy to this. In the late 1990s, when millions of state workers were laid off, SOEs were required to set up employment agencies to find work for the laid-off workers. When it was discovered that agency workers can serve as buffers to the vagaries of the market, they were used in a big way, and they still are.

What is your assessment of the field of Chinese labour studies today, in China as well as abroad? In your opinion, is there any empirical and/or analytical gap that still needs to be filled and what should be done to address it?

Kaxton Siu: Due to the rise of China as a global powerhouse over the past twenty years, there is a great wealth of research about Chinese labour today. However, there is a tendency to consider the development of China and the making and remaking of the Chinese working class over the past decades as unique and exceptional. But is the Chinese experience really that exceptional? To answer this question, we should compare China to other similar socialist countries, such as Vietnam. Unfortunately, not much research has been done to compare labour conditions, industrial actions, trade union reforms, as well as modes, sequencing, and trajectories of economic reform in China and these countries. Another empirical gap is related to the recent household registration reform and the parallel change in the urbanisation process happening in China. Since the mid-2000s, a growing number of migrant workers have moved with their spouses and children from the countryside to industrial cities. In 2014, this phenomenal shift in migration patterns has led the Chinese government to reform their household registration systems. Now, thanks to the reform, it is said that it is easier for migrant workers to stay in the urban areas where they work. There, they are encountering new modes of housing arrangements, new forms of community relations, integration into new social networks in cities, and new household organisation strategies. Exactly how this process of integration happens and how the mobility of the families of migrant workers affects workers' outlooks on their working and family lives are worthwhile topics for further research. Yet these major shifts have barely been studied, nor has there been research done on how the new surge in married migrant couples with children affects labour relations inside the factories.

Sarah Swider: In China, some of the most interesting labour questions are about the relationship between labour politics and regime stability, especially given the significant rise in labour protests in the last few decades (Chan et al. 2010). Authoritarian regimes are generally believed to be unable to tolerate political mobilisation and protest (Tilly 2001), but China's variant of authoritarianism has encouraged, and sometimes stimulated and directed it. Some studies suggest that China's regime longevity has been because of, not despite, social protests, as it contributes to legitimacy, creates a carefully managed outlet for anger, and shapes and exploits cleavages among groups (Perry 2007; Tang 2016). This compels us to ask, under what conditions is this less likely to happen? What segments of labour are more difficult to control or more likely to push the boundaries? What issues or subjectivities are more likely to allow groups to overcome cleavages and fragmentation, and what forms of organising and protest are less likely to be controlled/co-opted? More generally, the rise of precarious work and the persistence of informal work across the globe means that most of the world's workers are beyond the formal economy and outside of state welfare and protections. We need a new paradigm to understand this reality and it will require us to rethink the relationships between the state and the economy, between production and redistribution, and between the productive and reproductive spheres; all of which might prove to be fertile ground for reimagining work, labour politics, and the future(s) of workers.

Anita Chan: In the past couple of decades, Chinese labour studies outside China have expanded rapidly, from only a handful of scholars working on the issue to a few dozen. However, there is an over-concentration on the study of migrant labour, with an overwhelming focus on Guangdong province. This imbalance has led to an excessive emphasis on labour resistance because a disproportionately large percentage of labour protests have been taking place in the South. In my view, it is time that we begin to branch out to explore new areas, new sectors, and new locations where labour protests are not that prevalent. In the instances where we find that workers in different places are more compliant, then it would be our task to explain why.

MADE IN CHINA - **BRIEFS**

APR/JUN 2016

Wukan villagers during clashes with the local police. PC: Foreign Policy

He Xiaobo Released on Bail, Zeng Feiyang's Mother Attempts to Sue Official Media

On 8 April, He Xiaobo, one of the labour activists taken into custody in early December 2015, was released on bail after being charged with embezzlement. A forty-two-year-old former migrant worker, He is the director of the Nanfeiyan Social Work Service Centre, an NGO based in Foshan, Guangdong, that specialises in providing legal aid to victims of work-related accidents and occupational diseases. Another two labour activists, Zeng Feiyang and Meng Han, of the Panyu Migrant Workers Centre, an NGO based in Guangzhou, remained under detention with the charge of 'disrupting social order'. In late December, Chinese state media publicly accused Zeng of having embezzled money from factory workers, having affairs with several female workers, and writing 'vulgar' messages to women online. His mother Chen Wenying later attempted to sue the official *Xinhua News Agency* and *China Central Television*, demanding one million yuan in compensation for defamation, but in April she dropped charges due to the unrelenting pressures she and her family had been subjected to in the wake of the lawsuit.

(Sources: **Guardian**, **Quartz**, **South China Morning Post**, **Xinhua**)

(Left) Labour activist He Xiaobo. (Right) Policemen patrolling a street in China.

New Foreign NGOs Law Passed

On 28 April, the National People's Congress, China's legislative body, passed the long-awaited Law on the Management of Foreign NGOs' Activities within Mainland China. The new Law, which comes into effect on 1 January 2017, fills a grey area in the Chinese legal system, stipulating that any foreign group wishing to operate in China must register with the public security authorities. This means that the Ministry of Public Security and its local branches down to the county level will formally be in charge of supervising all activities of foreign NGOs in China. The passage of the Law signifies increasing restrictions on the activities of foreign NGOs (see also the Compendium on pp. 60–67 in the present book). Not only will they be barred from engaging in political or religious activities, or acting in a way that damages 'China's national interests' or 'ethnic unity', but criminal measures can also be taken against individuals who are suspected of having engaged in activities that violate these broadly-worded principles. As most foreign NGOs operating in China do not have any official registration, no official data are available on their numbers. However, according to one estimate, more than seven thousand international organisations are active in the country today. In light of this widespread presence, the Chinese authorities have argued that such regulation is long overdue, with an op-ed published in the *People's Day* on 4 May rhetorically asking: 'If you do not violate the law, what are you afraid about?' Still, critics maintain that the laws amount to a crackdown.

(Sources: **BBC**, **China Law Translate**, **Guardian**, **People's Daily**)

Henan Local Regulations Forbid Workers from Resorting to Extreme Measures to Pursue Back Pay

On 22 April, the local authorities of Zhengzhou, Henan province, released a set of 'Draft Regulations on the Construction Market', giving the public one month to provide feedback. The Regulations, which aimed at 'standardising the management of the construction market, protecting the order of the construction market, and guaranteeing the legal rights and interests of the actors involved', attracted public backlash because in their initial formulation they included provisions calling for the punishment of those construction workers who adopted 'extreme measures' when fighting to claim unpaid wages. In particular, this early draft explicitly prohibited acts such as climbing on cranes or buildings and threatening to jump—relatively common occurrences in the construction industry in China—saying offenders would be handed over to the judicial system. It also banned workers from using force or money to convince others to join protests. A draft subsequently released for public comment in May no longer included such provisions.

(Sources: **Caixin English**, **Caixin Chinese**, **People's Daily**, **Dahe.cn**, **Zhengzhou People's Congress Website**)

A Chinese construction worker.

PC: XINHUA

Walmart Employees Campaigning against Flexible Scheduling

On 16 May, Walmart announced a new flexible scheduling system—the so-called 'comprehensive working hour calculation system'—to be implemented across its retail stores in China, and asked its employees to sign a written declaration in which they agree to the new system. In contrast to the current standard eight-hour working day for full-time workers, with the new system Walmart will be able to schedule any number of hours, as long as they add up to 174 hours per month. Not only would the new system reduce workers' overtime payments, but it would also introduce an erratic work schedule. The *Jinan Daily* quoted a Walmart worker as saying: 'We are comfortable with the eight-hour working day. After switching to the new scheduling system, if management requests us to work twelve hours today and four hours tomorrow and if we sign the agreement, then we cannot refuse. This system will bring extreme uncertainty.' Walmart has previously attempted to implement this scheduling system but failed due to the resistance of its employees. The current opposition against the new scheduling has been led by an unofficial Walmart Chinese Workers Association (WCWA) founded by several current and former Walmart workers in 2014. With the hope of securing the support of the All-China Federation of Trade Unions (ACFTU), on 28 May the WCWA sent an open letter to the ACFTU co-signed by more than eight hundred Walmart workers. On 14 June, the Guangdong branch of the ACFTU issued a statement in which, without naming Walmart, it reiterated that the use of the comprehensive work hour calculation system in the retail sector is inconsistent with the existing regulations, and any labour dispute caused by the implementation of such a system must be reported to the union for timely intervention. For further details, see Anita Chan's chapter on pp. 50–55 in the present book.

(Sources: **Jinan Daily**, **Sixth Tone**, **The Nation**)

Mine Murders Uncovered in Mongolia

On 31 May, prosecutors in Inner Mongolia announced the indictment of seventy-four people for the killing of seventeen mine workers. The killings were for the purpose of faking mining accidents in order to blackmail mine owners running unlicensed operations into paying compensation. The compensation payments ranged from five to eight hundred thousand yuan. In a scheme that brings to mind the plot of the movie *Blind Shaft*, directed by Li Yang, these suspects lured victims from poor villages, and paid them a higher than average daily wage to work in the coalmines. The victims were then murdered within days. The actual number of victims is likely to be higher, as corpses were quickly cemented and disposed of. The killing of these seventeen people was discovered in January 2015, when the police were investigating a mining accident and found that some of the victims were actually alive. Newspapers have reported on similar schemes in the past. For instance, in 2009 the police discovered that several people from a village in Leibo county, Sichuan province, were involved in buying or kidnapping people with severe mental problems only to sell them as slaves or to kill them in the mines in order to get compensation.

(Sources: **China News**, **Caijing**, **The New York Times**)

(Left) Miners pushing a cart of coal. (Right) Bloggers Li Tingyu and Lu Yuyu.

Social Media Archivists of Protests in China Detained

On 16 June, Lu Yuyu and his partner Li Tingyu, chroniclers of protests in China on their website *Wickedonna*, were detained in the southwestern city of Dali, Yunnan province, where they lived. They are accused of 'picking quarrels and provoking troubles', a charge that is often used to silence activists in China. Since 2012, the couple has been gathering and posting text and images from Chinese social media, such as *Weibo* and *Baidu Tieba*, to document protests in China—providing what is arguably the most comprehensive daily updates of social upheavals across the country, including many labour protests. After dropping out of university, Lu became a migrant worker and in 2012, while in Shanghai, he had his first taste of political activism, publicly showing his support for five young people who were arrested in Guangzhou for holding up placards that called for president Hu Jintao to disclose his assets. At the time, Lu held up a similar poster in one of Shanghai's busiest shopping districts, until the police intervened and expelled him from the city. Over the years, he continued to be harassed by state security for his activism and documentation work. His accounts on Chinese social media have been deleted more than one hundred times. In a profile published by *The Week*, Lu was quoted as saying: 'As long as I am not in jail, I will continue to do it.' Amnesty International has called for the couple's immediate release.

(Sources: **The New York Times**, **The Week**, **Amnesty International**, **Wickedonna**)

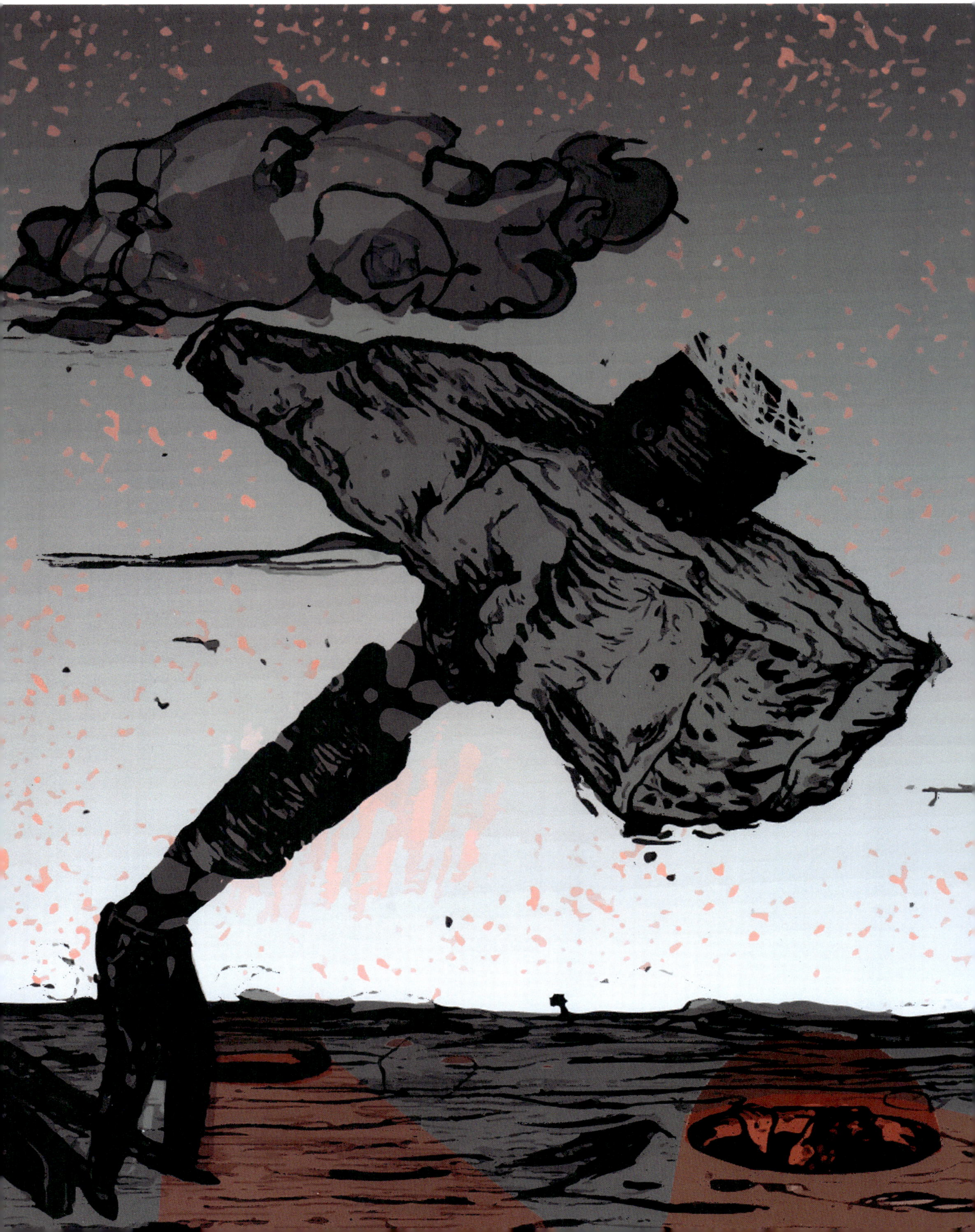

HAMMER TO FALL

Revisiting Chinese Labour NGOs: Some Grounds for Hope?

Ivan Franceschini

In the past decade, scholars have put forward several scathing criticisms of Chinese labour NGOs that go well beyond the usual concerns about the lack of transparency and internal democracy. Still, many things have changed in the past few years and now the time may be ripe for a reassessment of the role of these organizations.

Wu Guijun, a worker and NGO volunteer, was detained for over a year in 2013. PC: HKCTU

In the past decade scholars have put forward several scathing criticisms of Chinese labour NGOs that go well beyond the usual concerns about the lack of transparency and internal democracy. Some have criticised them for being nothing less than 'anti-solidarity machines' that, by putting too much emphasis on an individualistic view of rights, hinder the development of a labour movement among Chinese migrant workers (Lee and Shen 2011); others have noted how these organisations are also working for the benefit of the party-state, which they assist by minimising social conflict and orienting reforms in a way acceptable to the authorities (Froissart 2005). In a previous article, I myself joined the ranks of the critics, highlighting how Chinese labour NGOs suffer from a substantial lack of 'social capital', due not only to their strained relations with the party-state, but also to the considerable difficulties they face in gaining the trust of the workers (Franceschini 2014). Although these criticisms could be deemed ungenerous given the difficulties that these NGOs face under the constraints of the Chinese political system, they were grounded in years of observation and participation in the daily operations of these organisations. Still, the time may be ripe for a reassessment of Chinese labour NGOs.

Less Incorporation and More Repression

Since their appearance in China in the mid-1990s, in spite of their minimal size and lack of coordination, labour NGOs have always had to face the suspicions of the party-state. Already in 2009, an internal document by the Guangdong Politics and Law Committee of the Communist Party categorised labour NGOs as civic agents who intensify labour conflicts, carry out covert investigations of factories, and receive funding from overseas entities to intervene in the 'contradictions among the people' (*renmin neibu maodun*), endangering social stability, the security of the state, and even the international image of the country (China Labor News Translation 2010). More recently, in February 2015, Li Yufu, Vice-President of the official union, stigmatised labour NGOs for their connections with foreign donors (Lin 2015). Noting that 'the trends in the field of industrial relations are complex and intricate, and labour contradictions have already entered a phase of intensification and multiplication,' he denounced the fact that 'the interferences by hostile foreign forces are getting stronger, in the futile attempt to use industrial relations to break through.' According to Li, these forces 'resort to some illegal "*weiquan*" labour organisations and individuals to vie with the unions for workers, and so doing they break the solidarity of the working class and the unity of the unions.'

As Jude Howell has noted, what we have witnessed in recent years is a paradoxical development in which the party-state has pursued the 'incorporation' of some NGOs for welfaristic purposes, while simultaneously repressing others (Howell 2015). If the attempts at incorporating Chinese labour NGOs seem to have been a feature more of the latest years of the Hu and Wen administration than of the current leadership, repression has indeed intensified, reaching a climax last December. In the past few years, Chinese labour NGOs have been increasingly exposed to a wide array of threats and intimidations by the state security apparatus. This repression has taken many forms. Besides the usually non-confrontational praxis of inviting labour activists to 'have a cup of tea' (*he cha*), public and state security officers have often put pressure on landlords to repeatedly evict NGOs from their premises and have not refrained from liaising with other branches of the state (family planning offices, tax offices, social security offices, schools, etc.) to harass not only the activists, but also their families. In the worst cases, this repression took the semblance of an authentic police persecution. It happened in 2013 to Wu Guijun, a worker and NGO volunteer who was detained for over a year for joining a strike against the relocation of the company he worked in, and it happened in the past year to Zeng Feiyang and his colleagues (see the briefs on pp. 11, 41, and 77 in the present book).

Worth noting is that, while this repression eventually led some labour NGOs to shut down, many others simply changed name and revised their strategies. In the interviews that I carried out in 2014 and 2015, most of my interviewees stated that the number of labour NGOs active in China had grown since 2012—an *annus horribilis* in terms of political repression—but that the organisations had become smaller in size. Even more important is the fact that the new organisations that emerged in that period were mostly founded by activists of NGOs that fell victim to state repression. Although they were working independently from each other, these activists maintained friendly relations with their former colleagues, a development that in the long run may end up fostering solidarity and trust among organisations, laying the foundation for a tighter and more effective network that may even be able to exert some influence at a policy level. From this point of view, atomisation is not necessarily is a signal of impending annihilation. Still, it remains to be seen whether these new groups will be able to survive the latest assault by the party-state and the new restrictive regulations.

Labour NGOs and Migrant Workers' Struggles

Another significant development concerns the way labour NGOs deal with migrant workers' struggles. Until a few years ago, labour NGOs steered clear of collective disputes and politically sensitive cases—a modus operandi which attracted much criticism from the international academic community. Still, recently some organisations have displayed a remarkable willingness to engage with labour strikes and protests, effectively promoting collective bargaining (*jiti tanpan*) as a tool to solve labour disputes. This can be seen not only in many ordinary disputes related to unpaid employers' social insurance contributions, severance pay, overtime, and housing contribution schemes, but also in various high-profile cases that involved several hundreds if not thousands of workers, such as the Yue Yuen strike in Dongguan in 2014 and the struggle of the Lide employees in Guangzhou in 2014 and 2015 (Chen 2015; China Labour Bulletin 2015). That such events remain politically sensitive is proven by the severity of the consequences for the activists involved. In 2014 an NGO worker involved in the Yue Yuen strike was detained for a month after trying to convince the workers to elect their representatives to bargain collectively with the management, and Zeng Feiyang and his colleagues paid dearly for their involvement in the Lide campaign, which was played up by the Chinese state media as a case in which greedy activists neglected the interests of the workers in order to achieve money and fame (Zou 2015).

Duan Yi, a prominent labour lawyer based in Shenzhen, recently argued that labour NGOs are transitioning from 'service-oriented' (*fuwuxing*) and 'rights protection-oriented' (*weiquanxing*) to 'labour movement' (*gongyunxing*) organisations (Duan 2015). Yet, such a conclusion may be premature and even dangerous. It is premature because most labour NGOs still focus on providing services to migrant workers and, at most, deal with individual disputes of very limited social and political impact, such as cases related to occupational health and safety. It is dangerous because the term 'labour movement' evokes spectres of worker upheaval, which have been haunting the Chinese leadership since the early 1980s. According to my interviews, few labour activists identify their organisations with the 'labour movement' label. As an NGO leader in Shenzhen told me:

> Some scholars say that we are 'labour movement organisations'. I don't agree completely. I think that it would be more appropriate to define us as 'comprehensive organisations' (*zonghexing*). Why? Because our organisation carries out service work, rights-protection work, and even some work with strikes simultaneously… Sure, you can also talk about labour movement, the expression is not bad, but in my opinion it is not complete, it doesn't cover all facets. Moreover, this expression easily catches the attention of the government. If you talk about labour movement, the Party, who started to establish itself exactly through the labour movement… gets alarmed. Why? Because this is the way in which they came to power. For this reason, I prefer to use the term 'comprehensive' to define us and the other labour NGOs that engage with collective bargaining.
> [Interview, September 2015]

Lexical quibbles aside, it is undeniable that in recent years some labour NGOs have started to experiment with new strategies to engage more closely with migrant workers and have proved themselves willing to face the wrath of the authorities in order to push the boundaries of the political discourse and praxis. Although these organisations are still far from being 'independent trade unions', they are becoming more responsive to the real needs of migrant workers. In this respect, it is significant that the input for this push toward collective disputes and collective bargaining has come not only from foreign donors (which nevertheless played a fundamental role in this shift), but also from the workers themselves. In this regard, the experience of a southern labour NGO established in 2012 with the aim of carrying out cultural and recreational activities for female migrant workers is particularly interesting. As one of the leaders, herself an injured migrant worker, told me:

> At the end of 2012, many controversies between labour and capital arose in the factories around us and these female workers came to our centre to ask for information… During the winter, we organised a meeting during which we asked them to vote on what kind of activities best fit their interests. They chose trainings in law, collective bargaining and communication techniques. Their choices were completely different from what we expected! On this basis, since the end of 2012, we have rearranged our work, starting to deal with the rights of female workers and with collective bargaining. [Interview, April 2015]

Some Grounds for Hope?

In all likelihood, it was the very fact that labour NGOs were increasingly willing to deal with collective disputes, engage more closely with the workers, and promote a confrontational model of collective bargaining very different from the official narrative of 'collective negotiation' (*jiti xieshang*), that triggered the latest crackdown against them. Organised groups that didn't work as 'anti-solidarity machines', but actually promoted labour organising were highly menacing to the party-state and the official union, especially in light of the current slowdown of the Chinese economy. For this reason, Zeng Feiyang and his colleagues, who were at the forefront of this new trend, were made into a public example for all labour activists in China and abroad. Still, although the situation in China today is very grim, even in this bleak hour there may still be reason to look at the future of Chinese labour NGOs with some optimism. As described above, even in a context of further atomisation of these organisations, activists from NGOs targeted by state repression are breaking off to establish their own groups, a development that in the future may foster the emergence of a stronger solidarity network. Moreover, some activists are also adopting 'guerrilla' tactics, working on an individual basis and bringing aid in areas where no labour NGO is present. It remains to be seen how far the party-state is willing to go to fight this wave, if labour NGO activists will find a way around the new restrictions on foreign funding, and whether the migrant workers will remain silent or will finally start to speak up for those who have been risking everything to fight for their rights.

Ivan Franceschini

Ivan Franceschini is a Marie Curie Fellow at Ca' Foscari University of Venice and at the Australian Centre on China in the World working on a project on Chinese labour in a global perspective. From 2006 to 2015, he lived in China, where he worked as a journalist and as a consultant in the field of development cooperation. His research interests focus on Chinese labour and civil society.

A group of Walmart worker activists stages a protest at a Walmart store in Shenzhen on 29 June. On their shirts is written: 'Implement the spirit of President Xi's speeches; Walmart employees stand up; oppose the elections of puppet unions.' PC: WCWA

The Resistance of Walmart Workers in China: A Missed Opportunity

Anita Chan

Recently, Walmart workers in China joined hands with their international counterparts to move forward in the struggle against the American retail giant. This development has momentous implications for the Chinese labour movement, which is finally linking up with the outside world without going through any intermediary. Yet, this achievement urgently needs international support to be maintained.

On 21 June, the Walmart Chinese Workers' Association (*wo'erma zhongguo yuangong lianyihui*, WCWA) announced in its blog that it had joined hands in cyberspace with its American counterpart, OUR Walmart (Organisation United for Respect at Walmart), to discuss how to move forward in their struggle against the company. In a show of solidarity, the WCWA also launched a campaign in support of American Walmart workers' fight for a fifteen US dollar minimum wage. This marked a new stage in recent Chinese labour history. This time the news was not about a leader of the All-China Federation of Trade Unions (ACFTU), the official government trade union, shaking hands with a leader from a foreign trade union. Nor was it Han Dongfang, the well-known director of the Hong Kong-based China Labour Bulletin, shaking hands with the world's trade union leaders. Instead, a group of workers had themselves, through persistent efforts to break through Chinese walls, finally succeeded in reaching out to co-workers overseas. This appeared to be the culmination of a number of breakthroughs over the last decade, but then, after a few months of hard struggle, the movement encountered a setback. In this article, I will outline the background of the struggle of Walmart workers, illustrate its significance, and analyse the causes of its ultimate failure.

Zhang Jun: Electrician and Labour Activist

Walmart in China has more than four hundred stores in 169 cities, and employs around one hundred thousand people. The WCWA is an online network linking up a large number of Walmart employees across the country. It was set up in 2014 by two Walmart workers: Zhang Jun, an electrician then employed at a Walmart store in Yantai City, Shandong Province, and Zhang Liya, who was working in a store in Shenzhen. Their original intention was to create a platform where Walmart workers could exchange experiences, air grievances, and provide moral support to each other.

Zhang Jun was involved in union organising even before he started working at Walmart. In fact, he had helped organise the first democratically-elected workplace union born out of a strike in China (Chan 2015). The year was 2006. A group of sixty women workers in a small Danish electronics company named Ole Wolff felt aggrieved at the fact that the manager refused to pay social security contributions and agitated to set up their own union. Zhang, the husband of one of these workers, was then a blue-collar worker in a factory nearby and became their legal consultant. They struggled for four years against management and the district-level trade union to keep their union going. At one point, Zhang was exchanging texts with one of the ACFTU's deputy chairs, who flew to Shandong to personally instruct the provincial union to recognise the Ole Wolff union. The fight ended in 2010, when Ole Wolff deliberately relocated the factory to South China. In the meantime, Zhang had lost his own job and in March 2011 he became a Walmart worker in his neighbourhood.

2006: A Year of Significance

The chain of events that led to the emergence of the WCWA can be traced back to 2006. At that time, Andy Stern, the president of the

A group of Walmart worker activists stages a protest at a Walmart store in Shenzhen on 29 June. On the back of their shirts is written: 'Walmart employees stand up; boycott the comprehensive working hour system; oppose cheating and keep protecting our rights.' PC: WCWA

Service Employees International Union, one of the biggest unions in the United States, was launching an international campaign against Walmart. He had come to China a couple of times seeking to persuade the ACFTU to join the global anti-Walmart campaign and it so happened that the ACFTU at the time was under strong pressure from the party-state to contain the rising number of strikes in the country. This instigated the ACFTU to do something that it had not done since the 1950s—organise workers.

Up until that point, whenever it had wanted to set up a branch in a company, the ACFTU had gone directly to the management to establish a workplace union that managers would be able to control. This time, however, the ACFTU experimented with organising Walmart workers 'underground'. In less than two months, the ACFTU was able to set up about one and half dozen Walmart union branches, holding surreptitious night-time union committee elections and founding ceremonies (Chan 2006). But after two months, the ACFTU changed its mind and signed a memorandum of understanding with Walmart, which effectively allowed the company to set up management-controlled unions in more than one hundred stores. Since then, Walmart union branches have been staffed by human resource managers, who have signed so-called 'collective agreements' in the name of the workers (Chan 2011). Yet, as of today the ACFTU still boasts of its high unionisation rate in China's Walmart stores.

Still, the initial spate of democratic elections in 2006 had unintended consequences. Some workers who had participated in those elections wanted to get their unions back. In the following years, when some of the workplace union branches were due for new elections, they fought to register as candidates. Walmart management, with the tacit support of the local unions, put a variety of obstacles in their way. In 2015, Zhang Liya was fired for trying to run. He then sued Walmart, lost the first appeal, and is now waiting for the ruling of the second. In September 2014, Zhang Jun and Zhang Liya decided to establish the WCWA, which grew out of a series of online chat groups in which Walmart workers shared their experiences and gave each other advice on how to deal with problems in their workplaces all over China. In 2016, Zhang Jun quit his job at Walmart.

The Latest Struggle: the 'Comprehensive Working Hour System'

In mid-May 2016, Walmart announced that it was going to use a 'comprehensive working hour system', which is very similar to American Walmart's 'open work hour system' (see the brief on p. 42 of the present book), allowing extreme flexibility in the allocation of work hours. This meant that there would be no more overtime and thus no more overtime pay, which workers have been relying on to supplement the low income. Suddenly the number of people in the WCWA's online groups jumped to around ten thousand.

Drawing from Zhang Jun's experience at Ole Wolff a decade ago, one of the WCWA's strategies was to hold the trade union responsible for its failure to stop Walmart's flagrant abuse. The WCWA sent appeals for help to different levels of the ACFTU, including two open letters signed by a thousand workers addressed to the union headquarters (WCWA 2016). They also lodged a series of complaints about Walmart's violations of the Chinese labour law and the company's heavy-handedness in forcing workers to sign a consent form for the new working hour system.

Some managers, who were under intense pressure from upper levels of Walmart to collect these signatures, reportedly locked some workers who refused to sign in storage rooms, and threatened them with demotion and layoffs. Other workers were inundated by management phone calls and texts, and two workers even suffered mental breakdowns due to the incessant hounding from their superiors.

On 14 June, the Guangdong Province Federation of Trade Unions made a sudden public newspaper statement that a Walmart-style work hour system can only be used by workplaces that operate a special roster system (Xu 2016). Retail stores were not eligible to apply, and using it is a violation of the labour law. Blatantly missing from this statement was any mention of Walmart, or of the fact that some Walmart workers were in rebellion. For a while, it seemed the workers had gained a small victory. But because the union had not taken any concrete action besides these generic declarations (Huang 2016), the announcement did not deter Walmart from continuing to force workers to sign off on the new work hour system.

Strike as the Last Option

Having exhausted all possible channels to stop Walmart's coercion, workers in a Walmart store in Jiangxi province called 'Nanchang August First Walmart Store' 'fired the first shot'. On 1 July, starting at seven in the morning, seventy workers, all wearing the red Walmart uniforms with protest signs stuck on their backs, went marching up and down the store yelling slogans like 'Boycott Walmart's Comprehensive Working Hours System!' and 'Defend Our Rights to the End!' The news of the strike immediately spread through the WCWA network. Supportive messages poured in and the Nanchang August First Store was hailed as a model store by the aggrieved Walmart workers.

That the first strike broke out in this particular Walmart store is itself of great symbolic significance. 1 August was an important day and place for the city of Nanchang in Chinese Communist history. That day in 1927 the Nanchang Uprising led by key Chinese Communist Party leaders rose up against the Nationalist Party. The Nanchang Walmart workers prided themselves for having this privilege of starting a rebellion against the world's largest retailer in a store that bears this historically iconic name. They cried in unison: 'At this store, we are carrying on the glorious tradition of the Chinese Communist Party!'

A group of Walmart worker activists stages a protest at a Walmart store in Shenzhen on 29 June.
PC: WCWA

But still why this particular store? Indeed, for Walmart workers in China this store has a glorious past in its own right that has nothing to do with Chinese history. In 2006, this was one of the stores that were able to hold a genuinely democratic union election under the ACFTU's tutelage. An ordinary worker armed with self-taught knowledge of the labour law by the name of Gao Haitao ran as a candidate and was elected as the union chairman (Chan, 2011). He fought with Walmart management over a number of workplace issues. When Walmart issued a blanket collective agreement for all store unions to sign, Gao demanded some changes. The struggle became heated and the news passed upward to the ACFTU headquarters in Beijing. As a model of a courageous trade union chairman, Gao was invited to Beijing to meet with high-level union officials, but when he continued to resist signing the collective agreement, the ACFTU abandoned him and, in the end, he was fired. This case was widely reported in the Chinese press (China Labor News Translations 2008).

According to information circulated online in the WCWA network, the Nanchang store today is staffed by a sizeable number of older workers. Some of them must have fought alongside Gao years ago. It is thus not surprising that when the campaign against the new working hour system began, it was workers in this Nanchang store who came out first to declare that none of them had signed nor would sign the consent form.

On the second day of the strike, city authorities finally appeared at the store to find out what the protest was about. They then left and said that they would consider their complaints. In early July, one other store in Nanchang, one in Harbin, and one in Chengdu went on strike. Morale was then high among Walmart workers across the country.

Splits in the Movement

While activist members of the WCWA were immersed in daily struggle in the stores, some labour NGOs based in Guangdong Province entered the fray. Zhang Zhiru, the leader of a labour NGO based in Shenzhen, was particularly vocal in claiming a leading role in the struggle of Walmart workers. On several occasions, he publicly criticised the two WCWA founders for being too timid and cautious in dealing with the union and the authorities. He encouraged Walmart workers to set up a new group, the 'Walmart Workers Coordinating Committee' (*wo'erma yuangong xietiao huiyuanhui*), which purportedly would be a structured organisation strong enough to demand Walmart to come to the bargaining table.

Zhang Jun and his colleagues reacted with strong statements warning the members of WCWA about these attempted 'interferences from external powers' (Wechat 8 July 2016). This split had a devastating effect not only on the morale of the Walmart workers, but also on the relationship among labour NGO activists themselves, who had to take sides with one or the other while they still were right in the middle of one of the worst crackdowns against NGOs in recent history.

A Walmart worker in Chengdu holds a sign in support of American Walmart workers' fight for a 15 USD minimum wage.

Arguably, behind what at first seemed to be a strategic divergence—Zhang Jun's idea of cooperating with the unions against Zhang Zhiru's advocacy of a more confrontational type of collective bargaining—is the issue of funding. As international funds are rapidly drying up—a situation that is bound to get worse with the enforcement of the new Foreign NGO Management Law in January 2017 (see the compendium of the Law on pp. 60-67 of the present book)—some NGOs are becoming desperate to find new sources of sustainment. In order to attract the attention of foreign donors and secure their financial support, now more than ever they need to claim credit for workers' struggles, especially in high profile cases.

The open confrontation in the chatrooms between two sides, with a continuous exchange of venomous accusations of greed, official collusion, and corruption, filled the workers with consternation. Participation in the WCWA network went into free fall. The damage was so serious that an activist in a labour NGO privately told me that he believed that this clash between workers and NGOs—as well as among NGOs themselves—in the end had done more harm to the labour movement than the government crackdown. Before, labour NGOs were somehow united against a common enemy, now they are rift apart by mutual suspicion.

Taking advantage of this confusion, Walmart went on the offensive, forcing workers to sign the consent form and lashing out at the recalcitrant workers who refused. The retaliation has been relentless,

A group of Walmart worker activists stages a protest at a Walmart store in Shenzhen on 29 June.

A Missed Opportunity

with some employees being fired. The only thing die-hard activists can do now is to try to sue Walmart for wage theft and unfair treatment and dismissal. Despite the initial announcements that Walmart was breeching the law, local unions and the higher echelons of the ACFTU have not lifted a finger to help the workers.

What seemed to be a promising protest movement involving large numbers of workers coordinating on social media collapsed as quickly as it had begun. This exposed the shortcomings in totally relying on the social media as an organising vehicle. Co-ordination is still difficult and unsustainable. But a bigger lesson learned by workers and labour NGOs alike is that foreign funding—as well as the lack thereof—can have a corrosive effect on labour solidarity. Unfortunately, there is every reason to believe that this is bound to get worse in the near future.

Anita Chan

Anita Chan is Visiting Fellow at the Political and Social Change Department, the Australian National University. Prior to that, she was Research Professor at University of Technology Sydney. Her current research focuses on Chinese labour issues. She has published widely on Chinese workers' conditions, the Chinese trade union, and labour rights issues. On Walmart, she published the edited volume *Walmart in China* (2011). Her other recent publications include the edited books *Labor in Vietnam* (2011) and *Chinese Workers in Comparative Perspective* (2015).

Southern China Countryside
PC: Paz Lee

What Does Wukan Have to Do With Democracy?

Luigi Tomba

In September 2011, the village of Wukan, Guangdong Province, made international headlines for its violent protests against the illegal sale of land by their corrupt village elite. Villagers were successful in both toppling the existing village leadership and electing, in their stead, the moral leaders of the revolt as their new village committee. A few months ago, the original leader of the protests was arrested on unclear corruption charges, an event that led to violent clashes between villagers and police. Is Wukan's sad story an example of a conscious democratic challenge to the existing system?

In September 2011, the village of Wukan in Eastern Guangdong province became the centre of a media storm and made international headlines for its violent protests against the illegal sale of land by their established, and corrupt, village elite. Village leaders had taken it upon themselves to sell large chunks of village land without consulting the villagers, formally the collective owners of the land-use rights. Villagers in Wukan were successful in both toppling the existing village leadership and electing, in their stead, the moral leaders of the revolt as their new village committee. What was more important, in the tightly controlled Chinese system of village elections, was that villagers were allowed to cast a secret ballot.

Yet, despite international media calling Wukan the ultimate example of a democratic trend in rural China (Wong 2016), the situation of the villagers changed little. The government claimed that part of the land-stealing controversy was resolved 'according to the law', which took some of the wind out of the sails of the collective protests. Ultimately, however, the land-use rights were not returned to their owners. The new leadership rapidly split and members of the newly elected village committee were then investigated for petty acts of corruption and were themselves forced to write 'confessions'. The original leader of the protests, Lin Zuluan, was re-elected in 2015 with ninety per cent of the votes, only to be arrested on unclear corruption charges in mid-2016 (Birtles 2016). As it so often happens in these corruption cases, facts and circumstances are hard to ascertain. An *Al Jazeera* series of reports exposed the banality of village in-fighting between 2012 and 2015, along with the progressive re-assertion of state control over the conflict-ridden village (Lee and Leong 2013). The arrest of Lin, seen by many as a moral beacon in this complex story, led to new violent clashes with the police, and to the almost inevitable analysis of the end of Wukan's 'democratic experiment'.

Is Wukan's sad story an example of a conscious democratic challenge to the existing system, as it has often been argued? Is every conflict in China that attracts the attention of the media a new step towards an inevitable democratic future? The battles in the streets, with national flag-bearing villagers throwing stones at riot police are generated much less by a desire to change the political system than they are by the exclusion of countless villagers from the spoils of economic growth and urbanisation. Villagers have seen the value of their land grow and the profits of urbanisation being appropriated by greedy local elites in the name of national development. Villagers' slogans are invariably about the redressing of a wrong, not a call for a rather distant idea of democracy. In a competition with the predatory urban governments, the cards are stacked against the village collectives, often leaving little alternative to violence. And these conflicts are everywhere, potentially much more significant for prosperity, stability, and justice in China than for its democratic future. Arguing that the story of Wukan is about China's transition into a liberal democracy would be forgetting the structural conditions that have led to this local conflict in the first place.

Urbanisation and Land Ownership

To explain some of these conditions, let's take a step back. One of the pillars of China's authoritarian system, and the main remnant of its socialist planned past, is the public ownership of land. In the cities, this takes the form of 'state ownership' while in the countryside the collectives (the villages) can claim the ownership of use rights over agricultural land. Villages are not formally considered to be a level of 'government', but are instead a level of 'self-administration'—a subtle but important distinction that contributes to explaining why villages committees are the only part of the governance structure where leaders can be elected, not appointed.

In this context, urbanisation inevitably necessitates the 'conversion' of collectively owned land into state-owned land. Urban administrations reap significant advantages from conversion, as the price of expropriation or acquisition of rural land is invariably a small fraction of the price that they can obtain when they lease the land on the market. The competition is very intense and a matter of survival for both villagers and urban governments. Various estimates suggest that, on average, villagers end up being significantly short-changed. According to a report by Jiang Ming at Peking University, the market price of expropriated land is, on average, more than fourteen times higher than the cost of compensation (Tomba 2014). There are, of course, substantial variations, and some strategically located peri-urban villages have successfully negotiated handsome compensation packages through unified and collective bargaining, especially when, because of rapid urbanisation, some of these 'urban villages' have ended up owning land in central areas of Guangzhou or Shenzhen. Yet, in general, these remain the exception rather than the rule, and local governments use violence and even local thugs to evict village residents (Sargeson 2013).

City governments can be only partly blamed for having such an aggressive stance. This is because growth in their territory, their capacity to provide services to an increasing population, and their implementation of higher-level government policies remain highly dependent on land. Because of the centralised taxation system, land fees are among the few components of an urban government's revenue that stay local. This has turned cities into aggressive agents of expropriation as, according to the law, rural land can only be turned into 'construction land' once it has been converted to state-owned land and their inhabitants relocated or given an urban household registration (*hukou*). Despite central attempts to limit expropriation in the name of the preservation of the already limited amount of arable land in the country, the dependence of local governments on land sales has continued to grow over the last decade. On average, more than one quarter of urban governments' budget depends on land fees, and in some cities it is as high as forty or fifty per cent. In 2012 alone, income from land fees grew nationwide by more the forty-six per cent.

The Plight of Chinese Villagers

Villagers, for their part, have experienced expropriation since the 1980s. In the early period, it was easier for them to justify the state's intervention with the needs of economic development. Yet, after three decades of successive expropriations, the cases of neighbouring villages and the declining attraction of urban welfare (an urban registration was often offered in exchange for land-use rights) have made it more difficult and expensive to convince farmers to give up their land. With a much greater flow of information, they now know how much governments speculate on the land that is taken away from them, and they are no longer ready to sacrifice their interests in the name of national development.

Many 'rural' villages on the outskirts of large cities are also no longer relying on agriculture. Despite the legal limitations, they have often built significant collective industrial economies on their land and are now living from rent paid by factories, as well as the income generated by a growing army of migrant workers who need accommodation, food, and services. They no longer see their land as a munificent concession of the socialist state but as a long-held entitlement, and have created complex local institutions to control their collective economies. Shareholding cooperatives have been set up, for example, that spread from Guangdong to many other parts of the country, turning villagers into shareholders of their village corporation. Shares (that cannot be sold outside of the collective) have now replaced land, and traditional village elites have consolidated their capacity to decide on important aspects of the village economy with limited consultation with the villagers.

These are concerns that Wukan's villagers are familiar with and clearly not only theirs. About two-thirds of the estimated 187,000 collective conflicts a year across the country have something to do with land. Last year, land also replaced corruption as the main area of dissatisfaction in the government's work among Chinese citizens (Forsythe 2015), probably suggesting that, while the centrally engineered anti-corruption campaign is generating positive vibes, the aggressive stance of local urban governments (and the growing prices of real estate) is increasingly becoming a focal point in China's public opinion.

Wukan as Symptom of a Rural Malaise

When we think of Wukan in these terms, the democratic content of the violent resistance to the government's attempt to re-establish control over the village is hardly an indication of a growing democratic awareness, or a strong opposition to the existing institutions. Rather, the grievances stemming from the long-term infringement of local interests and the perception of being cheated by the local government contribute decisively to strengthening the resolve of these villagers. Yet, they hardly see the change of the current institutional arrangements as a solution to their grief. Much of the contestation has to do with the corruption of some officials. The election of their own leaders was supposed to return the land that was originally sold without their consent. The autonomy and special rules in the Wukan elections are part of the concessions resulting from the bargaining process in which local governments invariably engage when conflicts arise. By keeping that autonomy local—the result of specific negotiations, not a rule change—they very efficiently deny the possibility that a more democratic arrangement can emerge, that the legitimacy of higher-level leadership is affected, and that, eventually, the Wukan experience is systematically replicated.

This incident, and the massive contestation in the village between 2012 and 2016 is a very visible sign of China's rural malaise. Urbanising China is a massive attempt to nationalise its territory, to absorb collective economies that have in the last two decades been at the centre of China's industrialisation. It is driven by the structural needs of urban governments and observed with continuous apprehension by central authorities, always ready to tailor their intervention to the different realities of urbanisation in the country, to quell conflicts when they risk spilling beyond their local dimension. To look at Wukan as an experiment in local democracy would be too generous an evaluation for the current authoritarian government.

Luigi Tomba

Luigi Tomba worked at the Australian National University for over fifteen years. Since 2017, he is the director of the China Studies Centre at the University of Sydney. While his early research focused on China's labour reform, Luigi's best-known work is on urbanisation, the social engineering of a Chinese urban middle class, and land reform. His most recent book, *The Government Next Door*, won the 2016 Joseph Levenson Prize.

The Foreign NGOs Management Law: A Compendium

Ivan Franceschini, Elisa Nesossi

> *Recently, people from the State Security who had summoned me to 'have a tea' said to me: 'Us from the State Security are still quite civilised, but with this coming law that will regulate NGOs you will have to deal with the Public Security [i.e. the police]. You have to understand that their work methods are rather savage.' Actually, this was also a pressure of kind, you can read it as some sort of well-intentioned warning.*
> (Interview with a Chinese labour activist, Shenzhen, June 2015)

On 1 January 2017, the highly controversial Law on the Management of Foreign NGOs' Activities within Mainland China entered into force. As defined in Article 1, the Law was introduced with the aim of 'standardising and guiding all the activities carried out by overseas NGOs within China, and protecting their rights and interests.' From January 2017, those foreign NGOs that have been operating in the People's Republic of China in a legal limbo are required to act according to the principles established by this Law. Although some scholars have argued that the Law can be interpreted as a positive development in China's process of legal development and acceptance of international standards (Sapio 2016), we fail to see how this can be the case (see also the Forum on pp. 68–73 in the present book). At this stage it appears to us that the limits imposed by the Law on the practice of foreign NGOs significantly outweigh its alleged benefits. A number of provisions within the Law are extremely vague and urgently require further explanation by the relevant authorities. Still, on this matter we are unable to share the optimism of long-time observer of Chinese civil society Shawn Shieh who, in a valuable exegesis of the Law that appeared earlier on his personal blog, noted that some flexibility may be allowed in the implementation phase (Shieh 2016). Here below we offer our short analysis of the legislation in the form of FAQs to explain its scope and significance. For the translation into English of the contents of the Law, we wish to acknowledge our debt to the excellent version that appeared on *China Law Translate* (China Law Translate 2016).

What is an NGO and what kind of activities fall within the scope of the Law on the Management of Foreign NGOs' Activities within Mainland China?

The Law broadly defines NGO as 'non-profit, non-governmental, social organisations lawfully established outside Mainland China, such as foundations, social groups, and think tank organisations' (Art. 2) that can operate in fields such as 'economics, education, science and technology, culture, health, sports, and environmental protection, and in areas such as poverty alleviation and disaster relief' (Art. 3). In carrying out their activities, these organisations are required to abide by Chinese laws, and not to endanger China's national unity, security or ethnic solidarity, as well as not to harm China's national interests, the common good of the society and the lawful rights and interests of citizens, legal persons, and other organisations (Art. 5). Furthermore, they must not engage in or fund for-profit activities, political or religious activities (Art. 5).

Be aware that:

The range of activities NGOs can engage in, as listed in Articles 3 and 5, exclude issues that may be deemed politically sensitive, like work for the protection of labour rights and human rights (in particular civil and political rights). Article 5 is particularly vague and potentially problematic. Firstly, the meaning of 'political activity' remains unclear. In fact, the specific work in the allowed fields of operation for foreign NGOs as well as numerous policies encouraging charity and volunteer services are political at some level, and as such, might be excluded from the protection of the Law. Secondly, while it is reasonable to expect that a foreign NGO would not violate China's key national interests like national security, national unity and ethnic unity, it is important to understand the context in which these terms are phrased within Chinese law and how they may be broadly applied to incriminate a wide range of activities within society. Indeed in recent years, there have been numerous examples of NGO workers and activists having been incriminated under the existing criminal laws for endangering China's national security and interests, and in the future, in view of this Law, these circumstances might well extend to foreign NGOs. Thirdly, expressions like 'ethnic solidarity' and 'the common good of society' remain extremely vague and easily resonate with crimes concerning the disruption of public order frequently used to incriminate various categories of citizens who are considered a potential threat to social stability.

Do foreign universities fall within the reach of this law?

Article 53 of the Law states that 'where foreign schools, hospitals, natural science and engineering technology research institutions or academic organisations carry out exchanges or co-operation with Mainland Chinese schools, hospitals, natural science and engineering technology research institutions or academic organisations, it is handled according to the relevant national provisions, unless these activities violate the principles listed in Article 5.' This provision—which was inserted only in the final version of the Law and is one of the very few concessions made by the legislators to the critics—indicates that certain forms of educational exchange could be exempted from the registration requirements imposed on foreign NGOs, and that other laws should govern these kinds of activities instead.

Be aware that:

Much clarification is still needed in relation to what constitutes 'exchanges' and 'co-operation'. As some commentators have mentioned already, it is unclear whether exchanges and co-operation may include programmes between foreign schools and Chinese entities which do not operate schools (for example, third party providers of abroad programs or student internships), and unilateral programs of foreign schools (e.g., a faculty-led short-term summer program that is organised without affiliation with any Chinese partner). It is also unclear whether a foreign university that goes to China to recruit, or to meet with its alumni, is required to either register as a representative office of a foreign NGO or work with a Chinese co-operative body and secure an approval and record filing for temporary activities from relevant Chinese authorities.

What are the organs in charge of the registration and supervision of foreign NGOs?

According to the Law, the Ministry of Public Security (MPS) and the provincial public security bureaus (PSBs) are in charge of the registration of foreign NGOs carrying out activities within Mainland China (Art. 6). The PSBs at the county level or above are required to supervise and manage the activities of foreign NGOs and to provide services for their activities (Art. 7) (note that the Law refers to public security departments as 'registration and management organs'). In order to register with the public security authorities and establish a representative office, foreign NGOs should receive the consent of Professional Supervisory Units established under the State Council (Arts. 6 & 11). Once registered, they will be supervised first by the PSBs, then by a Professional Supervisory Unit at the local government level and by any other supervisory authorities responsible for national security, finance, foreign affairs, customs or tax (Art. 43).

Be aware that:
Foreign NGOs' supervision by the public security authorities is one of the most problematic aspects of the legislation. Currently, Chinese NGOs are supposed to register with the Ministry of Civil Affairs, but most of them—especially those that work in politically sensitive areas—are in fact refused registration and therefore are informally supervised by the State Security. Very few foreign NGOs are registered within China and, given their unclear legal status, their activities are informally monitored through their local partners. Giving control to the public security (rather than the Ministry of Civil Affairs) reflects the Law's emphasis on security, rather than a willingness to facilitate meaningful co-operation. It signals that, according to Chinese authorities, foreign NGOs have the potential to threaten social stability and security and, for this reason, they should be kept under control by one of the most politically powerful ministries within China. It remains to be seen whether the MPS—which lacks any relevant experience in managing civil society organisations—actually has the capacity to manage NGOs.

How to register a representative office in China?

In order to carry out any activity in Mainland China, foreign NGOs should register and establish a representative office. The Law sets out the following five requirements that a foreign NGO should satisfy in order to register and establish a representative office within China: a) it should be legally established outside of Mainland China; b) it should be able to independently bear civil liability; c) the objectives and scope of activities defined in its organisational charter should be beneficial to the development of social welfare; d) it should have continuously carried out substantive activities outside of Mainland China for two or more years; e) other requirements provided by other laws and regulations (Art. 10). A foreign NGO that meets the above criteria should submit an application for registration within thirty days after having received consent by a Professional Supervisory Unit listed in a directory published by the public security organs (Arts. 11, 12). The application should include the following materials: a) a written application; b) supporting documents and materials certifying that the NGO complies with the requirement outlined in Art. 10; c) proof of identity, resumé and materials or attestations showing proof of no criminal record for the proposed chief representative; d) materials showing the proposed premises for the representative office; e) materials showing the sources of capital; f) documents of consent from the professional supervisory unit; g) other documents and materials required by law or by administrative regulations. If the registration is granted, the foreign NGO representative office will obtain a registration certificate that it will use to register for taxes, get an official seal and establish an account at a bank in Mainland China (Art. 13).

Be aware that:
First, some of the criteria included in Article 10 are extremely vague and may easily exclude some foreign NGOs from the possibility of registering within Mainland China. Indeed, it remains unclear according to which standards an activity can be deemed 'beneficial to the development of social welfare' and what the

'other requirements provided by other laws and regulations' could be. Second, the Law does not specify whether a foreign NGO has the right to appeal decisions by the public security authorities and Professional Supervisory Units if registration is not granted. Finally, foreign NGOs are supposed to choose a local Professional Supervisory Unit from a list published by the public security organs 'together with the relevant departments' (Art. 11). This will clearly limit their choices and introduce an additional layer of supervision and control that will further restrict their ability to operate in China.

Is it possible to operate without a representative office?

Unregistered foreign NGOs that wish to conduct temporary activities within China should legally file a record (Art. 9). Foreign NGOs that have not registered and established representative offices or filed a record to carry out temporary activities are not entitled to carry out activities within Mainland China, and must not entrust or fund, or covertly entrust or fund, any unit or individual in Mainland China to carry out activities within the country (Art. 9). Temporary activities can be carried out only in co-operation with state organs, mass organisations, public institutions, or social organisations (Art. 16). It will be the Chinese partner unit who will have to file with the public security organs for the proposed activity at least fifteen days before activities are carried out (except for emergency situations) (Art. 17). The Law provides that 'temporary activities' cannot last for more than one year and that where 'there is truly a need to extend the period', a new filing shall be made (Art. 17). Beside this, the law clearly states that 'units and individuals in Mainland China must not accept retention, funding, agency, or covert agency to carry out foreign NGOs' activities in Mainland China, from foreign NGOs that have not registered a representative office or filed to carry out temporary activities' (Art. 32).

Be aware that:
This process entails the establishment of a closer relationship between the Chinese partner organisation—which needs to be officially sanctioned, for instance the official trade union, a university, or an NGO with a regular registration as a social organisation—and the public security authorities. This will inevitably lead to a closer scrutiny of the local partner by the police organs. Given the fact that most Chinese NGOs, especially in politically sensitive fields, cannot register as social organisations, the restrictions imposed by Article 32 of the Law make it almost impossible for international entities to fund most local NGOs, severely curtailing the ability of local civil society organisations to access foreign funding and putting even more pressure on Chinese activists (as highlighted by the quote which we added at the beginning of this compendium). The parameters for renewing a one-year permit for temporary activity remain unclear and it is not clarified whether multiple temporary activities can be carried out either simultaneously or in subsequent years.

Can a foreign NGO establish more than one office in Mainland China?

The Law establishes that the representative office of a foreign NGO in China can carry out activities only within their registered operational scope and region, and it cannot establish branch organisations within China, except as otherwise provided by the State Council (Art. 18).

Be aware that:
Prohibiting the establishment of branches and restricting the work of NGOs only within their registered region impose very serious operational limitations on the type and scope of activities that can be carried out. This provision has the potential to limit multiple

partners' co-operation and diversification of activities. The option for approval by the State Council is left extremely vague and it remains completely unclear what the scope and significance of exception might entail.

What are the planning and reporting requirements?

There are two types of reports that a representative office has to submit annually to the Chinese authorities: an activity plan and an annual work report. First, the NGO representative office is required to submit to the Professional Supervisory Unit before the end of each calendar year an activity plan for the following year, including a description of project implementation, use of funds, and other similar content (Art. 19). Within ten days of approval, the representative office has to file the plan with the public security authorities (Art. 19). When variations of the activity plan are necessary, these must be promptly filed with the public security authorities (Art. 19). Second, foreign NGO representative offices are required to file annual work reports to Professional Supervisory Units before 31 January each year (Art. 31). These reports shall include content such as audited financial accounting reports, and reports on the situation of activities, as well as personnel or institutional changes (Art. 31). When dealing with 'temporary activities', foreign NGOs must send written reports to the public security authorities within thirty days of concluding temporary activities. These reports must include information on the state of activities and the use of funds (Art. 30).

Be aware that:
While planning and reporting are very reasonable requirements for an NGO to operate legally, the Law however is fairly vague on the level of detail required by the annual plan. It is unclear the extent to which such planning will allow a degree of flexibility for the implementation of ad hoc activities or activities in an emergency situation. In case of both temporary and planned activities, it remains unclear how reports will be used, whether they will be simply filed by the relevant authorities or whether they will constitute the basis for approving future activities by the same NGOs.

What funds can be used to support activities within Mainland China?

The Law explains that foreign NGOs are allowed to use the following funding: a) funds from lawful sources outside of Mainland China; b) interests on bank deposits within Mainland China; and c) other funds lawfully obtained within Mainland China (Art. 21). Foreign NGOs and their representative offices must not fundraise within Mainland China (Art. 21). These funds—which must be used only in accordance with the registered scope of operations (Art. 23)—must be deposited in the bank account that is recorded on the official registration documents or, in the case of temporary activities, the bank account of the Chinese partner unit (Art. 22). Any other strategy to receive funding from abroad is explicitly forbidden (Art. 22) and wire transfers will have to be used in accordance with China's relevant provisions on regulation of foreign exchanges and payments (Art. 25).

Be aware that:
While these provisions might have been thought of as a way to control illegal money movements from outside and within China, they however present some contradictions and limitations. Article 21 allows for funding to be obtained within Mainland China but excludes the possibility of fundraising within the country. As the activity of fundraising is not defined in this Law, it potentially excludes a significant portion of funding that could come from within the country. It also creates opportunities for funding obtained lawfully to be considered illegal because it is attained through alleged fundraising. The Law also

excludes the possibility, or makes it extremely difficult, for Chinese citizens to donate to foreign NGOs operating in China, closing avenues for China's wealthy to contribute to international philanthropy.

What about accounting and taxes?

According to the Law, foreign NGO representative offices are required to implement China's unified accounting system, hiring accountants with Chinese professional certifications to carry out their accounting (Art. 24). Mainland Chinese accounting firms are required to audit foreign NGOs' financial accounting reports (Art. 24). Tax registration, tax declarations, and payment of taxes must be dealt with in accordance with the law (Art. 26), but it is explicitly stated that foreign NGO representative offices enjoy tax and other policy benefits according to the law (Art. 36).

Be aware that:
There are at least two main problematic issues concerning the required system of accounting and taxes. In terms of accounting, foreign NGOs are financially accountable to their donors, which generally impose strict accounting reporting standards. The imposition of carrying out accounting within China according to China's unified accounting system may either benefit the process of accounting for international donors, or hinder the process if the two systems are completely different, imposing significant operational burdens on the foreign NGOs. The requirements concerning taxes are utterly vague. It remains unclear what taxation regime will apply to foreign NGOs and what benefits, if any, they could potentially enjoy. It is also left unspecified whether these accounting requirements and taxes provisions apply to foreign NGOs conducting temporary activities.

Who should staff a representative office?

The Law states that foreign NGO representative offices can hire employees in Mainland China as long as they follow local laws and administrative regulations, and that all the information regarding employed personnel must be reported to the professional supervisory units and to the public security organs (Art. 27). Representative offices can designate a chief representative and up to three representatives as required for operations, but they must not be: a) persons lacking or having limited civil capacity; b) persons with a criminal record; c) chief representatives or representatives of representative offices that have been de-registered or had registration certificates cancelled within the past five years; d) other situations provided by the law or regulations (Art. 29). As for the expatriate staff, the Law provides that 'the chief representative and other representatives that are foreign employees of foreign NGO representative offices may use the organisation's registration certificate, documents proving the representative's status, and other materials to process employment and work permits in accordance with the law' (Art. 38).

Be aware that:
The clause 'other situations provided by the law or regulations' included in Article 29 is extremely vague and may be broadly interpreted by the public security authorities to exclude anybody who is deemed inadequate according to undefined standards. The Law is also silent in relation to the conditions for hiring volunteers.

What does supervision and management by the Chinese relevant authorities entail?

The Law provides that public security authorities are not only responsible for the registration of the NGOs' representative offices, annual inspections and the filing of temporary activities, but they have also a duty to investigate and punish illegal activities carried out by foreign NGOs. When public security organs suspect that a foreign NGO is violating this Law, they may adopt the following measures: a) question the chief representative and other responsible persons from the foreign NGO representative offices; b) enter the foreign NGOs' domicile and venues of activities within Mainland China to conduct on-site inspections; c) question units and individuals related to the investigation, and request an explanation; d) examine and reproduce documents or materials related to the matters being investigated, and seal documents or materials that might be removed, destroyed, concealed or tampered with; e) seal or seize venues, facilities, or assets suspected of being involved in illegal activities (Art. 41). Public security organs can also make inquiries into bank accounts of units or individuals related to the matter being investigated and request the courts to freeze bank account funds in accordance with the Criminal Procedure Law (Art. 42). Other departments, such as those for national security, foreign affairs, finance, financial oversight, customs, tax, and foreign experts are to conduct oversight and management of foreign NGOs and their representative offices in accordance with the scope of their duties and relevant laws (Art. 43). The anti-money laundering departments shall supervise and manage the opening and use of bank accounts by foreign NGOs, Chinese partner units, and also of units or individuals in Mainland China who receive funds from foreign NGOs (Art. 44).

Be aware that:
It appears that while the Law is fairly specific on what the public security authorities and other departments can do in case of suspicious activities, it imposes very few limitations on their actions. For example, on the basis of a simple suspicion, the public security can indiscriminately get access to individuals, their properties and domiciles without any significance restriction been imposed by the Law.

What are the penalties for non-compliance?

If a foreign NGO representative office or a foreign NGO carrying out temporary activities in China do not comply with the clauses that govern registration, filing, scope of activities, funds, reporting, supervision and inspection, they and the Chinese partner units will be given warnings or ordered to suspend activities for a given period by the public security organs, have illegal assets or unlawful gains confiscated; where the circumstances are considered serious, their registration certificate or temporary activity permit documents will also be withdrawn by the registration management organs and the temporary activities shut down (Art. 45). The same penalty applies where the representative offices of a foreign NGO, a foreign NGO carrying out temporary activities, or a Chinese partner unit provide false information to obtain registration certificates for representative offices or to obtain an authorisation to carry out temporary activities; or where there are acts of counterfeiting, altering, buying and selling, renting, or loaning registration certificates or seals (Art. 45). NGOs that have been de-registered cannot re-apply to set up representative offices in Mainland China or carry out temporary activities for five years from the date of de-registration, cancellation, or closure (Art. 48).

Article 46 explains that in circumstances where NGOs carry out activities without registration or filing, the public security organs can stop their activities, confiscate their illegally obtained property and unlawful gains, give directly responsible personnel warnings, and, in serious circumstances, detain them for up to ten days (Art. 46). The same applies to circumstances where units and individuals in Mainland China know that a foreign NGO has not registered or filed for temporary activities, and co-operate with them or accept their retention or funding, or act as their agent or covert agent to carry out activities for them or accept and spend funds for a project (Art. 46).

More serious penalties are provide for those foreign NGOs and foreign NGO representative offices that: a) incite resistance to the implementation of laws and regulations; b) illegally obtain state secrets; c) create rumours, engage in defamation, or the publication or dissemination of other harmful information that endangers state security or damages the national interest; d) engage in or funding political activities or illegal religious activities; e) other situations that endanger state security or damage the national or public interest (Art. 47). In such circumstances, the public security organs should cancel their registration certificates or shut down temporary activities; where a crime is not constituted, they will detain the persons who are directly in charge and other directly responsible personnel for up to fifteen days; and where a crime is constituted, criminal responsibility is pursued in accordance with the law (Art. 47). The same applies where foreign NGOs or foreign NGO representative offices exhibit criminal conduct such as separatism, undermining national unity, or subverting national sovereignty (Art. 47). These organisations may be added to an unwelcome list by the public security department under the State Council and must not again establish representative offices or carry out temporary activities within Mainland China (Art. 48).

When foreign persons violate this law, relevant organs may lawfully order them to leave the country within a given period of time, deport them, or expel them (Art. 50).

Be aware that:
Besides including a number of very vague clauses that can be easily used to justify arbitrary actions by the public security authorities in the name of protecting social order and stability—for instance, the publication of any critical report can be easily considered as 'dissemination of harmful information'—one problem that emerges from these provisions relates to the use of administrative detention for the personnel of foreign NGOs for up to fifteen days. It is well known that the public security authorities generally implement administrative detention without any judicial supervision and is in strict contrast with international fair trial standards.

FORUM

Edited by Ivan Franceschini and Kevin Lin

Ellen David Friedman

Ellen has been active in the Chinese labour movement for the last ten years, teaching labour studies and helping to found the International Center for Joint labour Research at Sun Yat-sen University in Guangzhou (closed by authorities in October 2014). Prior to this, she spent thirty years as a union organiser for public sector workers in the US, and contributed to the 'left pole' of the US labour movement, primarily through the Labour Notes project.

Kevin Slaten

Kevin has been researching Chinese labour rights, politics, and civil society since 2008. Until recently, Kevin was the Program Coordinator at China Labour Watch. He was previously a Fulbright teacher in Taiwan and a junior fellow at the Carnegie Endowment for International Peace.

May Wong

May was at the China Desk for the Asia Monitor Resource Centre (AMRC) for nine years. In this role, she was one of the key people to develop an informal network of labour NGOs in Mainland China in the late nineties. In 2006, she started to work with *Globalization Monitor*, focusing on extensive supply chain research and action and using brands and Corporate Social Responsibility as leverage to support labour rights.

A Civil Society Under Assault
A Debate among International Activists

Edited by Ivan Franceschini and Kevin Lin

As outlined in the previous chapter, the Foreign NGOs Management Law will deal a hard blow not only to foreign NGOs in China, but also to those Chinese organisations that work in sensitive fields and that are almost entirely reliant on foreign funding. Labour NGOs are, therefore, likely to suffer the most from the new rules. This Forum attempts to make sense of the current situation by posing questions to three international activists with extensive experience in the field: Ellen David Friedman, Kevin Slaten, and May Wong.

In your opinion, will the Foreign NGOs Management Law have a significant impact on Chinese labour NGOs?

Ellen David Friedman: Of course, it already had while it was not even a law yet. In China, the law is often 'advisory'. A law may not be enforced, or be enforced in wildly varying ways, and is coercive as an unpredictable and threatening presence. NGO activists will tell you that the state can—and already does—manage the presence of foreign NGOs in innumerable ways. For example, a couple of years ago, NGOs and other non-commercial 'units' were ordered to report on all foreign-sourced funds. Of course, this was understood not merely as a neutral inquiry, but a signal. One way to understand this law is as a sign of intent; a downward notch by the state in tolerating foreign 'interference'. But actually, in my view, it is not really directed at foreigners but at Chinese citizens. It is relatively easy for the government to shut the door on foreigners, but the problem remains—workers live miserable lives, lack security or dignity or a future, have no way to make things better, and so will continue to organise, strike, and force employers and the government to negotiate with them. This is not provoked by foreign influence, not funded by foreign foundations, but by a dynamic inherent in the political-economic system. So, yes, with this law we can expect further pressure on Chinese labour NGOs and their relationships with foreign funders, but we don't have to wait for the law to see the government is already increasing repression.

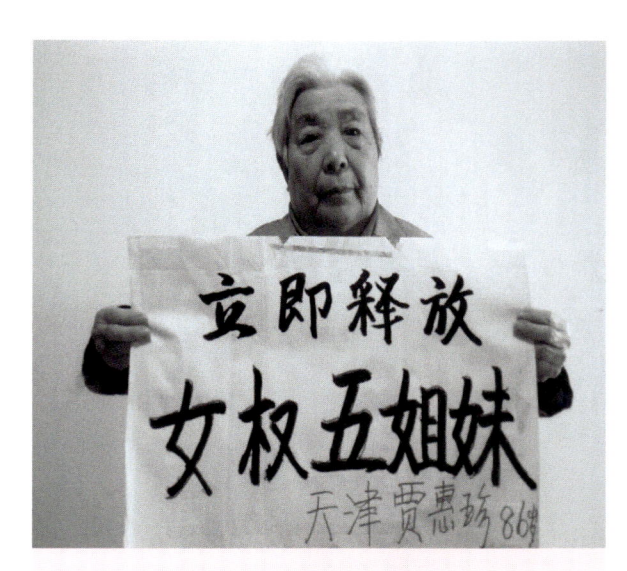

Eighty-six-year-old Jia Huizhen from Tianjin, China, holds a sign that says: "Release Feminist Sisters Now!" PC: 'Free Chinese Feminists' Facebook page

Kevin Slaten: Some of the labour activists and labour NGOs who have been most willing to walk the line of what is considered acceptable conduct under the Communist regime have been harassed, forcibly relocated, and now arrested. The repression has ramped up particularly over the past two years. It's important to note that this has all happened before the Foreign NGO Management Law was officially promulgated. It is difficult to imagine what actual new restrictions these regulations will create for labour NGOs. Most NGOs have been operating registered as businesses or unregistered altogether for years. So the authorities have long had the grounds to go after NGOs under the pretence of them operating outside of their organisational purview. Authorities have also carried out repression in the name of 'national security' and 'disturbing public order', which can be used by the government practically at will and without restraint. In this sense, the most significant part of the Foreign NGO Management Law for labour NGOs may not be the rules themselves but rather that the Law signals an intention by the government to more greatly restrict NGOs that are not under the thumb, or at least the close scrutiny, of the Party.

May Wong: As a Hong Kong labour activist and being treated as a foreign NGO, yes, I think that the law will have a significant impact on Chinese labour organisations because it puts lots of restrictions on the cooperation between foreign and local NGOs. This obviously aims at stopping local Chinese labour groups from getting overseas funds and making close contacts with foreign NGOs. For example, foreign NGOs, which fund mainland individuals or labour NGOs activities, or recruit local Chinese staff and volunteers, now need to apply for and get an approval from the authorities. This means that Chinese labour NGOs, which get foreign funds to support workers' rights in China, take greater risks. Labour activists could face long-term detention or imprisonment; in the worst case, they may be accused of being involved in activities that 'endanger China's national security' or 'harm China's national interests'. The law says that foreign NGOs must work with Chinese registered NGOs. However, most Chinese labour NGOs could not get official recognition as NGOs, and thus by law they cannot get foreign funds and work with foreign NGOs. Since it is impossible to get domestic funds to support labour rights in China, in the end the law will help to end Chinese labour NGOs.

What is your take on the latest wave of repression of labour NGOs? Why do you think it has taken place now? Is it an 'unprecedented' move by the Chinese authorities or part of a long-term trend?

Ellen David Friedman: I began working with labour NGOs in China around 2003, and believe I have observed three waves of repression since that time. Each has had some similar features. For example, whenever there is a crackdown, the offices of the NGOs will be visited by various local officials—from the water department, tax department, fire safety officers—and harassed about petty code violations. Often the landlord will abruptly cancel the lease, sometimes illegally, and evict the NGO. It is also very common over these years for government officials to 'drink tea' (*he cha*) with NGO staff or activists—to try and learn about their activities and deliver relatively polite warnings. But there have also been much more aggressive interventions by the government, often targeted at foreign funders, which impact on labour NGOs or university programs. In 2010, for example, Oxfam was bluntly forced to close programs at universities designed to expose students to public service experience. And sometimes the repression is violent—such as the knife attack that nearly killed labour NGO activist Huang Qingnan in 2007—which may have been initiated by bosses, but was done with little fear of state reprisal. So, no, I do not see this wave as unprecedented; far from it. At the same time, the repression is becoming deeper, broader, and more structured—the arrests of human rights lawyers, of the Feminist Five, and now of the Guangzhou labour activists, plus the targeting of foreign funders and other kinds of foreign influence—this appears to be a new stage.

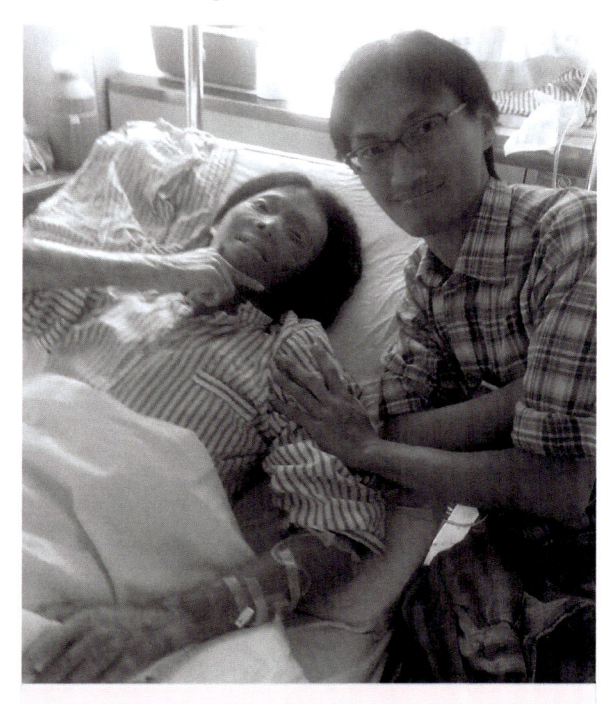

Shenzhen NGO activist Huang Qingnan (on the left) recovering in the hospital after a knife attack that nearly killed him in 2007.
PC: Inmediahk.net

Kevin Slaten: The tightening of space for labour NGOs seems to be at the intersection of at least two larger trajectories. One is the broad closing of space for civil society, especially those organisations and individuals who partake in activities that could be construed as challenging the authority of the Communist Party—which includes the All-China Federation of Trade Unions (ACFTU)—either through framing or organisational capacity. 2015 and 2016 witnessed broad harassment and arrests of feminists, lawyers, Christians, and other activists; the creation of new laws that further strengthen the government's basis for repressing voices in civil society, including laws around security, the Internet, and NGO management; and a clear intention of the Communist Party to reinstate its authority at every level of society. The other trajectory is the slowing of the economy. This is driven by overcapacity in real estate, infrastructure, and manufacturing, a long-term impending industrial shift as lower tech sectors head out of China, and a gruelling anti-graft campaign putting a drag on local economies which depended in part on a certain level of collusion between business and government. Widespread factory closures, lay-offs, and labour disputes have ensued, threatening a foundational thread of the Party's modern authority: a roaring economy and jobs. Some labour activists and NGOs exist at the intersection of these two trajectories. They are generally beholden to ideals that include fairness and justice, not beholden to the Party, which offends the first concern of the Party. The target population of labour NGOs also happens to be the group—workers—which is losing the most during the economic slowdown, which offends the Party's second concern. Given the framework above, in the long-term, either greater self-confidence on the part of the Communist Party or a return of rapid economic development could lead to the re-opening of space for labour NGOs. It is an open question when either of these factors will change anytime soon.

May Wong: The recent wave of repression against labour NGOs is an example meant to show the determination of the authorities to stop labour groups getting foreign funding. The Chinese economy has been slowing down and the export-oriented economy has been deteriorating. There have been lots of factory shutdowns, mergers, relocations to inner China or to other countries and thus many labour disputes and strikes to demand compensation. Labour NGOs in Guangdong have been using the recent provincial Regulations on Enterprise Collective Contracts to fight for the right of the workers to bargain collectively with factory bosses. The Regulations are not meant to be taken seriously, but labour activists really use them to empower the workers. The authorities fear that if they allow labour NGO to organise workers, the situation may get out of control. From this point of view, the crackdown is a way to stop the growing labour activism before the labour movement becomes stronger. Of course, this is not the first crackdown in China and, before this, the arrest of five women activists in March 2015 and the massive detention of lawyers also show that the authorities have changed their policy towards the development of civil society in China. Still, the crackdown is an 'unprecedented' move since China opened up its economy in the late 1970s, as it puts a halt on the growing labour activism and the overall growing civil society in mainland China.

In what way do you think the latest crackdown may change the landscape of civil society and what will it entail for the labour movement more generally?

Ellen David Friedman: In the last century or so, many countries adapted to the sharp inequalities of modern capitalism by establishing legal, enforceable channels for resolution of labour-capital disputes, including regulations for union elections, collective bargaining, arbitration, right to strike, and so on. Most of the progressive voices in China—labour activists, scholars, lawyers, and even a few trade union officials—yearned for that development, and were briefly optimistic around 2007 and 2008 that this might happen. But it did not. Now there is a dawning recognition that it will not, at least under the current government. So the inevitable result is that there will be continued extra-legal resistance by workers—strikes, sabotage, riots, mass petitions—that will encounter increased state repression. Civil society looks unlikely to develop. This means that it will be nearly impossible for workers to consolidate their knowledge, their experience of struggle, their trust of one another, in any kind of formal organisation; it won't be tolerated within the increasingly totalitarian framework. But, the direct resistance will of course continue, and I expect underground networks will inevitably continue to form—a harsh, but perhaps necessary, training ground for workers excluded from all other forms of self-determination.

Kevin Slaten: The crackdown may ultimately be aimed at trying to reassert the authority of the ACFTU among workers. By 'clearing out' the major potential organisational and principled challengers, the Party has ostensibly given the ACFTU an opportunity to become the hero for the massive proletariat created over the past two decades of neoliberal economic growth. To truly gain legitimacy among workers, the ACFTU would need to attain a much greater level of autonomy from the Party and representativeness for workers. But an autonomous union (or unions) would open up the door to a massive potential challenger to the Party, given the organisational potential of the union and the economic and political marginalisation of China's working class. Professor Eli Friedman discusses this predicament for the Party in his recent book, ***The Insurgency Trap***. It's worth mentioning that if the Communist Party ever arrived at a point where it was comfortable enough to allow the ACFTU to become more autonomous as a true organisation of Chinese workers, then the resulting political environment would also probably leave space for independent labour activists and NGOs.

May Wong: In the future, Chinese labour NGOs will face a tougher environment, but I am optimistic that these groups will be able to adapt. Even in the recent crackdown, it is possible to discern some positive signs. For example, despite all the dirty tricks played by the authorities, we see that the key detained activists fought the false accusations levied against them. This is a good sign for the sustainability of the Chinese labour movement, as it shows that these people have a remarkable commitment to their mission, which is fundamentally necessary to change the landscape of civil society in China. The authorities are well aware that labour activism in China is growing. For example, Meng Han, one of the activists detained in December 2015, was a worker representative in a labour dispute between security guards and a Guangzhou hospital, and had already been imprisoned for nine months in 2013. Roughly at the same time, Wu Guijun, a worker representative in a factory dispute in Shenzhen, was imprisoned for more than one year just because he took part in a strike. Instead of keeping silent after their release, both workers joined labour NGOs and continued to defend worker rights in South China. These two examples show that workers are more conscious about their class identity and more committed to organising their fellow workers. Imprisonment does not prevent them from upholding their mission.

How do you think the labour NGOs can best adapt to the new environment?

Ellen David Friedman: I am not at all optimistic. Of course it is up to those in the NGOs to decide their strategies, but their choices will become starker. If foreign funding is eventually choked off, will they look for ways to get these funds surreptitiously? That is very dangerous, but what are the alternatives? There really are not any domestic sources to fund labour NGOs. And who will carry on this work when NGO activists are surveyed, threatened, arrested, and immobilised? Some NGOs will try to change, and take up projects that are less sensitive—social enterprises, classes, cultural activities—but then the goal of promoting labour rights is lost. I expect that the state will largely succeed in disrupting and terminating the growth of labour NGOs in this period. But, the underlying problems will persist, and workers will still resist. So, out of this ferocious imbalance of power, something new will emerge. We just cannot see its outlines yet.

Kevin Slaten: It is not an easy environment in which to operate for people and organisations hoping to truly fight for the long-term interests of China's working class. Labour NGOs have a number of options. They can bide their time by occupying themselves with less risky activities, which are limited in scope and impact. Labour groups can cooperate with local authorities to participate in activities that are in line with official interests, including social stability and social services. Both of these paths lead to the continuation of labour's place in Chinese civil society, which is not all negative, even if it falls short of the hopes of political liberals inside and outside of China. Of course, despite the environment, labour NGOs can also choose to cross political lines, actively assist striking workers, and push for reforms through public advocacy. But they choose this road knowing that it carries a likely grave personal cost.

May Wong: The authorities should build up healthy labour relations by allowing space for workers and their elected representatives to resort to the various local collective consultation regulations to negotiate with bosses in order to improve wages and working conditions. They should also allow labour NGOs to support workers' rights where the official union remains inactive. I am optimistic that labour NGOs will find new ways to adapt to the new environment. After all, Pandora's box has been opened for a younger generation of Chinese migrant workers to develop their own ways to fight against capitalism for a better life, no matter how difficult the situation may be.

Walmart Workers on strike.
PC: Usilive.org and Controappuntoblog.org

JUL/SEP 2016

Walmart Workers on Strike

In July, the struggle of Walmart workers in China entered a new phase. Early that month, Walmart workers at retail stores in Nanchang, Chengdu, and Harbin staged wildcat strikes against the company's new working hour system (see Anita Chan's chapter on pp. 50-55 in the present book). Dozens of workers from each of these stores participated in the strikes, holding signs, and chanting slogans inside the Walmart premises. The strikes were coordinated via workers' online networks facilitated by the Walmart Chinese Workers Association (WCWA), an informal group led by former employees of the company. The *Financial Times* reports that there were forty such WeChat groups with about twenty thousand members, roughly a fifth of Walmart's workforce in China. The All-China Federation of Trade Unions (ACFTU) neither organised nor intervened in the strikes. Workers ended their protest only after management promised a response, but the company never stopped pushing for the new working hour system to be adopted in its retails stores. These strikes represent a rare instance of cross-regional labour organisation leading to work stoppages. Since July, individual Walmart workers have taken the company to arbitration on issues related to the new working hour system.

(Sources: **China Labor Bulletin, The Financial Times, Xinjing Bao**)

Second Anniversary of Zhou Jianrong's Suicide

On 17 July, Chinese labour activists commemorated the second anniversary of the death of Zhou Jianrong, a forty-nine-year-old worker at a Hong Kong-owned footwear factory in Shenzhen. Two years ago, Zhou committed suicide by jumping out of her dormitory after being fired for her role in organising a strike. Since May 2014, Zhou and her co-workers had been struggling with the management over the issue of compensation following the company's ownership restructuring. They were concerned they would lose out. In the protracted struggle, more than one hundred workers were fired by management. On 16 July, the day before the suicide, the company had fired another sixteen activist workers, including Zhou. In Shenzhen, it would have been extremely difficult for female workers over the age of forty to find any factory work, and the loss of her job deeply distressed Zhou. Two years later, her death is not forgotten. A candlelight vigil was held in the office of a labour NGO in Guangzhou with more than a dozen former worker representatives and activists from Zhou's factory. They proposed to mark 17 July as the 'Day of Suffering of Chinese Workers'.

(Sources: **Caixin, Radio Free Asia**)

(Left) Walmart workers stage a protest in a Shenzhen store at the end of June. (Right) Vigil to commemorate the second anniversary of Zhou Jianrong's suicide.

Mounting Concerns about the Impact of the Economic Slowdown on Wage Growth

In mid-July, China's National Bureau of Statistics issued a report warning that sustaining economic and wage growth will be a challenge in the second half of 2016. In particular, the report cited industrial overcapacity in the state-owned coal and steel sectors, and declining agricultural prices as contributing factors. In the first half of this year, inflation-adjusted disposable household income rose 6.5 percent, barely keeping pace with economic growth at 6.7 percent. However, in anticipation of slowing economic growth, the Chinese government has taken measures to moderate wage growth. The deputy director of China's Bureau of Social Security and Human Resources, Xin Changxing, maintains that if Chinese companies are to remain competitive, the frequency and scale of wage adjustment should be slowed. In the first half of 2016, only six regions in China increased their local minimum wage, compared to thirteen regions in 2015. The average minimum wage increase is also slower: only eleven percent compared to 13.5 percent in the previous year. Mirroring the minimum wage adjustment, local governments' annual guidelines for workplace salaries similarly propose slower wage growth. In addition, in August, the powerful National Development and Reform Commission released a document that described the relatively large amounts provided by the social insurance scheme as undermining the competitiveness of China's manufacturing industry. This comes after sixteen provinces slightly reduced the percentage of social insurance contributions in the first half of 2016 in an effort to drive down labour costs.

(Sources: **Caixin, Jinghua Shibao, The South China Morning Post, Zhongguo Jingji Zhoukan, 21 Shiji Jingji Baodao**)

Wukan Sieged and Conquered

On 19 June, hundreds of residents in the southern fishing village of Wukan, Guangdong province, returned to the street five years after protests had flared up against official corruption and land grabbing. The protesting villagers demanded the release of Village Chief Lin Zuluan, who had been detained on 18 June for his persistent advocacy for land rights. Lin had been elected as chief of the village committee and Party secretary after he and others led a massive village protest in 2011 that secured a concession to hold democratic village elections (see also Luigi Tomba's chapter on pp. 56-59 in the present book). The land issue at the heart of the protest, however, had become increasingly difficult to resolve. Frustrated, Lin attempted to mobilise villagers to collectively petition the government, but he was detained shortly afterwards. Following the detention of his grandson and having been denied access to his lawyers, Lin confessed to bribery charges. After his confession was taped and broadcasted on state television, he was sentenced to thirty-seven months in prison. For almost three months, villagers held daily public demonstrations. On 13 September, riot police broke into the village to detain thirteen villagers accused of inciting a mob and disrupting public order. The police were met with resistance by villagers, and with many injured; however, since this time the protest has subsided.

(Sources: **The Initium, The New York Times, BBC**)

(Left) A garment worker. (Right) Wukan villagers hold a demonstration in 2011.

Flurry of Legislative Activity on Civil Society Organisations

After the passing of the Charity Law and the highly controversial Foreign NGOs Law earlier this year, over the summer, the Chinese authorities have continued to move forward with the revision of legislation related to the management of civil society organisations. Since June, the Ministry of Civil Affairs has issued draft registration and management regulations for public comment for all three types of social organisations legally recognised in China: foundations (*jijinhui*), social service organisations (*shehui fuwu jigou*), and social association (*shehui tuanti*). As long-time observer of Chinese civil society Shawn Shieh has pointed out in his blog *NGOs in China*, 'these three sets of regulations form the heart of the regulatory system governing the registration and management of social organisations—China's equivalent of not-for-profit organisations.' Complementary administrative regulations in either draft, provisional, or final form have also been concurrently released. The rationale behind the new legislation is spelled out in an 'Opinion' jointly released by the General Office of the Communist Party's Central Committee and the General Office of the State Council on 21 August. According to this document, the overall goal of the reform is to see that by 2020 China will have achieved 'the complete and sound building of a Chinese-style social organisation management system that features unified registration, with each undertaking their own duties, coordination and cooperation, responsibilities according to level, and oversight on the basis of the law.' In the new legal and political environment, 'government and social organisations [will be] separate, powers and obligations [will be] clear, and self-regulation [will be] practiced in line with the law,' but at the same time 'Party organisations [will be] playing a more obvious role.'

(Sources: **China Law Translate 1, China Law Translate 2, NGOs in China, Central Government Website**)

(Right) Labour activist Zeng Feiyang signs a document in court.

Panyu Labour Activists Sentenced, Lu Yuyu Beaten in Jail

On 26 September, the Panyu district court in Guangzhou held separate hearings for labour activists Zeng Feiyang, Zhu Xiaomei, and Tang Huanxing. Zeng was sentenced to three years imprisonment, suspended for four years, for 'gathering a crowd to disturb social order', while Zhu and Tang received prison sentences of eighteen months, suspended for two years, for the same charge. The case of Meng Han, another activist who refused to cooperate with the judicial authorities, was sent back to the police for further investigation (he already had a previous conviction back in 2014 for organising hospital security guards). All activists worked for the Panyu Migrant Workers Centre, an outspoken labour NGO based in Guangzhou that has, over the past few years, distinguished itself for taking on several high-profile collective cases. After being arrested in a coordinated crackdown against labour activists in early December 2015, Zeng and his colleagues were formally accused of 'gathering a crowd to disturb social order'. While Zhu and Tang were released on bail after a few weeks, Zeng and Meng remained under detention for almost ten months. Worrying news has also emerged about blogger Lu Yuyu, chronicler of protests in China, and his girlfriend and collaborator Li Tingyu who have been detained since 15 June. On 31 August, Lu met his lawyer at the Dali Bai Autonomous Prefecture Detention Centre, and told him that he had been beaten by officers and was suffering from sleep deprivation after having been exposed to strong light at night. Amnesty International has called for urgent action in support of Lu and Li.

(Sources: **Amnesty International, China Labor Bulletin, The New York Times**)

EYE IN THE SKY

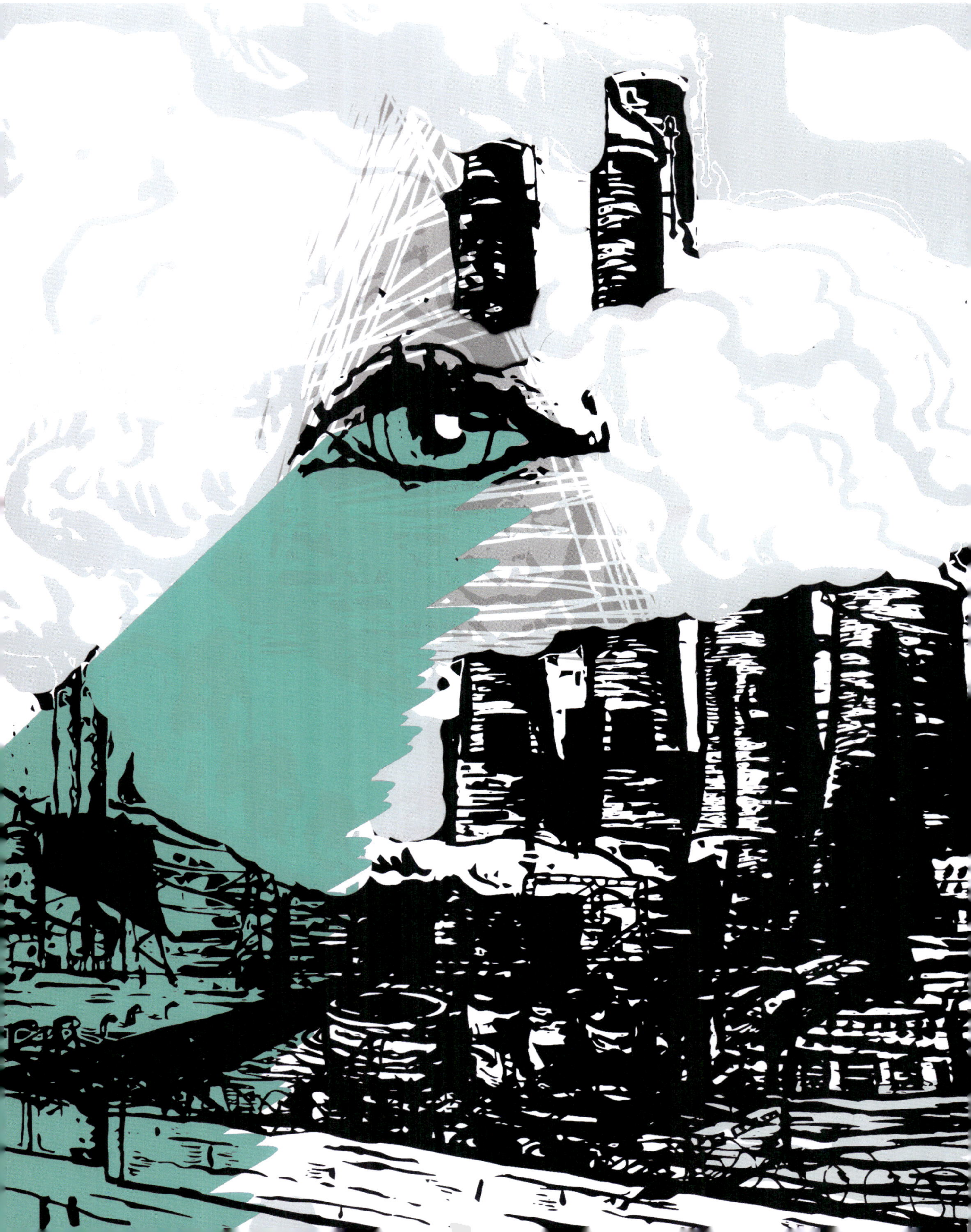

Portrait of Antonio Gramsci
PC: Unknown

The Neglected Side of the Coin:
Legal Hegemony, Class Consciousness, and Labour Politics in China

Elaine Sio-ieng Hui

Since China's opening up, the Chinese party-state has put great effort into reforming its labour laws. Taken at face value, the new laws and regulations adopted in these decades may easily be seen as a sign of the commitment of the party-state to advance labour rights. This article contradicts this view through an examination of how the labour law system in China has been utilised to build up hegemony and dampen workers' class consciousness.

This article is based on two of the author's publications: 'The Labour Law System, Capitalist Hegemony and Class Politics in China', *The China Quarterly* (226): 431-455; and *Hegemonic Transformation: The State, Laws and Labour Relations in Post-Socialist China*, Palgrave Macmillan, New York (forthcoming).

Since China's opening up in 1978, the Chinese party-state has put great effort into reforming the labour law system. During the 1990s, the 1992 Trade Union Law, 1994 Labour Law, and the 1995 Arbitration Law were enacted. In 2001 and 2004, the revised Trade Union Law and Provisions on Minimum Wage were promulgated respectively. In 2007, the Labour Contract Law was passed. All these events may be easily taken at face value as a sign of the commitment of the party-state to advance labour rights.

This article, however, argues that the labour law system is a vital vehicle through which the Chinese party-state has constructed capitalist hegemony with regard to state-capital-labour relations in the country. While Marx and Engels, as well as Lenin, mostly focussed on the oppressive nature of the state, in *Prison Notebooks* Gramsci advanced the idea that the power of the ruling class is organised by the state in both political society and civil society through 'coercion' plus 'hegemony' (Gramsci 1971). He contended that the coercive machinery of the state helps sustain the domination of the capitalist class, but at the same time it has to acquire the active consent of the working class by establishing what Joseph Femia termed 'its own moral, political and cultural values as conventional norms of practical behaviour' in order to sustain its class rule (Femia 1987, 3). The ideological ascendency of the capitalist class over the subaltern classes is what Gramsci called 'hegemony'.

For years, Chinese migrant workers have carried out contentious actions to strive for defaulted wages, compensation for workplace injury, overtime payment, and so forth. Recently, democratic enterprise trade union elections, decent wages above the minimum wage rate, compensation related to factories' closure or relocation, and payments of social insurance have also been key demands of migrant workers. Some studies point out that migrant workers have manifested a growing level of class consciousness over time (Chan and Pun 2009). Workers' class consciousness and capitalist hegemony are two sides of the same coin. Hegemony is the endeavour of the ruling class to constitute workers' worldviews and values in such ways that the latter may criticise, but not challenge fundamentally, the legitimacy of the capitalist economy and the party-state, and that they may resist, but not take rebellious actions to transform the socio-political and economic systems. In other words, through establishing capitalist hegemony, the ruling class aims to forestall the emergence of workers' class consciousness, which is a cardinal factor in inducing system-changing initiatives. Focussing on the often-neglected side of the coin, this article examines how the labour law system in China has been utilised to build up hegemony and dampen workers' class consciousness.

The Double Hegemony Buttressing Market and Party-State

The labour law system has been given a greater role in the mediation of industrial relations in post-reform China. The concept of '*yifa zhiguo*' (rule of law) was added to the Chinese constitution in 1999 and the notion of '*yifa weiquan*' (defending rights according to the law) has been widely promoted by the party-state (see also the Forum on the rule of law on pp. 98–105 in the present book). The labour law system has produced a *double hegemony*, which seeks to deflect radical worker opposition against both the market economy and the party-state. Concerning capital-labour relations, despite complaining about poor income, many workers still approve of the meagre wages offered by their employers. As one female worker whom I interviewed back in 2013 remarked: 'I go to work according to the schedule; it is fair and just, so long as my employer does not underpay me.' Another male worker I interviewed noted that 'labour laws must have been passed for good reason. They were made by professionals; they, thus, must have taken into consideration national and social needs.' Many workers have taken labour laws as a yardstick for measuring employer behaviour—if employers do not violate the Labour Law, then paying workers low wages is not unjust. This 'normalising mechanism' embedded in the labour law system does not simply legitimise low wages, but also covertly endorses market principles such as waged labour, private property rights, surplus value extraction, commodification of labour, and so forth.

Another mechanism—which I define as a 'countervailing mechanism'—is incorporated into the labour law system to strengthen capitalist dominance. Despite its pro-capital essence, the labour law system provides aggrieved workers with a platform for resolving labour disputes, such as mediation, arbitration, and litigation. Being unaware of the many limitations of this system, because of the countervailing mechanism, many workers believe that the market economy is not structurally exploitative, and that their hardships are a result of erratic misdeeds from idiosyncratic employers. In one of my interviews, a migrant worker commented: 'Some factories are really bad… But when my employer is problematic, I can simply complain to the labour bureau or sue the boss. There was no law when we first worked in the cities; now things have improved.' For some workers, the juridical sphere is autonomous from the capitalist economy, and labour laws are a useful tool for remedying misbehaviour occurring in the economic realm.

Concerning state-labour relations, the abundance of labour laws in China, which on paper are very comprehensive and seemingly try to constrain and regulate employers, has convinced some workers that the party-state protects workers. They, thus, do not attribute worker misfortunes to the state's pro-capital bias. As a worker I interviewed noted: 'In the past, there were no regulations on wages, and we just earned a little. But now, enterprises must follow the laws and pay us the minimum wage. Our situation is much better now...' This 'concealing mechanism' embedded in the labour law system induces some workers to believe that the Chinese political regime is 'autonomous' from the market economy and is willing to curb economic misdeeds. Hence, they do not fundamentally challenge the party-state's legitimacy.

The concealing mechanism usually goes hand in hand with another mechanism—the 'transmuting mechanism'—to protect the Chinese Party-state from workers' radical challenges. Due to the decentralised politics of China, the central government delegates the task of capital accumulation to local governments, while it focuses its attention on maintaining political legitimacy and social harmony (Lee 2007). Some workers, therefore, perceive government corruption and its pro-business bias as being caused by local governments or officials. In the words of a worker I interviewed: 'I think the central government doesn't have any problems; it has legislated many labour laws to protect workers. The problem lies with the local governments who protect businesses too much.' In brief, the transmuting mechanism shifts the target of workers' contempt from systemic state-capital collusion to local governments.

An Uneven Influence

Through the aforementioned four mechanisms, the labour law system has been able to impose double hegemony on some workers. However, the double hegemony has influenced Chinese migrant workers in an uneven manner. Some workers have granted *active consent* to the ruling class through the mediation of the labour law system, while some others have rendered *passive consent*. Some, however, have given *no consent* at all.

Those workers who have rendered active consent to the capitalist leadership approve of the official legal discourses and labour law practices (see also the chapter by Ivan Franceschini on pp. 84–87 in the present book). Most of them perceive of economic reforms and economic growth in a positive light. They endorse the state's development strategy of 'letting some people get rich first', which is akin to the liberal 'trickle down economics' theory, believing that economic progress fuelled by the state's pro-business policies will eventually benefit other members of the society. Many of them believe that employers would have been above reproach had they paid workers wages according to the labour laws. The market economy and the wealthy class are thought to have created jobs for workers and prosperity for the country, rather than exploiting labour.

Workers who have rendered passive consent to capitalist leadership have neither completely assented to it, nor fundamentally challenged it. Some workers do not place full trust in the labour law system because of the gap between their work experiences and the unfulfilled promises of the official legal rhetoric. However, the labour law system is still able to elicit passive consent from them because, as Joseph Femia put it, their 'spontaneous discontent is contained by the pre-existing categories of the dominant ideology' (Femia 1987, 137). This means that, even though they disapprove of the juridico-political and economic system, their criticism is constrained by the ideational framework produced by the ruling bloc. Although these workers discredit the labour law system, their criticism usually targets implementational issues rather than asymmetrical power relations embedded within the system. Many of them maintain that the central government has good intentions to protect workers with labour laws; they attribute the failing labour law system to the fault of local governments or officials.

Some workers have given no consent to the ruling class at all. These workers have formulated radical challenges to both the market economy and the party-state; and they refuse to follow the ruling bloc's leadership. They are relatively immune to the normalising mechanism of legal hegemony. They do not see legal minimum wages as fair or just; instead they measure their wages against how much their employers earn. In addition, they are not influenced much by the countervailing mechanism. Some of them understand that the legal and the economic are not independent from each other; that the law-making process and legal content are biased towards employers; and that workers and capitalists are on unequal footing within the legal realm. Moreover, the concealing mechanism and the transmuting mechanism have little effect on them. They see through the intricate relations between government and businesses, and do not construe the party-state as wholly autonomous from the capitalist class. They do not simply blame the local governments or officials, but censure the central government or the party-state en bloc.

Precarious Hegemony

The differing degrees in which the impact of this legal hegemony on workers expose its fragility and precariousness, which are the results of a number of factors. At the economic level, unbalanced economic development and growing social inequality have laid the material foundation for worker contestation to capitalist leadership. At the associational level, the Party-led trade unions are unable to secure short-term material concessions for workers and, hence, worker allegiance to the ruling bloc. At the legal level, the party-state has failed to consistently uphold the legal ideals it has reproduced; the discrepancies between legal ideals and legal reality have produced disenchantment. In July 2015, more than two hundred rights-lawyers and legal assistants were detained by the government without following proper legal procedures. In December of the same year, seven labour NGO activists were arrested—five of them were formally charged at a later date for 'gathering a crowd to disrupt public order' and 'embezzlement'—and they were denied many legal rights, such as the rights to communication with lawyers and families. Some of the detained activists were made to confess their alleged crimes on television. These incidents have aroused tremendous concern at both the international and national level. Still, it is important to highlight the fact that the greater the discrepancies between the government's rhetoric and the legal reality is, the easier it is for workers to become distrustful of the juridico-political system and to overcome the deception of the legally-mediated double hegemony.

Elaine Sio-ieng Hui

Elaine Sio-ieng Hui is an Assistant Professor in the School of Labor and Employment Relations at Pennsylvania State University. Her research interests include critical state theories, legal theories, class consciousness, civil society, social welfare, and labour relations in China.

Wu Tingshan, a worker in Shenzhen interviewd for the documentary *Dreamwork China* in 2011

Chinese Workers and the Law: Misplaced Trust?

Ivan Franceschini

In recent years, much has been written about the 'rights awakening' of Chinese workers. But what kind of rights are we talking about? Do they respond to an entirely subjective concept of justice or do they somehow coincide with the entitlements provided by the labour legislation? On the basis of a survey carried out among 1,379 employees of Italian metal mechanic companies in China, this article will attempt to answer three key questions: how do Chinese workers perceive the labour contract? How much do they know about labour legislation and how does this knowledge affect their trust of the law? What do they think about going on strike as a strategy to protect their rights?

A fuller set of data can be found in the author's book: *Lavoro e diritti in Cina: Politiche sul lavoro e attivismo operaio nella fabbrica del mondo* (Labour and rights in China: Labour policies and worker activism in the world factory), Il Mulino, Bologna, 2016.

One fascinating question concerning labour activism in contemporary China regards the attitude of Chinese migrant workers towards the law. In recent years, much has been written about the 'rights awakening' (*quanli de juexing*) of Chinese workers. But what kind of rights are we talking about? Do they respond to an entirely subjective concept of justice or do they somehow coincide with the entitlements provided by the labour legislation? And what is the relationship that binds legal awareness (*falü yishi*), rights consciousness (*quanli yishi*), and solidarity (*tuanjie yishi*)? That these elements do not necessarily go hand in hand is highlighted by the following testimony by a labour activist whom I interviewed in Shenzhen in 2014:

If ten [young migrants] come to me saying that their rights have been violated, they usually want to sue the company, but don't know how. Although I suggest that they sue the company together, they generally choose to do it separately. I don't think of this as a contradiction. If legal consciousness and solidarity consciousness are so low, how can they have such a high awareness of rights protection (*weiquan yishi*)? For example, if one of their fathers had his rights violated, he would choose to stay silent. If the son has his rights violated, he will explode and fight. If he didn't sign a labour contract and gets fired, he will ask for double wage as compensation. But they don't know anything about these compensations, they only know that their bosses have deceived them.

[Interview, Shenzhen, October 2014]

It is with these and other questions in mind that a few years ago I undertook a survey among the employees of nine Italian metal mechanic factories (either joint ventures or wholly foreign owned enterprises) in three Chinese cities: Shenzhen, Yangzhou, and Chongqing. In three rounds of interviews—respectively in 2012, 2014, and 2015— I was able to conduct 1,379 questionnaires at the gates of the various factories, without any knowledge or interference by the management. The workers in my sample were mostly men (74.2 per cent); 24.5 per cent of them were born before 1980, 45.4 per cent in the Eighties, and 30.1 per cent in the Nineties; and their educational level was medium-high, with 32.7 per cent of the workers having graduated from middle school, 22.1 per cent from high school, 20.2 per cent from middle technical school, and 18.9 per cent from higher technical school.

Were all these workers migrants? Actually, only 63.7 per cent of the respondents had a rural household registration (*nongye hukou*), the traditional parameter to determine a worker's status as an internal migrant. Still, taking the *hukou* as a parameter that defines the identity of Chinese workers today may be quite treacherous, as many 'urban' employees of the factories in Chongqing and peri-urban Yangzhou were local farmers whose status had been 'upgraded' following the new policies of forced urbanisation adopted by the local authorities. Similarly, only thirty-three per cent of the workers came from a different province—with the significant exception of Shenzhen, where only 11.3 per cent of the workers were from Guangdong—a finding that mirrors the growing importance of intra-provincial migrations in China.

In my survey, I attempted to measure the awareness of these workers regarding some key aspects of labour law, as well as their expectations towards wages and work hours. Yet in this article I will focus on three questions: how do Chinese workers perceive the labour contract? How much do they know about labour legislation and how does this knowledge affect their trust of the law? What do they think about going on strike as a strategy to protect their rights?

Labour Contracts

At the cornerstone of the discourse of the party-state on 'harmonious labour relations' (*hexie laodong guanxi*), labour contracts can provide some interesting insights on the way Chinese workers relate to the labour law and the relevant propaganda. 97.2 per cent of the workers in my survey had signed an individual labour contract, a clear proof of the commitment of the authorities to enforce the labour contract system, at least in the industry I considered (in other sectors, for instance the construction sector, the rate is remarkably lower, and according to official data from the National Bureau of Statistics in 2015 only 36.2 per cent of all migrant workers had signed a labour contract with their employer). But how many workers believed in the importance of the contract as an instrument to protect their rights? A question I asked is whether the workers had read the clauses of the contract before signing it. Only 26.7 per cent of them had read them carefully (*zixi yuedu*), while 46.5 per cent just had had a quick look (*suibian kan*), and 26.8 per cent had signed without reading (*qianming eryi*). This seems to display a certain disinterest in the labour contract, as if it were an irrelevant piece of paper. Yet, when directly asked whether they considered contracts as an effective tool to protect their rights, 22.3 per cent of the workers responded affirmatively (*keyi*) and 49.2 per cent was relatively optimistic (*hai keyi*), compared with only 7.3 per cent who expressed disbelief (*bu keyi*), and 21.2 per cent who did not know how to answer. In essence, almost two thirds of the workers trusted the capacity of labour contracts to protect them.

I then asked whom they thought was the main beneficiary of a labour contract. Although the Labour Contract Law that came into force in 2008 is rather favourable to workers when it comes to the resolution and severance of labour relations, somehow unsurprisingly 82.5 per cent of the respondents believed that a labour contract benefitted both employer and employee, while only 3.5 per cent declared that the worker was the one to benefit the most. Still, there was a significant minority of workers (12.8 per cent) who believed that the labour contract benefitted only the company. This was because in the eyes of some workers a labour contract is a significant restraint to mobility, and mobility—i.e. 'voting with your feet' (*yi jiao toupiao*)—often is the only way to resist corporate exploitation. As a migrant worker whom I interviewed in 2011 for the documentary *Dreamwork China* said:

A contract? It is like this: if you sign it, you cannot leave for the next three months. If you don't sign it, you can leave whenever you want, even before a month. If it is an annual contract, you have to work for at least three months or you cannot quit. This is the labour contract. [Interview, Shenzhen, January 2011]

Legal Knowledge and Trust towards the Law

This relative confidence in labour contracts opens some further questions about how Chinese workers perceive the labour law. Without going into too much detail, I found that the workers in my sample to have a selective knowledge of the provisions of the labour legislation, exemplified by the 1995 Labour Law and the 2008 Labour Contract Law. In particular, they were very aware of clauses that affected their direct economic interests—such as those that regulate the way overtime wages are calculated (90.6 per cent of the workers were aware)—while knowing very little about other aspects of the labour legislation, which they probably perceived as less relevant to their income. For instance, just 17.5 per cent of the workers knew that they were supposed to work no more than thirty-six hours of overtime a month. Similarly, only 25.1 per cent of the workers could write down the correct local minimum wage (on the whole, though, I found that the higher a worker's basic wage, the less likely he/she is to know the correct minimum wage). Even more important, I found a clear divide between the knowledge of individual rights—generally low but still existing—and that of collective rights. Many workers had no clear idea about what a trade union is (11.4 per cent had never heard the word 'trade union' before), and 98.2 per cent of the respondents had no idea of what 'collective negotiation' (*jiti xieshang*)—the Chinese watered-down version of collective bargaining—was.

In spite of (or maybe due to) this highly selective knowledge, when I asked the workers whether they believed that the existing labour legislation was able to protect them, most of them were quite optimist. 5.7 per cent were absolutely sure that it could (*wanquan neng*) and 49.6 per cent were slightly less sure, but still quite positive about it (*yinggai keyi*). On the contrary, 34.1 per cent were dubious (*yexu neng*) and 10.5 per cent were definitely sceptical (*bu neng*). If these results display a considerable confidence in the law, it is interesting that this perception does not derive from a personal experience with the Chinese legal system. In fact, only 3.3 per cent of the workers in the sample had dealt with a labour dispute by legal means before. This apparently confirms what Mary Gallagher and Yuhua Wang found out in a previous study, that 'non-users [of the legal system] tend to have vague but benevolent notions of the legal system and its effectiveness' (Gallagher and Wang 2011, 204).

Perception of Strikes

How do strikes figure within such a 'benevolent notion' of the legal system? My survey shows that trusting the law and resorting to strikes are not necessarily mutually exclusive. While China has ratified the International Covenant on Economic, Social, and Cultural Rights, which at article 8.1 (d) binds the government to ensure 'the right to strike, provided that it is exercised in conformity with the laws of the particular country', the Chinese legislation does not mention the right to strike at all, consigning it to a grey area (Chang and Cooke 2015). Since even Chinese scholars have not reached a conclusion on the legality of industrial actions in China, I therefore did not expect the workers to have a clear idea on this issue. Yet, when I asked them whether they believed that going on strike was legal or illegal, I was surprised to find out that 38.5 per cent of the respondents said that it was legal, compared with only 13.9 per cent who believed the opposite (the rest did not know). That such a high percentage of workers expressed the belief that strikes are legal is quite impressive. It means that many workers in China believe that the law—and therefore the apparatus of the party-state—will support them in the event of a strike. This may be taken as a hint of the extent to which the work of propaganda and legal dissemination undertaken by the Chinese authorities in the past two decades has succeeded.

Still, the idea that going on strike is 'legal' does not mean that Chinese workers are willing to protest at the slightest perceived violation of their rights. The right to strike is often framed by the workers in moral rather than legal terms, as a last resort after all other avenues of redress have failed. As a young respondent said: 'In a situation in which there is no choice other than going on strike, you cannot say that it is illegal. Still, the workers do not want to go on strike without reason' [Interview, Shenzhen, April 2012]. Nevertheless, when I asked what they thought about going on strike as a strategy to protect their rights, 43.3 per cent of the respondents were either favourable or extremely favourable, compared with only 26.8 per cent who were against or absolutely against it (29.8 per cent did not know).

Conclusions

The data presented in this article show that when discussing the 'rights awakening' of Chinese workers it is important to consider what we mean by the term 'rights'. In particular, more attention should be paid to the way these workers respond to the official discourse on labour rights promoted by the party-state through the labour law and other relevant policy documents. As I have attempted to show, the official discourse is deeply rooted in the mind of the workers in my sample. This can been seen in two respects: the workers' conviction that labour contracts and the labour law can protect them; and their selective knowledge of the labour law provisions, strongly unbalanced towards individual rights with direct economic implications. This 'benevolent notion' of the legal system even affects the perception of strikes, which are considered 'legal' by a very significant portion of the workforce. This means that many Chinese workers believe that the apparatus of the party-state will support them in their decision to go on strike—at least as long as they have a 'reasonable' motivation to do so. If these findings do not provide a definite answer to the wider theoretical questions outlined at the beginning of the article, they nonetheless warrant some further attention when discussing the 'awakening' of the Chinese working class.

Ivan Franceschini

Ivan Franceschini is a Marie Curie Fellow at Ca' Foscari University of Venice and at the Australian Centre on China in the World working on a project on Chinese labour in a global perspective. From 2006 to 2015, he lived in China, where he worked as a journalist and as a consultant in the field of development cooperation. His research interests focus on Chinese labour and civil society.

The Labour Contract Law, 2007

Chinese Workers and the Legal System:
Bridging the Gap in Representation

Aaron Halegua

A decade ago, the Chinese authorities adopted a set of new laws to grant increased legal protections to workers and easier access to the legal system to enforce their rights through litigation. Since then, Chinese workers have increasingly turned to labour arbitration and courts in the hope of resolving their grievances. But how do they fare in this process? And are they able to find legal representation?

In 2007, the Chinese authorities issued the Labour Contract Law to grant new legal protections to workers and the Labour Dispute Mediation and Arbitration Law to make it easier for them to enforce their rights through litigation. In the decade that followed, Chinese workers have increasingly turned to labour arbitration and courts in the hope of resolving their grievances. But how do they fare in this process? Are they able to find legal representation? In China, as elsewhere, a significant 'representation gap' exists between workers' legal needs and the available legal services.

A new report that I authored, *Who Will Represent China's Workers? Lawyers, Legal Aid, and the Enforcement of Labour Rights*, takes an in-depth look at the landscape of enforcing worker rights in China, with a particular focus on trends in labour rights litigation and the availability of legal representation (Halegua 2016). The report draws on over one hundred interviews, observations from litigation proceedings, and an extensive review of published and unpublished written materials. The executive summary lists seven 'key findings', including that the number and diversity of labour disputes is rising; mediation has become the predominant means of resolving labour disputes; workers are often unsuccessful in litigation; and represented workers achieve better outcomes in litigation.

Finding competent legal representation to assist in the litigation process remains a challenge for workers, however. Due to economic and political considerations, private lawyers and law firms are reluctant to represent workers. 'Barefoot lawyers' have been essentially banned and labour NGOs are significantly constrained in the current political environment. More workers are represented each year by the government-sponsored legal aid system, which pays private lawyers a set stipend to handle cases regardless of the outcome. But many workers are still turned away and those who receive a lawyer are often dissatisfied with the quality of the representation.

In addition to describing the above trends, the report takes an initial step towards quantifying the representation gap and other aspects of labour litigation. In collaboration with the Chinese data analytics company Legal Miner, over thirty thousand publicly available court decisions were collected and then analysed to determine how many workers have a legal representative, the identity of these representatives (licensed lawyers versus other providers), and the average length of the court proceedings. A significant number of workers, roughly forty percent, had no legal representation in court. However, plaintiffs who make it all the way to court are only the tip of the iceberg in terms of workers who need legal assistance but are unable to obtain it.

In light of this representation gap, the penultimate section of the report sets forth eight practical strategies to narrow the chasm and improve the enforcement of labour rights. Some proposals seek to decrease the 'demand' for legal services by reducing labour violations in the first place. Others are designed to increase the 'supply' of quality legal representation for workers. In the remainder of this article, I discuss three of these strategies that have received less attention: (1) strengthening anti-retaliation measures; (2) imposing criminal sanctions and establishing personal liability for employers; and (3) encouraging the growth of a plaintiffs' bar.

The first two strategies address the 'demand' side of the representation gap. One crucial reason for the prevalence of noncompliance with labour standards, and thus the large number of aggrieved workers, is the lack of adequate deterrents for employers. The labour inspectorate in China, which enforces labour laws, employs just one inspector for every thirty thousand workers. For the most part, investigations only occur in response to a worker filing a complaint. Furthermore, even when violations are detected, a fine against the employer is only imposed in 3.4 percent of cases. Accordingly, measures are needed to both encourage workers to come forward with violations and raise the penalties for employers who are not in compliance—which the first two strategies do. The third strategy—growing a robust plaintiffs' bar—most directly addresses the 'supply' side of the representation gap, but a heightened threat of litigation against employers could also lead to increased compliance.

Anti-Retaliation Measures

Employer retaliation against workers who complain about unfair or illegal working conditions is commonplace—not only in China, but also other countries. In the United States, for instance, over forty-four percent of the nearly ninety thousand charges filed with the federal anti-discrimination agency in 2015 contained an allegation of retaliation, making it the most frequent complaint. This agency even made combating retaliation a 'national priority'. As for China, a survey of Foxconn employees revealed that over forty-seven percent of workers experienced retaliation after raising a complaint. Eighty percent of Guangzhou workers feared that suing their employer would result in their termination. If workers are too afraid to complain about violations, employers will not be held accountable. With nothing to fear, employers will continue violating the law.

The Chinese government may consider adopting anti-retaliation protections for workers who protest employer violations of discrimination, workplace safety, and other labour laws. The concept of an anti-retaliation measure is not foreign to China. Indeed, similar protections already exist for trade union officers, workers who complain to the labour inspectorate, and certain witnesses. The best model may be the fairly robust anti-retaliation provisions to protect whistle-blowers that China promulgated in 2016, which includes a broad list of actions that constitute retaliation.

Labour advocates might propose that any amendments to the Labour Contract Law, which is rumoured to be revised in the near future, include an anti-retaliation provision. This would provide an opportunity not only to explicitly prohibit retaliation, but also establish procedures for handling complaints and set meaningful penalties against violators. In light of speculation that the other amendments will be designed to increase the flexibility of employers, and may even broaden the grounds upon which employees can be terminated, it is particularly important to make explicit that workers cannot be fired for challenging illegal conditions in the workplace.

Criminal Prosecutions and Personal Liability

Another strategy to deter employer noncompliance is to hold them personally accountable for any violations, including through criminal prosecutions. In 2011, China amended its Criminal Law to establish criminal penalties—including fines and imprisonment—for the malicious non-payment of wages. Where an employer has been ordered to pay a 'comparatively large sum' of wages, but instead chooses to transfer assets or otherwise evades payment, he may be held criminally liable. The Chinese government has already demonstrated some willingness to undertake these prosecutions: 753 cases were prosecuted in 2014 and nearly one thousand and two hundred in 2015, an increase of fifty-eight percent. But while Shenzhen alone brought ninety-three cases in 2014, Beijing did not prosecute its first case until 2013 and is reported to only undertake about forty per year.

Labour advocates should engage local governments to increase both the number of criminal prosecutions and their impact. Chinese officials complain that the most significant obstacle to achieving more prosecutions is the poor evidence that workers bring to the government. Accordingly, one potential area for cooperation is for the government to educate lawyers and labour NGOs about the types of cases and evidence they seek, and for these advocates to then identify cases that are ripe for prosecution—thus resulting in more prosecutions. Another aspect of this type of cooperation would be for labour advocates to assist in publicising the prosecutions that occur. If employers are aware that these prosecutions are happening, and with increasing frequency, they are more likely to be deterred from committing similar violations.

An additional prong of this deterrence strategy is to create civil liability for individual employers. At present, an individual does not have the capacity to be an 'employer' under Chinese labour law. Therefore, a judgment for unpaid wages can only be issued against the corporate entity that employed a worker and may only be enforced against the assets of the corporation. The individual employer has little to fear. Labour law scholar Xie Zengyi writes that this lack of individual accountability has a lot to do with the poor implementation of labour law in China (Xie 2015). Therefore, labour advocates should propose establishing such individual liability so that judgments can be enforced against the personal assets of the individual employer.

Plaintiffs' Bar

Given their current reluctance, the emergence of a bar of Chinese lawyers committed to representing workers would significantly help to narrow the representation gap and improve the enforcement of labour rights. If the compensation structure were properly aligned, attorneys could become entrepreneurial and zealous advocates for workers. The report recommends reforms in three areas—contingency fee arrangements, aggregate litigation, and fee-shifting provisions—that would help create such incentives.

Contingency fee arrangements—by which the lawyer only collects fees if the client recovers money—are generally banned in labour cases. Workers are therefore required to pay legal fees upfront, which many cannot afford. Permitting contingency fee arrangements would allow lawyers to represent workers with strong cases, regardless of whether they could afford to pay. Moreover, as contingency fees are often calculated based on a percentage of the compensation awarded to the worker, they may allow attorneys to earn more money in cases where there are sizeable recoveries.

Bringing collective or class litigation is difficult in China. But aggregating small, individual claims can be an effective way to make litigating those cases economically viable for a lawyer. For instance, a China Labour Watch report discovered that seventy thousand workers at Pegatron attended a fifteen-minute meeting each day for which they were not compensated (China Labour Watch 2016). Litigating the claim of one worker may not be worth a lawyer's time; but if one lawsuit could be brought on behalf of all workers, who are collectively owed over eleven million US dollars, the case would be quite attractive. Therefore, labour advocates should promote the adoption of measures to facilitate collective and class labour cases.

A final reform to help encourage the growth of a plaintiffs' bar is a properly structured fee-shifting scheme. Shenzhen already permits workers to be awarded legal fees when they prevail in labour cases, but several aspects of that system limit its utility and impact. Due to restrictions on contingency fees, plaintiffs must still front the legal fees before a court can require the employer to reimburse those fees. In other countries, fee-shifting schemes can deter employers from dragging out litigation because the amount of the fees is calculated based on the number of hours worked by the plaintiff's counsel. In Shenzhen, the legal fee is tied to how much the worker actually paid his lawyer and is capped at five thousand yuan per procedure—hardly enough to deter most employers. But if this system were modified, it has great potential to help narrow the representation gap.

Conclusion

As the Chinese government considers rolling back some of the labour protections previously granted to workers in the Labour Contract Law, it becomes even more important to ensure that whatever rights still exist are adequately enforced. For a more comprehensive discussion of the landscape of labour rights enforcement in China and other proposed strategies for narrowing the representation gap, readers are encouraged to access the full report (Halegua 2016).

Aaron Halegua

Aaron Halegua is a practicing lawyer, consultant, and research fellow at the NYU School of Law. He has published a variety of book chapters, journal articles, and op-eds on labour and employment law issues in the United States and China. More information on his work is available on his website: http://www.aaronhalegua.com.

Entrance to the tomb of Cangjie, legendary inventor of writing. As an expression of gratitude and civic virtue, Guomindang general Zhu Qinglan restored this tomb in 1939. The Guomindang and Republican flags are clearly visible above the entrance. Baishui County, Shaanxi, 19 September 2016. PC: Thomas DuBois.

China's Religion Law and the Perils of Counting Consciousness

Thomas David DuBois

The academic study of Chinese religion overlaps with, and sometimes confronts, the work of rights advocates. These encounters can be uncomfortable for both parties. Scholars, diplomats, and jurists often have very different ideas of what rights are worth protecting, and what counts as religion. As recent revisions to China's religions law show, ideas about religion in China are changing quickly.

Nearly two decades since China launched its campaign against Falungong, issues of religious freedom remain among the most sensitive and stubborn points of contention between the Chinese government and the international human rights community. Even as the legal protection and regulation of religion has taken on an increasingly global character, China has withstood criticism to stand by certain core principles of how it defines legitimate religious expression.

As a historian of Chinese religion, I occasionally find myself in the unexpected position of explaining and even defending the logic behind China's religion policy. The basic reason is that historians such as myself aim to investigate trends and processes, rather than to engineer them. Our job demands the separation of advocacy from the dispassionate task of understanding what happened and why.

Part of this is the realisation that ideas of human rights and freedoms are themselves products of history. Even within the Western world, the genesis and application of religious freedom legislation is by no means static or universal. Looking to China, there is a world of difference between seeking to understand, and seeking to transform, between asking 'what does China value?' and 'why doesn't China value what we want them to?'

Religion in the Eyes of Advocacy

There is, of course, a great deal of common ground between these two premises, and the best way to find it is by understanding the faults in the ground we stand on. The most effective rights advocacy is that which is able to draw a line between universal ideals and culturally specific practices. Religious freedom is a very good example. Religious freedom is a very laudable ideal, and in some jurisdictions also a legally actionable one. The 1998 passage of the International Religious Freedom Act (IRFA) required the U.S. State Department to annually assess the state of religious freedom in every country, and left open coercive options up to and including sanctions for the worst offenders offenders (U.S. Department of State 1998). Recently, a number of other countries, including Canada, the United Kingdom, Italy, France, and the European Union have followed suit (Hurd 2015), introducing legislation that advocates the promotion of religious freedom at home and abroad.

However, the difference between an ideal and an actionable program is very significant. Putting an assessment of religious freedom into practice forces a general principle through a very specific set of gateways and criteria that will suit some situations better than others. While most states, including China, avow support for the ideal of religious freedom, they differ quite significantly when it comes to defining it. The difference between these views derives less from religion itself than from the place of religion in history. Winnifred Fallers Sullivan (2005), Elizabeth Shakman Hurd (2008, 2015) and many others have written extensively and persuasively about the ways that the American legal understanding of religious freedom, including the specific criteria by which IRFA makes its judgments, derive from very specific moments in US history. In contrast, the French view that public space must remain secular has played out most recently in the ban some French cities have levied on Islamic swimwear (aka the 'burkini'), and derives from the deeply egalitarian tendencies of the French Revolution (Decherf 2001).

China, of course, has its own very long, and at times very violent history of organised religion (a term that already presents something of a problem when used historically), and this view will undoubtedly shape how the current Chinese state understands not only the limits, but also the definition of religious freedom, specifically the question of freedom from whom and to what end. While the American view heavily favours the rights of churches to be free from an oppressive state, the Chinese state advocates freedom of the individual conscience from an oppressive clergy, or from foreign interference.

Heresy and the Freedom of Religion

If we want to see what Hurd calls the 'historical contingency' of how states understand religious freedom, we need look no further than the difference between these two views. Throughout the history of the United States, flight from religious oppression has been a consistent source of new migrants. Not surprisingly, the American legal protection of *confessional* freedom—that is, the right of organised religions to exist—is very near absolute. In contrast, the history of China has included some very painful experiences with organised religion itself. Because the imperial state saw itself as a moral entity that mediated between the sacred realm and the human world, rebellion or other anti-state activity oftentimes started with a competing view of the supernatural, otherwise known as heresy. I use this term very deliberately. As early as the fourteenth century, the legal code of the Ming dynasty demarcated three realms of religion: 'proper' (*zheng*), 'illicit' (*yin*) and 'perverse' (*xie*). The final category was strictly banned precisely because it was real, and thus a source of danger on many levels—as a moral danger to be sure, but also as a gateway for dark magic and demonic forces to infiltrate the realm. For the next five centuries, the imperial state excluded this realm of *illegitimate religion* from religious choice, in the same way that freedom of speech would not extend to libel or an incitement to violence (DuBois 2012).

Similarly, because official memory often equates Christian mission with imperialism, the Chinese state remains especially vigilant to what it would call foreign domination in the name of religion. Of course, China's experience of Christianity was in reality extremely broad, and included the foundation of many of the country's first modern schools, hospitals, and orphanages. Yet, while the tendency to equate mission with foreign oppression is unquestionably biased, it is by no means new. The country's first modern charity regulations, enacted in late 1920s Shanghai, aimed to curb the influence of foreign benefactors by making it difficult for missions to channel donations to Chinese counterparts (DuBois 2015). Chinese Christians themselves developed a resentment towards the tendency of some foreign missions to view native clergy as churches in perpetual training (Young 2013). Fears in the early years of the People's Republic of China (PRC) that Chinese Christians might already have been brainwashed into acting as a foreign dominated fifth column drove the new government's violent confrontation with the Catholic clergy during the 1950s.

We need not be unduly dismissive of the fact that many of these fears were politically created or exaggerated, because the narrative of history shapes national character regardless of its origin. Part of the Chinese political view of religion in fact comes not from China, but from the experience of the early Soviet Union, which faced in the Russian Orthodox Church a much larger, more politically powerful and more deeply rooted religious enemy than anything that any Chinese state had seen for a thousand years. It was in part from the Soviet experience that China adopted the idea, or at least the rhetoric, that religious freedom was less freedom of a clergy than freedom from it (Gong 2014). The fact that indices of religious freedom used by diplomats and advocates alike often disproportionately emphasise the rights of clergy and clerical organisations should alert us to the potential for conflict down the line.

Religion and Law in China

At the same time, the 'China first' view—that everything the Chinese government does or says grows out of China's cultural particularism—has its limits. Not everything can be explained by culture, and certainly not everything should be excused by it. Part of the problem is that there is no culture without power. Whatever its legitimacy, the argument that Asians culturally value stability over democracy (aka the case made for 'Asian values') would likely have gained wider acceptance had it not originated from Malaysia's Mahathir Mohamad and Singapore's Lee Kwan Yew, two of the region's most deeply entrenched political dynasts (Sen 1997). And there is no doubt that just as China has made an art of mobilising the idea of historical victimhood to further its interests, it promotes the idea of cultural difference to deflect human rights criticism, conveniently selecting the elements of culture that are useful at the time (Browne 2016).

The point here is not to dissuade the promotion of human rights, religious or otherwise, but to understand where the Chinese state is likely to be the most sensitive of criticism, especially in those areas where they would believe themselves to be in the right. A good first step would be to take seriously China's own pronouncements on the issue, especially as they have evolved over the past few years. Beginning with Article 88 of the 1954 Constitution, China's successive legal reforms have all voiced various iterations of support for religious freedom, consistently defined as the freedom of *belief* (*zongjiao xinyang de ziyou*) (Constitution of the People's Republic of China 1954). This wording is worth noticing—it was copied directly from previous Chinese constitutions, and before that appeared in Japanese constitutions as early as 1889. As written, the freedom being promised is closely in concert with Article 18 of the Universal Declaration of Human Rights, which demands 'freedom of thought, conscience and religion' (United Nations General Assembly 1948).

So far so good, as long as religion is defined strictly as individual belief and conscience.

The difficulty begins with the life of religion as a social entity. The same article of the Universal Declaration that speaks of the freedom of thought, also demands that religion find free expression 'in community with others and in public or private, [manifested] in worship, observance, practice and teaching.' In contrast, the PRC's stance has always been that religion be banned from public life. This assessment featured prominently in the 1982 document titled 'The Basic Viewpoint and Policy on the Religious Question During Our Country's Socialist Period' (*zongjiao wenti de jiben guandian he jiben zhengce*, more commonly known as 'Document 19'), which is widely seen as the key moment of rehabilitation for religion in the post-Mao era (Central Committee of the CCP 1982). Since the 1994 passage of the 'Rules for the Regulation of Sites for Religious Activities' (*zongjiao huodong changguo guanli tiaoli*), China has set aside sites specifically demarcated for religious activity, while at the same time insisting that the rights of religious expression end at the door of the church, mosque or temple. Even with these restrictions in place, only a set number of religions are legally accepted, and each of these is corralled into a Patriotic Religious Organisation (*aiguo zongjiao xiehui*), overseen by the State Administration of Religious Affairs (*guojia zongjiao shiwuju*). Very little is left to chance.

China has produced a steady stream of laws, regulations and legal pronouncements on religion (Zhuo 2008). The first full religions law, the 'Regulations on Religious Affairs', was promulgated in 2005, with draft revisions released in September of 2016. Placing the 2005 law and the recent revisions side by side shows continuity in the desire to physically separate organised religious activity from public spaces (DuBois 2016). It also reveals some more recent changes: a growing concern over the spread of information (especially over the Internet), and desire to exert greater control and oversight over the internal finances of religious groups and activities. But even as restrictions on religious activity tighten, the space given to what the law calls 'legitimate' religion is, if anything, growing. Some have even suggested that the Xi Jinping regime may be signalling the emergence of a new and less virulent stage in the campaign against Falungong (Ong and Xie 2016). We should take these trends seriously especially as recent legal reforms suggest that the Chinese state seems genuinely interested in developing and expanding the role of 'social organisations', i.e., civic groups, charities and NGOs.

What is most striking is what the laws neglect. Even if they reveal a certain recalibration of policies towards organised confessional religion, none of the laws as written deal in any way with the real religion of China: the holy trinity of country, party and civic virtue. As early as 1974, Joseph Kitagawa first suggested that the worship of Mao Zedong satisfied all of the hallmarks of religion—an organised regimen of worship, a sacred text and a deified founder—an idea that has continued to reverberate with scholars of Chinese religion (Kitagawa 1974). However, I am speaking instead of one variety of what Jose Casanova (1994) has famously called 'public religions', the sort of religion that exists within and undergirds the life of the public sphere. Although the church of politics is no longer mobilised to replace personal loyalties (as in the past, or in Emilio Gentile's 2006 portrayal of *secular religion*), China's civic religion indeed remains ubiquitous, written into slogans, pictures, commercials and dramas in every conceivable space. If the techniques of dissemination have changed, much of the content—respect for historical paragons, admonitions to pursue knowledge, respect elders and love country—remains true to the moral education first advanced in the early Ming dynasty. Now as then, civic virtues are not optional.

Temple of Guandi, with the character for 'loyalty' in prominent gold paint. This temple shares a courtyard with the Communist Party Headquarters of Beixian Township, Shaanxi, 19 September 2016.
PC: Thomas DuBois.

Counting Consciousness

Returning to the larger problem, I find it striking how often not just the specialised perspective of rights advocacy, but the process of counting and categorising more generally, misrepresents the real state of religion in China. Again, this does not in any way deny the legitimacy of rights advocacy, or of the history of repressing certain religious groups in China—not only Falungong, but also Christianity, Islam, and Tibetan Buddhism. Rather, it simply takes note of how poorly the normative criteria used by diplomatic organs such as IRFA fit the actual practice of religion in the country, both the ubiquitous expressions of public ethics, and very often even the lives of those who consider themselves religious.

Many of the nation's Christians do indeed visit churches, but millions of others, like this elderly woman I recently spoke to in rural Shaanxi, lead a very private Christian life. Asked about the meaning of Christianity, she replied that her religion taught to be kind to others, not to cheat or steal, and to seek spiritual value in suffering (this last point is one that I deal with at some length in most recent book) (DuBois 2017). This woman's religious life, one that she has held dear for decades, is completely internal and individual. It resembles neither the public religion of Chinese nationalism, nor the organised, church-based religion that is the primary concern of the rights community.

Just across the street from this woman's house, other villagers were gathering for the funeral of a woman who had died of cancer. The scene was a hive of activity. Even with teams of specialists hired to do the cooking, perform the rituals, and play the music, there was a job for every member of the community, and importantly for this discussion, absolutely no reason or excuse for opting out. Every member of the community was assigned a task, with names and jobs posted on a large sheet of paper at the doorway of the courtyard. Although the activities would include scriptures and incense, few would have thought of the funeral as a religious function, or of their required presence as

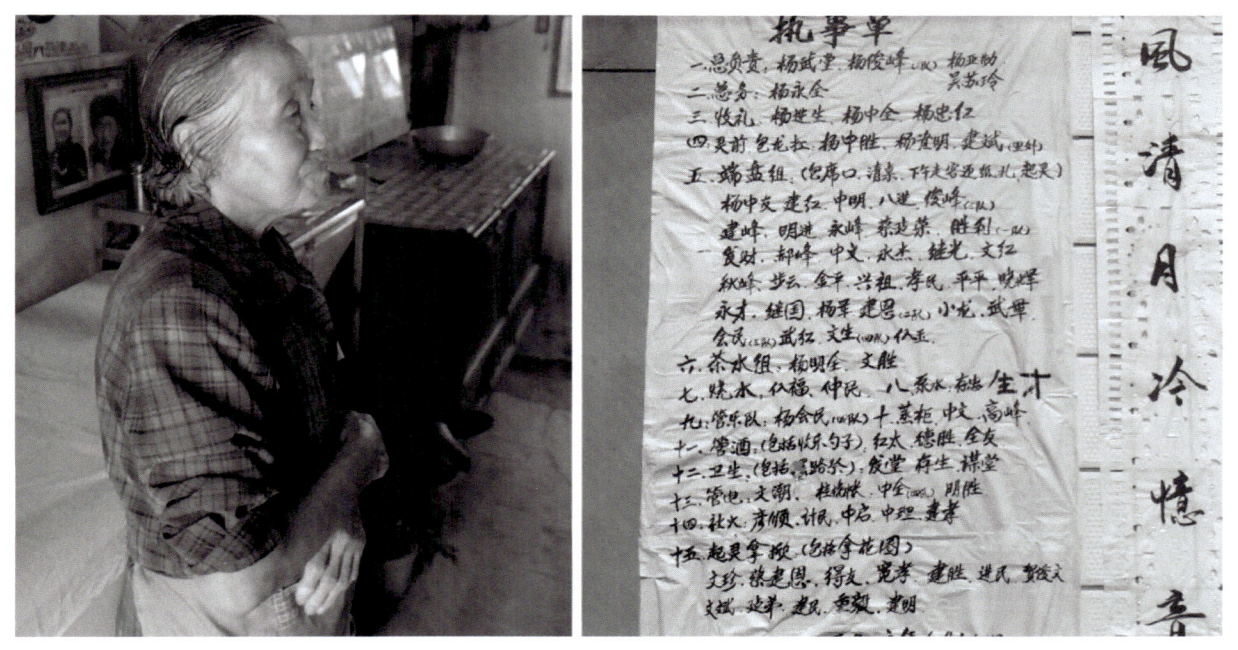

(Left) Christian woman in Gounan Village, Shaanxi, 18 September 2016. Photo by Micah Muscolino. (Right) Roster of duties at village funeral, Gounan Village, Shaanxi, 18 September 2016. PC: Thomas DuBois.

an imposition of religious freedom (the lone Christian had happily taken her place peeling sweet potatoes with the other old women). If anything, they would have described the gathering of the community as good-neighbourliness, or simply common sense.

The difference in vision is not simply one between scholars and advocates. The problem of a field of vision clouded by categories is likely to apply to any overly normative approach to beliefs and ethics. This would include the problem of surveying values, or as the title suggests, counting consciousness. Surveys, such as the often-cited Pew Values Surveys or the big data approach taken by scholars such as Fenggang Yang at the Center on Religion and Chinese Society can produce very useful points of reference, but can also be dangerously misleading (e.g. Gutting 2016) if taken too literally, or read without appreciation of the background issues. Like religion, ideals such as democracy and human rights in reality contain within them a very wide spectrum of ideas and understandings. Simply comparing how respondents in countries as diverse as Korea, Singapore and Vietnam answer the same questions about these exceedingly complicated concepts cannot tell us much if we do not know what these ideas mean on the ground and in history (Doh 2011). In these cases, survey data alone may obscure more than they reveal, a case of bad information being worse than no information at all. In the end, no amount of surveying can replace a deep and substantive appreciation of history and values in practice.

Thomas David DuBois

Thomas David DuBois is the author of *Sacred Village: Social Change and Religious Life in Rural North China*, and *Religion and the Making of Modern East Asia*. His most recent book, *Empire and the Meaning of Religion in Northeast Asia*, was published by Cambridge University Press early in 2017.

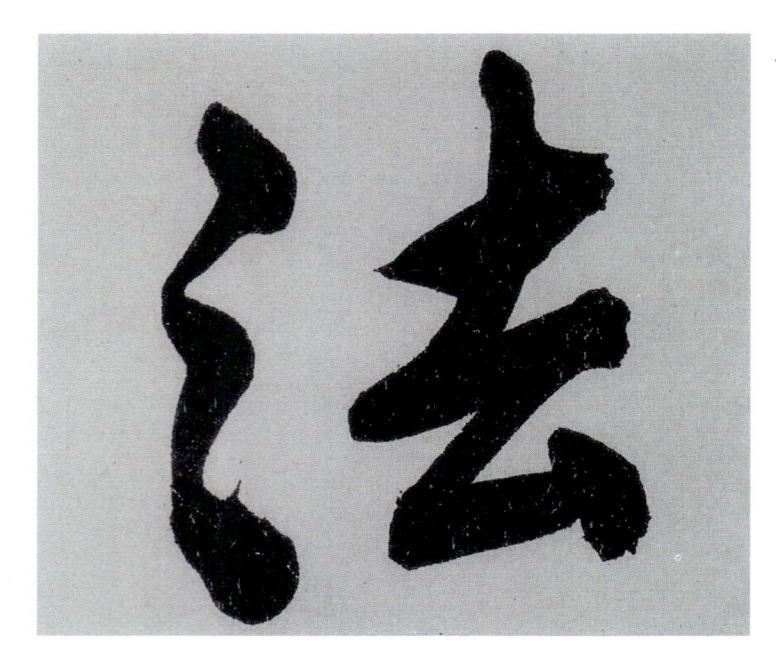

FORUM

Edited by Elisa Nesossi

Joshua Rosenzweig

Joshua is a Business and Human Rights Strategy Advisor/Analyst at Amnesty International's East Asia Regional Office in Hong Kong, where he has lived since 2008. An observer of all things Chinese for more than twenty-five years, he has more than a decade of experience researching, analyzing, and teaching about human rights developments and criminal justice in China. The views expressed in this piece are his own and do not necessarily represent the views of Amnesty International.

Ewan Smith

Ewan is a Lecturer at Trinity College (Oxford). He is admitted to practice in New York, where he worked for Debevoise and Plimpton.
In 2005, he joined the Foreign and Commonwealth Office and worked on UK policy towards the Middle East and China. From 2009-2014 he was posted to Beijing, where he analysed developments in Chinese leadership politics and government policy, with a particular focus on the reform of the legal system and the fight against corruption.

Susan Trevaskes

Susan is a professor of the Griffith Criminology Institute at Griffith University (Australia) and an Adjunct Director of the Centre on China in the World at the Australian National University. Her main research interests include the death penalty, policing, drug crime, public shaming events, and justice system reform in China.

Interpreting the Rule of Law in Xi Jinping's China

**Edited by Elisa Nesossi,
with the participation of Joshua Rosenzweig, Ewan Smith, Susan Trevaskes**

以 法 治 國

Yifa zhiguo, the Chinese expression often translated as 'rule of law'.

With its ample resonance both within China and internationally, 'rule of law' (yifa zhiguo) is an expression that can justify the most disparate justice reforms. It is both a political value worth defending and a reason for consternation; it is an ideal that is inherently troubling for its interlocutors, advocates, and critics. For this reason, even the term 'yifa zhiguo' has been translated differently, with 'rule of law', 'rule by law', and 'ruling the country according to the law' being the most frequent renderings in the English language.

While the rule of law has become a key component of the Chinese legal-political vocabulary since the onset of the reform period, under Xi Jinping's leadership it appears to have increased in importance. Since Xi Jinping took the helm in 2012, he has chosen to adopt exactly this expression to shape his policy and justice agendas. But the authoritarian way in which the concept has been used thus far has, in many quarters, produced a palpable sense of surprise and dismay over the future of the Chinese legal system. The current leadership is shaping what at first glance seems to be quite incongruous goals—fighting corruption and the erosion of institutional credibility; fighting criminals and dissenters who threaten stability; and guarding against national and international security threats—all under the same rhetorical and ideological rubric. During the last year, the rule of law has served the practical function of maintaining social stability and controlling dissent. It has equally justified anti-corruption campaigns targeting party officials, and the repression of civil society and human rights activism. Although their activities remained well within the legal or constitutional rights of Chinese citizens, lawyers, labour activists, and people working for NGOs became key targets of repression.

Through a discussion between three experts on the historical and ideological development of socio-legal issues in China—Joshua Rosenzweig, Ewan Smith, and Susan Trevaskes—this Forum aims at reframing our understanding of Xi's 'rule of law' agenda and enriching our sense of the meaning of this contested expression in the contemporary political context.

The expression 'yifa zhiguo' may be translated in different ways. The most common renderings in English are 'rule of law', 'rule by law', and 'ruling the country according to the law'; however, each of these translations carries different connotations. How would you best translate 'yifa zhiguo' and, in your view, what is the meaning of this expression in contemporary China?

Joshua Rosenzweig: I think that part of the reason why this expression has so many different translations is that the meaning can be very context-dependent. As with other ideologically significant phrases, there are hegemonic uses that serve to reinforce existing power structures and there are counter-hegemonic uses that work against those structures—often deliberately, sometimes less so. Most people probably have a particular understanding of what they mean when they use the phrase at any given point, but once those usages become part of the public discourse, they can be understood in ways that were not necessarily intended. Put simply, I think that the differences boil down to whether or not one believes that law has any autonomous moral authority of its own, separate from political power. When Chinese officials speak of '*yifa zhiguo*', they are thinking of law purely in terms of a tool of governance. Law establishes rules that reflect the morality that is assumed to inhere in political order, and a society that understands and follows those rules is, therefore, a good and just society. I do not think it matters too much whether you call this notion 'rule by law' or 'rule according to law'. When others talk about '*yifa zhiguo*'—or its cousin '*fazhi*'—it is clear that they are, in fact, thinking in terms of law as a source of authority that is distinguishable from power. As such, for them law reflects external standards that should set bounds for the behaviour of the regime, not just society. I think this is closer to what many people mean when they think of rule of law. Because the difference comes from different understandings of '*fa*', so the same phrase can connote different things to different people.

Ewan Smith: Neither rule of law nor '*yifa zhiguo*' has a fixed meaning: both expressions refer to a range of contested ideas. There is a partial overlap between the English and the Chinese phrases. Sometimes, '*yifa zhiguo*' means something similar to rule of law. For example, if the words are used casually, to describe an alternative to arbitrary government, the 'rule of law' is the best translation because it is familiar. In contrast, 'rule by law' and 'ruling the country according to the law' are unfamiliar expressions that jar the reader. They draw attention to the fact that '*yifa zhiguo*' means something different, unfamiliar and even dissonant to rule of law. In some contexts, it is important to underline these differences by translating '*yifa zhiguo*' in this way. It would be unwise to offer an all-purpose definition of '*yifa zhiguo*', just as it would be unwise to give an all purpose definition of the rule of law. It might mean the same thing A.V. Dicey, or Lon Fuller, or Tom Bingham meant when they said 'rule of law'. But in official discourse, this is unlikely.

Susan Trevaskes: '*Yifa zhiguo*' is probably best translated as 'governing the nation [or country] in accordance with the law.' This is a concept that developed in the mid-1990s drawing on basic ideas about socialist rule of law from the 1980s. It began in the 1990s as a slogan that stood for greater emphasis on the use of law and regulations in state administration. It does not mean a separation of the Party from the state. To the contrary, governance in China since the 1990s has seen the embedding of the Party within the state through party groups (*xiaozu*) planted in all areas of government which comprise members holding key positions (such as a governor of a province). The Party delegates authority to state institutions for routine governance while continuing to lead exclusively over political, ideological and institutional matters.

In your opinion, to what extent has the use of the concept 'yifa zhiguo' changed in Xi Jinping's China in comparison to the Jiang Zemin and Hu Jintao eras? Can you please highlight both continuities and changes?

Joshua Rosenzweig: I do not think that Jiang Zemin or Hu Jintao had substantially different understandings of the concept of '*yifa zhiguo*' compared to Xi Jinping. But Xi Jinping seems to have given the idea a bit of a renaissance and made it a more prominent part of his agenda. One reason is that Xi Jinping sees rule-based governance as a way to impose discipline and centralise control over the party-state bureaucracy. The stress of the previous decades had been on promoting economic growth and maintaining social stability, and there was a tacit understanding that as long as these results were achieved there would not be too many questions from above about who was getting rich on the side or what methods were employed to maintain stability. But corruption, inequality, and 'rigid stability' tactics contributed to a growing sense of popular injustice that needed to be addressed in some way. Moreover, given the daunting task of reorienting China's economy, the country's leaders need to be able to count on the bureaucracy to respond to its directions instead of playing by its own rules. Another reason for the prominence of '*yifa zhiguo*' under Xi Jinping is that China's current leadership is trying to restore the party-state's ideological dominance by flooding the public discourse with its own messages and squeezing out any alternative usages. The promotion of '*yifa zhiguo*' in the 1990s coincided with the re-emergence of a relatively autonomous arena for discussion and debate of public affairs in which matters of law and justice formed an important part. For a while, ideas about human rights, procedural justice, and constitutionalism flourished and shaped critical notions of how law might function in China. Recognising the challenge posed by these alternative ideas, Xi Jinping has taken steps to isolate and excise these views from the public discourse and 'unify thinking' around orthodox views of law and justice.

Ewan Smith: Hu Jintao came to power less than a year after China acceded to the

Jiang Zemin, Hu Jintao, and Xi Jinping have guided the Chinese Communist Party for almost three decades. PC: *South China Morning Post*

World Trade Organization. During Hu's administration, the '*yifa zhiguo*' policy was often presented as necessary step towards compliance with rule of law obligations, and as an instrument to achieve bigger economic objectives, such as the '*xiaokang shehui*' or 'moderately prosperous society'. Over time, we see more and more language presenting the rule of law as something that is instrumentally good. In the official discourse, rule of law became an 'essential guarantee' of policy goals as diverse as 'socialist material, spiritual, and political culture', the 'three represents', and 'scientific development'. In his explanation of the Decision of the Fourth Plenum from 2014, Xi mirrors this language. He describes the rule of law as a 'fundamental requirement' for 'safeguarding social harmony and stability', 'guaranteeing the long-term peace and order of the Party and the country', and '[promoting] the sustained and healthy development of our country's economy and society'. But one important change under Xi has been a decidedly voluntarist turn in the use of the rule of law, especially with the advent of the current anti-corruption campaign. Under Xi, the rule of law has been partially subordinated to an agenda that seeks to contain power 'within the cage of regulation' (*ba quanli guanjin zhidu de longzi li*). It is not a tool that can rectify institutions. Instead, it is one of a series of tools that can rectify individuals.

Susan Trevaskes: The use of '*yifa zhiguo*' in the Xi Jinping, Hu Jintao, and Jiang Zemin eras is essentially the same, but Xi has given it a new twist, emphasising the idea of Party leadership through the rule of law. The Resolution of the historic Fourth Plenum of the Eighteenth Party Congress in 2014 states that the Party's leadership [over and through government] and socialist rule of law are identical. Crucially, the document insists that the Party will now 'implement its leadership role through the rule of law'. The meaning of '*yifa zhiguo*', or at least the purpose to which it has been put to use by Xi Jinping and close colleagues, is to accentuate a particular relationship between the party-state and the people. After a decade of Hu Jintao's 'Harmonious Society' (*hexie shehui*) and 'Stability Maintenance' (*weiwen*) in the 2000s, it had become apparent to the incoming Party leadership that rigid Stability Maintenance operations were severely undermining judicial and political credibility, and could not be sustained as a long-term political solution. To win back the hearts and minds of people whose trust in the law had been seriously eroded by party corruption, Xi Jinping and Li Keqiang began talking about accountability, transparency, clean government, and so on. But this new platform required a substantial reinvigoration of centralised Party power in order to regain the capacity to limit corruption at the local level on the one hand, and to deal with perceived threats to national security on the other. Hence, we find Xi Jinping bringing Party supremacy back into political fashion. The ideological role of '*yifa zhiguo*' in Xi's China gives the Party rhetorical permission to govern China in such a way that it can deal with disunity, dissent, and crime using the weapon of the law.

How does history matter to the way in which 'yifa zhiguo' is officially intended today?

Joshua Rosenzweig: There are so many ways to approach this question, in part because there are different ways to think about 'history'. Let me focus on two. First, I would say that in contemporary China '*yifa zhiguo*' has always been contrasted positively against the idea of the 'lawless' and arbitrary years under Mao, especially during the Cultural Revolution. The Maoist period is a useful benchmark for legal and institutional progress because, especially for the majority of people whose lives have improved since the 'reform and opening', there are so many reasons to be satisfied with the relative stability and security that China's current legal system has to offer—even with its many flaws. But the utility of this referent is fading as time marches on, and there's reason to wonder whether Chinese citizens now in their twenties, thirties, and even forties will continue to evaluate the state of their legal system against the high point of legal nihilism under Mao. Second, I would say that history matters in the sense that, in the nearly forty years since the beginning of the reform period, China has experienced historical changes that I would argue are transforming the way that Chinese people think about the state-centred justice model that underlies the official agenda of '*yifa zhiguo*'. Several decades of socio-economic change have produced a society that is far more individualistic, diverse, and contentious than the authoritarian stability-harmony model acknowledges. It is within such a society that alternative ideas about rights, checks on government, and procedural rights have started to make sense. China's current leaders seem to want to ignore the passage of time and the demands that socio-economic change has brought. They want to force society to conform to their vision of society, rather than adapt to the changed realities of that society. I do not think this is a sustainable strategy.

Ewan Smith: History provides a reference point by which we can assess what it means to run the country according to law. While international comparison dominates the debate about the rule of law outside China, historical comparison is a much more important context for Chinese official discussion of '*yifa zhiguo*'. Every politburo member grew up during the Cultural Revolution, and this serves as a framing device for '*yifa zhiguo*'. Younger Chinese people grew up while a legal system was rebuilt from scratch around them. In the official discourse (especially the early official discourse) this sense of constant progress is offset against the type of arbitrary government that came before. In this way, history amplifies the importance of '*yifa zhiguo*', it relativises it, and it emphasises the extent to which it has already been achieved. More broadly, for reasons that I touch on above, historical argument sets the tone and tempo for political reform in Chinese official discourse. During the Seventeenth Politburo, one reason why China needed to implement the rule of law policy was because 'prevailing historical conditions' meant the time was right. Likewise, at least in the official discourse, 'prevailing historical conditions' will dictate when China is ready for more democratic and accountable governance.

Susan Trevaskes: The history of various discussions on socialist rule of law and a number of key political events in China have helped to shape '*yifa zhiguo*' as we know it today. We can break up the term '*yifa zhiguo*' into various parts—'*fa*' then '*yifa*' then '*yifa zhiguo*' to understand the influence of history. First, in terms of law (*fa*), from the early 1950s onwards, law in the People's Republic of China was seen as a manifestation of party policy. That is not to say that all laws were party policies, but that the intent of the law was basically in harmony with Party policy. After Deng Xiaoping came to power, the Party's ideas about the nature of law did not fundamentally change; law remained socialist in purpose and intent. As the scholar Harro von Senger noted in 1985, 'law does not serve the function of an autonomous force for shaping the social order, independent of the [Chinese Communist] Party norms. It serves rather as a vehicle for making casuistic elaborations to Party norms' (Von Senger 1989, 207). Second, the phrase '*yifa*' (in accordance with the law) has its origins in the 1950s, particularly during a brief period after 1954 when the Constitution was promulgated. It was taken up again with gusto in the early 1980s as a phrase attached to various party-state actions such as 'severely punishing in accordance with the law (*yifa yancheng*) or '[Party] Rule in accordance with the law' (*yifa zhizheng*). Stressing '*yifa*' in the 1980s was an attempt to changed public and Party mindsets from 'rule of man' to 'rule of law'.

This was a new consciousness of law based on the idea that law would institutionalised through courts and government agencies to create a basis for economic modernisation and a sound spiritual civilisation. Third, in terms of '*yifa zhiguo*' in the 1990s. It has been widely documented that the Party abandoned its aspiration of state-Party separation following the 1989 Tiananmen incident and the collapse of the Soviet Union. Therefore, progressively throughout the mid to late 1990s, the relatively simple message about the benefits of rule-of-law over rule-of-man was replaced with a more specific governance-based message about how the country should be ruled. This new political line required a new slogan, 'Governing the Nation in Accordance with the Law' (*yifa zhiguo*). '*Yifa zhiguo*' became the platform under which the institutionalisation of the Party-state was to take place in China. It was a catchcry about how good governance should be achieved: through introduction of new laws and regulations aimed at better supervising and limiting administrative powers. In the late 1990s, '*yifa zhiguo*' morphed into a political institutionalisation strategy, bolstering Party power to make concrete decisions about governance through Party groups and committees at all levels of government. President Jiang Zemin promulgated '*yifa zhiguo*' at the Fifteenth Party Congress as the Party's ruling paradigm and it was inserted into the Constitution in 1999.

In your view, what is the relationship between 'yifa zhiguo' and 'yide zhiguo' (ruling the country according to virtue) in today's China?

Joshua Rosenzweig: I think the ideas are meant to be complementary and acknowledge the two main strands of Chinese political tradition, Confucianism and Legalism. Even though these are often taken to be opposed, the reality is that for millennia Chinese leaders governed by mixing the two schools of thought. To me, the relationship between the two goes back to the assumption of a political regime that is inherently moral. The virtue of the regime's rulers is a manifestation of that morality but is also something that must be properly cultivated and reinforced. Law is necessary to guide virtuous behaviour among officials and society at large, but it too is intended as a manifestation of the moral regime. Both work together in a kind of balance that produces order and stability from the top down. I do not necessarily think this harkening back to traditions of Chinese political-legal culture is part of any great ideological shift under Xi, per se. These ways of thinking about power and the relationship between state and society are structural elements of Chinese culture that are being laid bare because the modern ideological garb that they have been wearing for over a century has begun to wear thin.

Susan Trevaskes: To understand the significance of '*yide zhiguo*' for '*yifa zhiguo*' we need to understand the Confucian mindset of the Party. Party leaders assume a paternal fosterage role in enlightening a politically and legally illiterate citizenry. Xi has been continuously enlightening China's citizens of the necessity of a strong Party to rule in their interests

The concept of 'rule of law' very often seems to imply a teleological march from Marxism to a more liberal system of governance. In your view, to what extent will the 'yifa zhiguo' agenda be able to promote the development of a different, more democratic, and accountable system of governance in China in the future?

Joshua Rosenzweig: In and of itself, the official legal development agenda associated with '*yifa zhiguo*' is not intended to lead to liberal democracy for China, and I think the sooner we all recognise that the better. For too long we have chosen to hear 'rule of law' every time a Chinese official speaks of '*yifa zhiguo*' or '*fazhi*', and we think that they are aspiring to achieve our version of legal and political culture, but they just lack the capacity or techniques to get there. So we have focused on helping them build that capacity and meanwhile our paths are still not converging—or to the e*x*te*n*t that they are converging, it might be because we are actually moving closer to them, rather than the other way around. The best thing '*yifa zhiguo*' really has going for it is the promise of stability and order. I do not see any hint of democratic innovation out of such a paternalistic system that puts limits on basic freedoms of expression and association precisely to stunt the development of a democratic (as opposed to populist) culture. As for accountability, I think that, so long as the system relies on self-regulation and sees the regime itself as the ultimate source of moral authority, there will not be much innovation there either. I would not say that either democracy or accountability is faring much better in Western countries right now, but I do not see any reason to hold out hope that China's current path is leading to something superior.

Ewan Smith: I do not agree that the rule of law should be thought of as a march. Political reform in China is controversial and no single idea leads inexorably towards liberalisation. If anyone is likely to think of the rule of law as a march towards a distant goal, it is the Chinese Communist Party. The Party's official doctrine embraces the Marxist theory of a historical materialism. Put simply, historical materialists believe social and political progress is achieved through historical and economic development. From this point of view, political ideas like the rule of law can be seen as waypoints on a longer march towards an inevitable, historical objective. It may also be politically convenient to think of the rule of law as something to be achieved gradually, in increments, alongside other economic objectives. Progress towards the rule of law is not the same as rule of law, and the more we think about where China is going, the less we think about where China actually is. This is not to say that the rule of law does not play an important role in Chinese politics. Eighty-five million party members spent the latter part of 2014 talking about a version of the rule of law because it was the topic of the Fourth Plenum and, in areas where there is limited political opposition, China has made rapid progress. The current reforms to the justice sector will make life more predictable for millions of people. Both of these examples suggest ways in which the 'rule of law' agenda might promote a more accountable system of government in China. At the same time, we ought to resist the temptation to overstate its importance. It is official state policy to promote '*yifa zhiguo*', but there is nothing fundamental about this. The policy yields to cardinal principles like Party leadership.

Susan Trevaskes: A number of basic elements of Xi Jinping's '*yifa zhiguo*' push may, in the future, become very helpful in improving greater transparency and accountability. But the concept of '*yifa zhiguo*' will not promote an overall improvement in the relationship between the party-state and society (or more precisely between the Party and 'the people'). This is because the very purpose of '*yifa zhiguo*' is to promote the idea that the law is a manifestation of the people's will and interests, and that the Party exists in order to protect the people's interests. Under the '*yifa zhiguo*' ideology, the people cannot enjoy any rights and interests outside the leadership of the Party whose role it is to develop and protect (Party-initiated) rights and interests.

OCT/DEC 2016

Rescuers after a mine blast that killed thirty-two miners in Inner Mongolia on 3 December. PC: XINHUA

Xi Stresses Party Leadership over State-Owned Enterprises

On 11 October at a high-level national meeting Xi Jinping reaffirmed the centrality of Party leadership over China's state-owned enterprises (SOEs). According to the official Xinhua News Agency, Xi emphasised that under a stronger leadership from the Party—'the root and soul' of SOEs in his words—SOEs should serve to implement the decisions of the Party, to promote national projects such as One Belt One Road, and to strengthen China's economic and social development and national power. Xi urged further reform of the management and supervision of SOEs in order to improve corporate profitability and competitiveness, and to increase the value of state assets. Xinhua reported that in 2016 central SOEs underwent merging and consolidation, and announced that next year the reforms will focus on cutting inefficiency and overcapacity of local SOEs. SOEs retain a dominant role in the Chinese economy: in the first half of 2016, the gross revenues of central and local SOEs (excluding financial companies) reached 21.39 trillion yuan, or more than sixty percent of the national gross domestic product. In the same speech, Xi pointed to state workers' rights to 'know, participate, express and supervise within the SOEs', and referred to the role of workers' congresses in the democratic management of the companies and in the resolution of labour disputes. This is likely in response to the state workers' protests early this year against the government's cutting of overcapacity in the steel and coal industries (see the chapter by Kevin Lin on pp. 20–23 in the present book).

(Sources: **South China Morning Post, Xinhua 1, Xinhua 2**)

Tougher Rules for Ride-Hailing Businesses in China

In October, some of China's largest cities—including Beijing, Shanghai, Guangzhou, Shenzhen, Chongqing, Tianjin, and Hangzhou—rolled out new regulations on internet-based ride-hailing businesses. China has thus become the first country in the world to create a formal legal framework for the sector. The regulations limit the pool of drivers and vehicles, citing concerns about traffic and safety. However, the criteria are discriminatory toward migrants in that they require drivers to have a local household registration or at least to be long-term, tax-paying residents of the city with a temporary residence permit of no less than six months. In recent years, Internet-based ride-hailing businesses have flourished, attracting migrants to work as drivers: in Beijing, more than eighty percent of the ride-hailing drivers are migrants from outside the city. The ride-hailing businesses have also led to protests by taxi drivers who see their businesses squeezed by unlicensed taxi and ride-hailing cars. But ride-hailing car drivers in China have held their own protests: for instance, in March, hundreds of Uber drivers in Hangzhou blocked roads and protested against entrapment by police. Uber China reportedly told its drivers not to clash with police.

(Sources: **Bloomberg, Caixin 1, Caixin 2, Caixin 3, The Financial Times**)

(Left) President Xi Jinping giving a speech. (Right) Cars impounded for 'illegal transportation'.

Meng Han Sentenced

On 3 November, Meng Han, the last of the labour activists detained in the crackdown of December 2015, was found guilty and sentenced to twenty-one months in jail by the Panyu district court in Guangzhou. While detained, Meng Han was denied access to his lawyer, and his parents were repeatedly harassed in their apartment by unidentified men. After the announcement of the sentence, friends and fellow activists held a fundraising initiative to collect money to support Meng Han's living expenses while in jail, and about thirty unionists and labour rights groups in Hong Kong organised a protest outside the Hong Kong China Liason Office demanding his immediate release. Days before the trial, the International Labour Organisation's Committee on Freedom of Association released its interim report in response to a complaint launched by the International Trade Union Confederation. In it, the Chinese government was criticised for its treatment of labour activists, who 'appear to have been arrested, detained and charged for being involved in a labour dispute and considers that the detentions of persons connected with their activities in defense of the interest of workers constitutes a serious interference with civil liberties in general and with trade union rights in particular.' Labour NGOs all over the country are under increasing pressure. In Beijing, the Migrant Workers' Home, a historic labour NGO that focuses on cultural activities for migrants, is facing eviction after more than ten years. The enforcement of China's Foreign NGO Management Law in January 2017 will make it increasingly hard for NGOs to gain access to vital financial support from abroad (see the Compendium of the Law on pp. 60–67 in the present book).

(Sources: **China Labour Bulletin**, **Jiliuwang**, **South China Morning Post, The Initium**)

Mine Blasts Kill Dozens

On 27 September, a gas explosion in a coal mine in Ningxia took the lives of twenty miners. Similar explosions killed thirty-three miners in the municipality of Chongqing on 31 October, twenty-one miners in Heilongjiang province on 29 November, and thirty-two miners in Inner Mongolia on 3 December. More recently, on 5 December a gas explosion resulted in the deaths of eleven miners in Hubei province. Being the world's top producer and consumer of coal, China has a tragic history of mine explosions. In recent years, authorities have been swift to crack down on unsafe mining operations. Commenting on the blast in Chongqing municipality, the State Administration of Coal Mine Safety said that despite the fact that the mine operation was fully licensed, it was still unsafe and illegal. In particular, the mine was too deep and the underground facilities did not have adequate ventilation. The State Administration has ordered all Chongqing mines to halt operations and conduct immediate safety inspections. China's national safety regulator has also warned coal mines not to operate beyond their daily capacities, as rising prices tempt mine owners to increase production. In several cases, safety officials have been fired and mine operators arrested.

(Sources: **Sixth Tone**, **South China Morning Post**, **Xinhua**)

(Left) Labour activist Meng Han. (Right) Xinjia Coal Mine in Badong county, which was the scene of the third fatal mining explosion in China within a week.

Parents of Left-Behind Children Face Prosecution

According to an official survey on the migrant population in China in 2016 released in mid-October by the National Health and Family Planning Commission, around sixty-one million children—more than a third of whom are younger than seventeen—currently live in the Chinese countryside without the daily care of their parents, who have migrated to other areas for work. These 'left behind children' are a serious social problem in China (see also the brief at p. 12 of this book). Earlier this year, Zhang Dandan a professor at Peking University, released the result of a survey of one thousand two hundred criminals in prison: about seventeen per cent of them had been 'left behind children'. Tragedies are common. Earlier this year, three children, who had been left in the care of their grandmother by their migrant parents, drowned in a pond near their home village outside of Nanchang, Jiangxi province. There have also been some instances of suicide. In January 2014, a nine-year-old child hanged himself in the house of his grandparents in Huayang, Anhui province, after learning from his grandmother that his mother, a migrant worker, was not going to come home for the holidays. In June 2015, in a village in Bijie, Guizhou province, a thirteen-year-old boy and his three younger sisters killed themselves after having been left alone for months by their migrant parents. To prevent such tragedies, in February 2016, the State Council ordered local governments to establish a database of these children and issued guidelines to improve the physical and psychological health of such children. In November 2016, the Ministry of Civil Affairs, along with the police, the judicial departments, and the Ministry of Education announced a clampdown on parents who leave their children behind. Parents who fail to provide their children with proper parental care for six months or longer can now lose their custodial rights at the request of their relatives, village officials, or civil-affairs authorities.

(Sources: **Caixin**, **CCTV**, **State Council**, **Zhongguo Qingnianbao**, **National Health and Family Planning Commission**, **South China Morning Post**, **The Paper**)

Strikes at Multinational Companies in China

The last quarter of 2016 witnessed a series of strikes among the employees of several multinational companies in China over ownership changes. First, on 8 November, dozens of employees went on strike at a bottling plant owned by Danone in Guangzhou that had just been sold to a local company after learning that the French multinational was refusing to offer severance payment according to the workers' years of employment on the pretext of the unchanged corporate name. After two weeks of strike, the company agreed to meet with the workers, but on that occasion the riot police entered the factory grounds and attacked the workers, with the result that several were injured. On 10 November, workers at a smartphone camera parts factory in Guangzhou owned by Sony went on strike for two weeks after the company announced the sale of the plant to a local company. They feared that working conditions and pay would suffer and jobs would be lost under the new ownership. To end the protest, the Japanese company paid off the workers with one thousand yuan each and fired dozens of strike leaders. Finally, on 23 November, protests erupted among workers in three plants owned by Coca-Cola in Chongqing, Chengdu, and Jilin province, when it was announced that the American company was going to sell all its bottling plants in China to a Chinese state-owned food giant. The workers feared that after the sale they would lose their jobs or get lower wages, so they launched these coordinated strikes to demand the disclosure of the details of the agreement and economic compensation.

(Sources: **Caixin**, **China Labour Bulletin**, **Nikkei**, **Red Balloon Solidarity**, **The Guardian**)

Danone's Chinese logo.

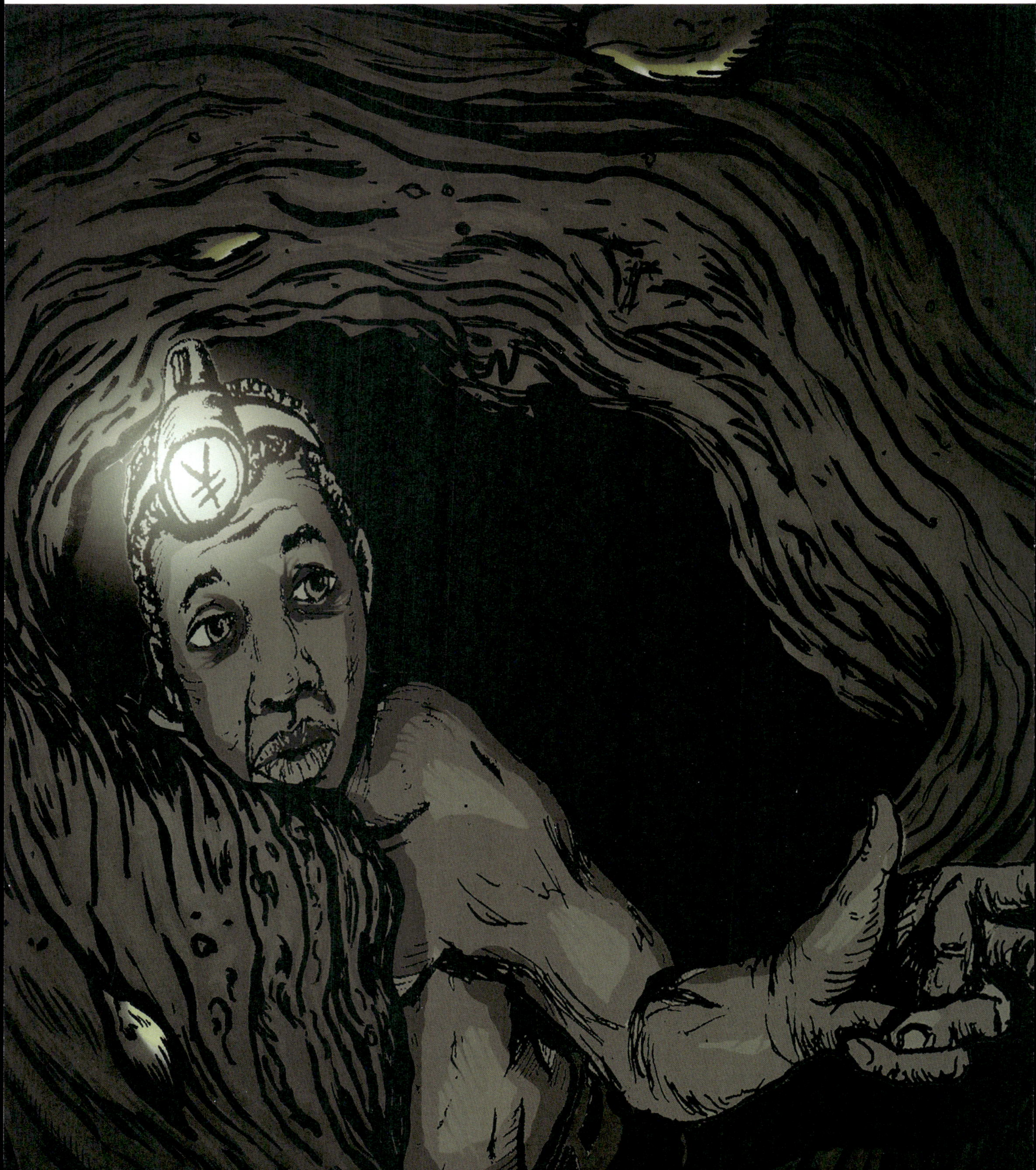

HEART OF DARKNESS?

Nkana mine in Zambia is one of the largest in Africa and has been in operation since 1932. PC: Wikipedia

Fighting the Race to the Bottom:
Regulating Chinese Investment in Zambian Mines

Mukete Beyongo Dynamic

Following the widespread privatisation of the Zambian copper mining sector in the 1990s, several state-owned companies from China began to invest in the country. While these companies have created jobs, built valuable infrastructure, and paid taxes to the government, China's increasing presence in Zambia has also given rise to a number of concerns. Some Chinese mining companies have been accused of maintaining lax safety standards, paying low wages to local employees, and of physically abusing their workers. Critics allege that this has triggered a 'race to the bottom' in labour standards. Still, such a perspective runs the risk of being over simplistic, as it largely overlooks the agency of local actors.

Copper mining remains the dominant economic activity in Zambia, a situation that has not changed since 1928 when large-scale mining was introduced in the country. According to a World Bank report released in June 2015, the sector today accounts for more than sixty-five per cent of Zambia's export earnings and eleven per cent of its gross domestic product (The World Bank 2015). However, while the World Bank detailed the benefits of the sector to the economy, another more critical report released at the same time by the Office of the Auditor General of Zambia found that the mining sector has seen the largest number of industrial accidents and fatalities in post-colonial Zambia (Auditor General 2015). For this reason, finding a way to mitigate risks to worker safety while increasing copper production has become a paramount public concern in the country.

The widespread privatisation of the Zambian copper mining sector in the 1990s led to the re-emergence of foreign mining companies in the country, including several state-owned companies from China. While these Chinese companies have created jobs, built valuable infrastructure, and paid taxes to the government, China's increasing presence in Zambia has also given rise to a number of concerns. Some Chinese mining companies have been accused of maintaining lax safety standards, paying low wages to local employees—especially if compared to other foreign mining companies—and of physically abusing their workers (Blair 2006). For these reasons, critics have accused the Zambian government of weakening its safety standards to attract foreign investors, of failing to monitor compliance with safety and labour laws, and of underfunding local regulators (Haglund 2008).

These critics allege that this has triggered a 'race to the bottom' in labour standards. By 'race to the bottom', they refer to a tendency where the government reduces the monitoring and enforcement capacity of public regulatory institutions, or enacts lax safety laws, in order to attract foreign investors. They not only argue that the Zambian government weakens safety standards through funding cuts, but they also claim that current regulatory standards are obsolete and that the government intervenes in the decision-making process of regulators to protect Chinese companies from paying penalties when they fail to comply with local regulations. Still, such a perspective runs the risk of being over simplistic, as it largely overlooks the agency of local actors.

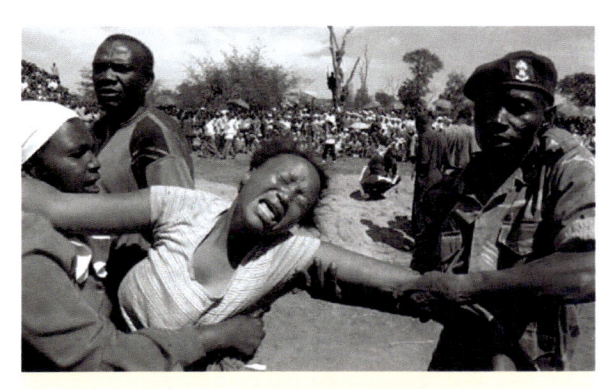

A woman in despair at the funeral of fifty-one workers who were killed at a Chinese-owned copper mine in Zambia in 2005. PC: Salim Henry

The Roots of the Discontent

In April 2005, fifty-two Zambians were killed in an accident in an explosives factory jointly owned by the Beijing General Institute for Research and Metallurgy (BGRIMM) and the Non-Ferrous China-Africa (NFCA) Mining Company—both state-owned companies—in Chambishi in Zambia's Copperbelt Province (BBC 2005). One year after the accident at the BGRIMM plant, five Zambians were shot and injured by gunshots fired by their Chinese manager while they were protesting against low wages and lax safety standards at the NFCA Chambishi mine. In light of this, it is not surprising that Chinese safety and labour relations in Zambian copper mines were at the centre of Zambia's 2006 presidential election. Indeed, in a keynote speech former Zambian president Michael Sata stated that '[Chinese] labour relations are very bad. They are not adding any value to what they claim is investment; instead of creating jobs for the local workforce, they bring in Chinese workers to cut wood and carry water' (Blair 2006).

Such high-level political attention fuelled the discontent. In August 2008, more than five hundred Zambian workers attacked a newly built Chinese-owned Chambishi Copper Smelter and burnt down the kitchen of a Chinese-resident. One Chinese and three Zambians working in the kitchen were seriously injured. The protesters claimed that they had been told that the management was going on vacation and abandoning collective negotiations in which workers had demanded changes in safety standards and a reduction in work hours. In another accident that attracted a lot of media attention in 2010, a Chinese supervisor at the Collum Coal mine in Southern Province shot thirteen Zambians. The workers at the mine were complaining against the state of safety standards in the mines and their low wages. These accidents and protests have raised serious debate about labour and safety standards in Chinese mines in Zambia and about the local government's ability to enforce their own regulations in these contexts.

The Importance of Local Actors

The claim that Chinese companies are creating a 'race to the bottom' in labour standards, while having certain merits, ultimately simplifies the processes at play in the formulation of safety and labour regulations in Zambia. It is based on a state/business-centred approach that ignores the role of non-state actors, such as trade unions, mine workers, local NGOs, and international organisations. The 2006 protest at the NFCA mine mentioned above is a good case in point. In June 2006, NFCA mine workers went on strike in protest against the company's refusal to implement a labour agreement it had agreed to with National Union of Mine and Allied Workers of Zambia to improve safety at its Chambishi mine. When five miners were shot in the protest, the popular reaction to the onslaught led to significant safety and labour relations reform at the mine (Sautman and Yan 2014).

In response, the NFCA launched the 'Safe Production Management System' in which Safety and Environmental Protection were restructured into a separate department. Moreover, in 2007, the NFCA introduced a company 'Safety Month' in commemoration of the incident, an event that is still being held every June. Nine years after the incident, in a company memo sent to all workers at the start of the 2015 Safety Month, the management suggested that commemorating the month of June on a yearly basis demonstrates the company's commitment to ensuring that its operations are conducted in a safe and risk-free environment. In an interview that I conducted in Chambishi Township in October 2015, a union leader at the NFCA mine told me that the 2006 protest positively changed safety and labour relations at the mine.

Furthermore, the 'race to the bottom' thesis suggests that the Zambian government is passive with regard to safety abuses in the country, or negligent of labour conflicts within Chinese mines because the authorities prioritise economic growth and investment over safety. This is far from the truth. For instance, during a parliamentary debate on 11 July 2007, in response to the 2005 BGRIMM accident, former deputy minister of Mines and Minerals Development, Maxwell Mwale, told the Zambian parliament that the government had increased the number of inspection vehicles, logistics, and staff at the Mines Safety Department (National Assembly of Zambia 2007). According to official data, inspections increased from two hundred and sixty in 2004 to 1,269 in 2014. Furthermore, a report published in 2009 by the International Labour Organisation also highlighted labour and safety reforms undertaken in Zambia since the incident (International Labour Organisation 2009). For instance, in 2006, the government introduced an integrated labour inspection form to streamline inspections and verification of compliance; forty-five new inspectors were hired; and the administrative powers of inspectors were increased.

In addition, in 2008, 2012, and 2015, the government revised the national Employment Act. A Minimum Wage Bill was introduced in 2012, fines for non-compliance with safety standards were increased, and labour inspectors were provided with more powers to enforce labour and safety laws. In November 2007, the government established a Labour Task Force through the Ministry of Labour and Social Security to enforce and ensure adherence to national labour laws. The number of members on the task force jumped from forty-five in 2007 to ninety-one in 2009. Moreover, a new Mines and Mineral Development Act was passed in 2015, providing officials at the Mines Safety

Department with stronger powers to enforce and ensure that mining companies maintain a safe and healthy working environment. According to official data, industrial accidents and fatalities in mining companies have declined since 2006: the number of accidents recorded by the Mines Safety Department fell from three hundred and fifty in 2005 to 123 in 2014, while the number of fatal accidents fell from eighty in 2005 to twelve in 2014.

Challenges Ahead

Ching Kwan Lee has claimed that 'Chinese investors [operating in Zambia] have had to climb a steep learning curve in dealing with types of politics not found in their own country' (Lee 2014, 29). The trend of injuries and fatalities in Chinese mines in Zambia recorded by the Mines Safety Department supports this claim. However, as a 2011 study by Human Rights Watch (HRW) has highlighted, Chinese mining companies in Zambia still have further reforms to make in order to strengthen their efforts to mitigate accidents (HRW 2011). These include improving the safety conditions of workers hired by subcontractors, reducing the number of casual employees, and cutting the number of working hours. A letter sent to HRW by officials from the China Non-Ferrous Metal Mining Company in 2011, and quoted in the same report, suggest that these reforms are gradually being introduced. Conversations between the author and mine workers at the NFCA mine indicates that as of October 2015, although safety and labour disputes between the NFCA and local unions have been normalised, some workers in Chinese companies contracted by the NFCA still work under unsafe conditions—most often without appropriate safety equipment. However, as one worker said, compared to 2006, before the BGRIMM accident and the NFCA Chambishi protest, there have been significant improvements in the enforcement of safety and labour regulations at the NFCA mine and the Chambishi Copper Smelter.

To conclude, the activities of Chinese mining companies have indeed threatened a 'race to the bottom' in labour and safety standards in Zambia. But local actors such as trade unions have organised protests, and pushed the issue into the public agenda. In response to these protests, some Chinese mining companies have altered their safety policies and normalised their relations with unions. Furthermore, under mounting public pressure, the Zambian government has introduced labour laws and established structures to strengthen its safety regulatory standards in the last decade. Nevertheless, notwithstanding the demonstrable success of these measures in reducing industrial accidents, the industrial relations system in Zambia still suffers from inadequate funding, limited human resources and capacity, and in some instances a lack of coordination among the relevant regulatory agencies.

Mukete Beyongo

Mukete Beyongo is a PhD Candidate at the Australian Centre on China in the World, the Australian National University. His research focuses on local responses to growing Chinese outbound direct investment in Zambia. He completed his undergraduate and postgraduate studies at the University of Yaounde II-Soa, Cameroon, and the Cherkassy State Technological University, Ukraine.

Small-scale miners in Ghana, PC: Francis Carmine

There and Back Again:
Conceptualising the Chinese Gold Rush in Ghana

Nicholas Loubere
Gordon Crawford

In mid-2013, the Ghanaian government initiated a crackdown on the estimated 50,000 Chinese nationals engaging in small-scale gold mining in the country. In both the media and popular discourse the Chinese miners were depicted as feeding into corruption, destroying the environment and stealing resources from marginal sectors of Ghanaian society. However, we still do not know much about who these miners were, the factors that compelled them to travel to such a distant land in the hopes of 'striking it rich', or how the spoils of this gold rush were distributed back in China.

On 15 May 2013, Ghanaian President John Dramani Mahama announced the establishment of an Inter-Ministerial Task Force aimed at bringing 'sanity' to the country's rapidly (and chaotically) expanding small-scale mining sector (Kaiman and Hirsch 2013). Over the course of the next month, the army and police proceeded to 'flush out' and deport nearly five thousand foreign nationals who were illegally engaging in small-scale mining—the vast majority of whom were Chinese, primarily originating from Shanglin County in the country's Guangxi Zhuang Autonomous Region (Crawford and Botchwey 2016). While there are still some reports of illegal miners setting up new operations 'deep in the bush' (Quartey 2013), most of the estimated fifty thousand Chinese that flooded into Ghana, mainly between 2008 and 2013, have either been deported or have left of their own accord (He 2013).

This brief but intense episode has much to tell us about the perceptions and outcomes of large-scale global migrations, and the ways in which scarce and valuable resources are allocated in the Global South. At the same time, it provides a way of understanding what the increasingly large presence of China on the African continent means for labour and livelihoods in both places. The sudden influx of these small-scale miners to Ghana also draws parallels with Chinese involvement in other gold rushes throughout history. Most notably, the mass exoduses to the United States and Australia in the nineteenth and twentieth centuries—both of which resulted in violent confrontations, strict immigration policies, and the demonisation of the Chinese as 'invaders' by local labour movements. Indeed, in contemporary Ghana, as in previous gold rushes, the Chinese migrant miners have been implicitly depicted as a homogeneous mass that is working in unison, collectively benefiting from the extraction of Ghanaian gold at the expense of poorer segments of the local population, and having a uniform (primarily negative) impact on the environment, economy, and lives of local people. This essay will begin by examining the sudden arrival and equally sudden departure of small-scale Chinese miners in Ghana. It will then go on to raise important questions for future research related to China-Africa migration dynamics, the labour relations and inequality existing amongst the Chinese, and the allocation of the extracted resources back in China.

The Gold Rush

Ghana is the second largest gold producer in Africa, and artisanal gold mining has been a traditional indigenous activity in the country for centuries. Particularly over the past few decades, small-scale mining has become an increasingly important way for poor and marginal segments of Ghanaian society to improve their livelihoods by supplementing low returns from farming. In recognition of the importance of this activity for poor rural people, in 2006, the government specifically restricted the sector to Ghanaian citizens, making it illegal for foreign nationals to engage in any small-scale mining activities (Yang 2013).

However, this attempt to reserve small-scale mining for Ghanaians was unsuccessful. From 2005, large numbers of Chinese miners began to arrive to Ghana, mostly from Shanglin County. Shanglin, whose population is primarily ethnically Zhuang (a minority group), has a long historical tradition of gold mining. Throughout the 1990s, Shanglin residents migrated domestically within China to engage in small-scale mining around the country. When the Chinese government tightened regulations on this type of activity, the Shanglin miners looked outward. In the late 2000s, stories of people 'striking it rich' in Ghana, combined with the increase in gold prices in 2008, resulted in a mass influx of Chinese miners establishing over two thousand mining operations (He 2013).

Small-scale miners in Ghana. PC: Francis Carmine

Most of the 'Shanglin gang' took up mining in the rural areas surrounding Kumasi, Obuasi, and Takoradi, compensating the owners of the land with usage fees, and often paying percentages to local government officials or tribal chiefs (Song 2013). In general, mining activities were financed by individual Chinese investors or small groups of partners, who borrowed and pooled larger sums from financial institutions in China in order to purchase excavators and large pumps for dredging (He 2013). The miners then employed workers from China who were promised set monthly wages, and local Ghanaians who were paid daily at a substantially lower rate than the Chinese workers (Song 2013). The Chinese involvement in the sector has resulted in a huge jump in the production of gold from small-scale mines in Ghana (Pichler et al. 2016). And at the height of the gold rush it was estimated that billions of yuan were being sent from Ghana to China—far more than the Ghanaian governmental revenue (He 2013).

Collusion and Pushback

The sudden influx of Chinese miners, and the expansion of their small-scale mining operations, was facilitated through cooperation (or collusion) with Ghanaians, many of whom benefitted individually from their relationships with the Chinese. This situation led to the widespread perception—particularly in the media—that the mining phenomenon was feeding into corruption, and that these corrupt activities were the reason the government had largely ignored (or even protected) the illegal miners. In many cases this perception was entirely justified, with Chinese miners bribing officials to 'turn a blind eye' or paying-off local chiefs in order to illegally gain access to land for mining. For instance, Ghana Immigration Service officials allegedly enabled entry into the country and then provided (false) work permits to Chinese miners for a fee. Ghanaian small-scale miners also reported that, if challenged, Chinese miners would 'threaten to call the minister or police commander,' suggesting close links to high levels of government facilitated by bribes (Crawford et al. 2016).

The Chinese mechanisation of the small-scale mining industry also had huge environmental impacts through the pollution of bodies of water and the clearing of large areas of agricultural land (Kaiman and Hirsch

Gold Mining in Ghana Figures

50,000+
Estimated number of Chinese miners in Ghana until 2013

2,000
Estimated number of Chinese small-scale mines in Ghana in 2013

5,000
Number of Chinese miners directly deported by the Ghanaian government

91 metric tonnes
Ghanaian gold production (2014) (second most in Africa after South Africa)

12 Cedis (about 3 USD)
Approximate daily salary for a Ghanaian mine worker

200 Yuan (about 29 USD)
Approximate salary for a Chinese mine worker.

2013). The introduction of new technologies and mining teams—replacing traditional techniques—meant that the Chinese miners were able to extract much larger quantities of gold than their Ghanaian counterparts. The increasingly visible wealth of the Chinese miners, particularly of the main investors, unsurprisingly resulted in a narrative of resource theft. The Chinese were depicted as stealing a vital livelihood resource from marginal Ghanaians, while also extracting the country's wealth and sending it back to China through illegal channels. In a 2014 interview conducted in Upper Denkyira East Municipality, a licensed Ghanaian concession holder who had worked with Chinese miners expressed the view that 'gold was sent direct to China' with 'so many ways' of doing so. He recounted one method where containers that brought machinery into the country were then used to smuggle gold back to China by cutting out part of the container, filling the inside with gold, and then re-welding it (Crawford et al. 2016).

While most interactions between the Chinese and Ghanaians were collaborative in nature, the negative perception of the Chinese miners was also exacerbated by the widespread reporting of some violent conflicts that coincided with their arrival. As the operations successfully began extracting gold, they also became targets for local bandits and armed robbery. This prompted the Chinese miners to arm themselves—often with guns purchased illegally from the local police (Hirsch 2013)—and engage in firefights with would-be thieves; resulting in the deaths of both Chinese and Ghanaians (Modern Ghana 2013). Finally, in mid-2013, the combination of these issues presented too large of a political challenge to the Ghanaian government, and President Mahama established the Task Force, stating: 'The government will not allow their [the illegal miners] activities to cause conflict, dislocation, environmental degradation and unemployment when in fact the sector should rather benefit our communities and our country' (Kaiman and Hirsch 2013). With that, the Chinese gold rush in Ghana was largely brought to an inglorious end.

Conceptualising the Chinese Migrant Miner

So what does this tell us about the perception of Chinese migrant miners in Ghana, and the role of Chinese migration to the African continent more generally? While the story has been reported on extensively—primarily from Ghana—the picture that has been presented fails to shed light on a number of important aspects of this episode of mass migration, resource extraction, and wealth production (for some). In general, depictions of the Chinese miners in Ghana have been essentialised representations. The miners themselves are largely described as a homogenous group composed of individuals with the same ambitions and having the same potential to 'strike it rich'. This perception of the Chinese as a uniform mass, rather than differentiated individuals and subgroups, follows classic tropes and popular representations of mass migrations in general and Chinese mining migration in particular, both historically and in contemporary discourse. Most notably—and notoriously—both the 'Chinese Exclusion Act' in the United States and the 'White Australia Policy' were the direct result of antagonism towards the sudden arrival of large numbers of Chinese miners, and their perceived ability to extract more gold than 'local' miners through collective effort. Moreover, it is well known that after the end of the gold rushes in the United States and Australia, the remaining Chinese were demonised by local labour movements and accused of undercutting wages. Similarly, the short-lived Chinese gold rush in Ghana has seen 'the Chinese' as a whole being blamed for causing widespread environmental degradation, feeding into corruption, increasing violence, stealing the livelihoods of poor Ghanaians, and capturing the country's resources.

While these problematic issues arising from the sudden influx of Chinese miners and the rapid expansion of mining activities should certainly not be underestimated, the current depiction of the Chinese in Ghana as a singular group tends to obscure as much as enlighten. In particular, these representations fail to explore the migratory and class dynamics that gave rise to the exodus in the first place. They also turn a blind eye to the ways in which different types of Chinese miners benefitted or lost out, and ignore the developmental impacts back in China. Little is known about the Chinese miners themselves, other than the fact that they mainly come from a single poor county in the Guangxi Zhuang Autonomous Region. Even less is known about the labour relations that operated within the small mining groups, or the social processes within China that gave rise to the wider migration phenomenon. While the mining groups are often described as collaborative efforts of 'partners' investing together (He 2013); hierarchical structures have also been observed, with individuals or small groups hiring wage labourers from China (Song 2013). This points to the likelihood that the individual Chinese miners in Ghana have benefited in significantly different ways—with some potentially even being exploited. After all, research on small-scale mining within China has shown that the contribution to the livelihoods of miners is highly differentiated, with wealthier investors profiting at a much higher rate than more marginalised individuals (Lu and Lora-Wainwright 2014). Research has also documented the ways in which poor Chinese migrant workers are often exploited through the withholding (and sometimes non-payment) of wages by 'labour subcontractors' (*baogongtou*) operating in townships and villages (Pun and Xu 2011).

Disentangling the Chinese Miner

Ultimately, this points to the need for research following up on the Shanglin miners who were chased out of Ghana three years ago. Future research should look to examine who these people are, how they went to Ghana in the first place, how the spoils of this gold rush have been distributed amongst the Chinese participants in this story, and what the remittances meant for socioeconomic development in marginal Shanglin County and its ethnically Zhuang population. By lumping the Chinese together, ignoring the different experiences of the miners, and disregarding the fact that these Chinese are themselves a minority group in their own country, we get a distorted view of this historical episode that does not properly reflect the developmental processes and relations at play. Rather than seeing the complex webs of relationships connecting peripheral rural China with the margins of Ghana—and thus producing patterns of resource extraction, accumulation, and inequality between, within and across the people involved in both places—the Chinese as a whole are depicted as uniformly (negatively) impacting on the environment, Ghanaian politics, and the livelihoods of the poorest. In this way, the Chinese miners are ascribed with causal abilities—they are seen as the origin of the negative outcomes rather than a symptom of wider systemic issues. This shifts attention away from the labour relations and unequal power that exist within the Chinese 'mass', resulting in the production of winners and losers among the miners themselves. It also obscures the processes implicit within global capitalism that prompt large numbers of precarious and marginal people to move from one place to another—and sometimes back again—in search of secure livelihoods amid increasingly low returns.

Nicholas Loubere

Nicholas Loubere is an Associate Senior Lecturer in the Study of Modern China at the Centre for East and South-East Asian Studies, Lund University.

Gordon Crawford

Gordon Crawford is Researcher Professor of Global Development in the Centre for Trust, Peace and Social Relations, Coventry University.

A Chinese Empire in the Making?
Questioning Myths from the Agri-Food Sector in Ghana

Jixia Lu

While China's expanding presence in Africa is often framed as a new project in empire building, the Chinese authorities explain their engagement on the continent as simple 'South-South cooperation'. Taking the agricultural sector in Ghana as a case study, this article challenges both narratives and argues that Chinese farmers in Africa are not a 'silent army' (either malevolent or benevolent), but instead are largely precarious individuals attempting to meet their livelihood needs.

Western media and research often frame China's expanding presence in African countries as a new project in empire building on the continent. The Chinese government, on the contrary, espouses a very different narrative—one which depicts Chinese companies and migrants as promoting development through beneficial South-South cooperation resulting in mechanisation and advanced techniques. In this way, in both academic research and popular discourse, discussions about China's developmental role in contemporary Africa often end up implicitly categorising all the activities of Chinese businesses and individual migrants in African countries as being either malevolent or benevolent extensions of China's expanding global influence.

This is particularly apparent in the agricultural sector. At present, most

'Mary tills her field'
PC: Felix Clay

media attention and research on Chinese agricultural engagements in Africa focus on aid or commercial investments by large state-owned enterprises (SOEs), neglecting the fact that on the African continent there is also a growing number of small-scale farms run by individual Chinese migrants and their families. Indeed, while doing fieldwork in Ghana (Cook et al. 2016), I only encountered one case of large-scale Chinese agricultural investment that involved modern mechanised technologies aiming to produce rice for the local Ghanaian market. I did, however, encounter a collection of small-scale Chinese farms that are filling a very different niche. They are characterised by strong personal networks and family relations, and target an expatriate population trying to make ends meet. Such endeavours do not fit neatly into the narratives espoused neither by the Chinese government nor Western media and research.

In this article, I will take Ghana as a case study to explore how Chinese migrants operate in the agri-food sector in Africa. In particular, I will argue that Chinese farmers in Africa are not a 'silent army' (either malevolent or benevolent), but are instead largely precarious individuals attempting to meet their livelihood needs. Moreover, these migrants are a symptom of, and a response to, wider global migration dynamics. In particular, many of these small-scale farmers have gone into Ghanaian agriculture in order to provide for the huge influx of Chinese migrant miners (see Loubere and Crawford in this issue). In this way, Chinese farmers in Ghana can be considered reflective of wider processes of contemporary globalisation.

Chinese Migration to Ghana

Although since the Mao era there have been groups of Chinese people dwelling in Ghana—many of whom had originally come over as aid experts—the last few years have seen a dramatic increase in the number of Chinese immigrants in the country. This is primarily due to the small-scale mining phenomenon and the fact that Chinese companies have entered a growing number of sectors, including mining, construction, and manufacturing, just to name a few. In addition, Chinese migrants maintain a significance presence in retail trade, fishing, small-scale mining, and timber sectors, much of it outside the law and without proper registration. It is, therefore, not surprising that data on the number of Chinese migrants in Ghana are limited and unreliable, with estimates varying between seven and twenty thousand (Mohan et al. 2014). Still, even these figures may be conservative if we consider that in August 2013 the *South China Morning Post* quoted the secretary general of the Chinese Mining Association in Ghana as saying that more than fifty thousand Chinese gold miners had poured into the country since 2005 (He 2013). Another article from *The Guardian* published roughly at the same time reported that 4,592 illegal Chinese gold miners had been deported from June to July 2013 alone (Hirsch 2013).

While Chinese miners in Ghana have often featured in the international media, China and Ghana have a longer history of engagement in agriculture than in mining. Cooperation in agriculture between China and Ghana goes back to the 1960s, and has continued to grow and develop over subsequent decades (Amanor and Chichav 2016). Today, China and Ghana officially cooperate in a number of sectors, including agro-processing, irrigation, infrastructure development, and agricultural technology (Amanor 2013). Chinese agronomists even teach at the University of Ghana. Yet, just as the information on Chinese migration is patchy and unreliable, data on Chinese investment in the agricultural sector are incomplete and often inaccurate. According to some estimates, Chinese investments in agriculture constitute about four per cent of total Chinese investments in the country, with the largest being in rice irrigation projects (Amanor 2015). In other words, compared with other industries, farming seems to be a relatively neglected sector for the Chinese in Ghana.

It is clear from our fieldwork that in Ghana there are only a few formally registered farms. According to a list provided by the Ghana Investment Promotion Centre, only twelve Chinese farms officially registered with the government between 1994 and 2013. Moreover, after attempting to get in touch with these farms, we found that only two of them were actually contactable. Both were registered as producing vegetables and one was said to rear pigs. However, while we were visiting the official farms we had contacted, we by chance met some other unlisted farms owned by Chinese individuals, as well as some unregistered farms owned by large Chinese SOEs with their own small vegetable and pig farms geared towards meeting their own consumption purposes, i.e. for their employees. To shed some light on why Chinese people migrate to Ghana to undertake small-scale agriculture I will discuss three of these small-scale individually-owned farms, two of them registered and one not. The three farms were between two and twenty hectares and, on average, they employed three Chinese nationals as managers and technicians and five to ten local people as manual workers.

Profiling Chinese Farmers in Ghana

According to our findings, many Chinese small-scale farmers in Ghana come from non-agricultural backgrounds. In the cases examined in this article, all three farm owners were from different provinces in southern China (Hunan, Guangdong, and Zhejiang), but only one of them migrated specifically for agriculture. Before setting up his farm, the owner of one of the farms had been trading agricultural products between China and Ghana. Another of the farm owners had been working in Ghana as an engineer in a Chinese company. Only the owner of the third farm came to Ghana specifically to set up a farm. However, his migration history was far more complex than those of the other people we met. For the past two decades he had been living and farming on the Northern Mariana Islands, a US Commonwealth territory in the middle of the Pacific Ocean where he had moved during the Cultural Revolution.

Despite their very varied backgrounds, though, all of them have learned about farming, livestock, agricultural management, and marketing in a remarkably challenging social, linguistic, and physical environment. Furthermore, they also have shown a willingness to convert to a new line of business if it proves to be more economically viable. Moreover, their motivations to start their farms were somewhat similar: all of them said they aimed to meet their own needs for vegetable consumption in the first instance. As a Chinese employee on one of the farms put it: 'The boss of our farm is about sixty years old. He was running a trade business in agricultural products between China and Ghana four years ago. Later on, when he found it difficult to find Chinese vegetables in the local market, though, he started his first farm.' In this way, the farm was established as a response to a particular market need, which itself arose due to the wider processes of global migration.

The Chinese farmers we interviewed stated that in order to successfully run a small farm in Ghana, they had to consider the following elements: land, water resources, access to markets, and labour. Among these aspects, land was the most significant and challenging element to consider. Generally speaking, the Chinese farmers had great difficulties securing the land of the size and quality they wanted within the existing legal framework. Part of the problem is that throughout Ghana there is a lack of clarity about land ownership, particularly between local chiefs and local governments. This is a major hindrance for those foreigners who want to invest in agricultural activities in Africa, because it is not always clear who owns the land rights. This meant that the Chinese farmers were often unable to operate in a technically 'legal' way, not necessarily because they are maliciously land-grabbing or exploiting local people, but rather because legality in this context is tenuous for everyone involved. For this reason, many Chinese migrants give up farming after one or two years.

That being said, although in the beginning the farms we examined encountered a lot of difficulties, those who stayed and persisted in earlier years were able to survive due to a sizeable Chinese community that provided a ready market, particularly the rapid influx of illegal miners after the increase in gold prices in 2008 (see the chapter by Loubere and Crawford on pp. 116–121 in the present book). However, due to the expulsion of a large number of Chinese gold miners in June 2013, the farms lost a significant portion of their market. The remaining Chinese farmers confirmed that they have been selling less than before and are, therefore, struggling. Besides the difficulties mentioned above, since their products are sold locally, they still need to compete in the local market, both among themselves and with Ghanaian farmers. This greatly tests the farmers' business acumen, patience, and resilience.

Dispelling the Misconceptions

The examples provided above suggest that Chinese 'land grabs' and agricultural 'cooperation' in Ghana in fact mostly consists of informal small plots of a few hectares producing vegetables to sell locally. While there are a handful of larger SOE farms, they are primarily operating for the consumption needs of the personnel employed by the company. More widespread are small individually-owned farms; however, the majority of these farmers are working hard to meet their own livelihood needs in an increasingly unpredictable and volatile market. This does not fit neatly into the western media discourses focussed on land grabbing and neo-imperialism, nor into the narrative of the Chinese government centred on the idea of mutually beneficial South-South cooperation.

From this perspective, Chinese agricultural workers in Africa are not an organised 'silent army' of labourers, but are actually diverse and fragmented. They are relatively marginal people moving from one place to another in an attempt to improve their livelihoods. Living independently with no support or even contact with the Chinese government, they struggle to ensure their survival in the local markets, facing the competition of local producers and sellers, and surviving in unstable and unclear legal situations. Quite clearly, there is no real prospect for these farms to become large-scale, highly mechanised or capital intensive, which is actually what most African governments yearn for in order to increase agricultural production. In other words, China's presence in the agricultural sector in Africa mostly remains in the realm of individual entrepreneurship, a far cry from the ambition of empire.

Jixia Lu

Jixia Lu is an Associate Professor at the College of Humanities and Development Studies, China Agricultural University. Her research fields include Chinese and international development, environment, health and development, development intervention and social change.

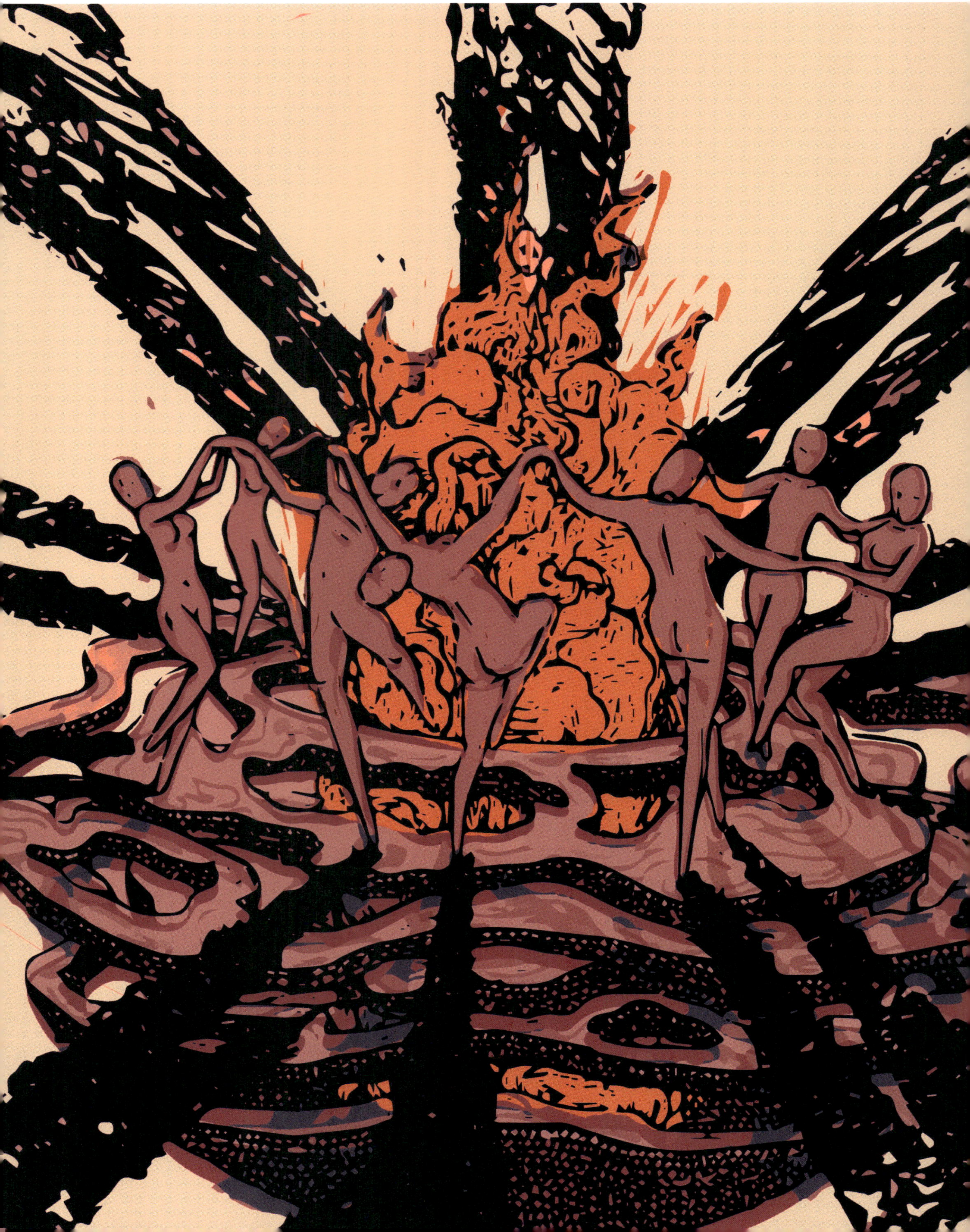

SOUL SACRIFICE

Paradise under Construction

Christian Sorace

A shot from Zhao Liang's Behemoth

> *From the earliest times, human civilization has been no more than a strange luminescence growing more intense by the hour, of which no one can say when it will begin to wane and when it will fade away.*
> W.G. Sebald

Zhao Liang's recent film *Behemoth* (*beixi moshou*) is a cinematic meditation on the *Anthropocene*—the current geological epoch marking 'a new phase in the history of the Earth, when natural forces and human forces become intertwined, so that the fate of one determines the fate of the other' (Zalasiewicz et al. 2010, 2231). Composed from documentary footage of natural and human life in their devastated forms, *Behemoth* offers a dystopian view of our present reality based on a script written by Zhao Liang that is loosely adapted from Dante's *Divine Comedy*. In an interview I conducted with the director via the popular Chinese social media platform WeChat this past July, taking a studied cynical tone, he described his art as a technique of making the ugly beautiful: 'Most of the time, I take some ugly affair and make it "look beautiful" on film. But isn't our world often packaged to appear beautiful in this way, especially politics?'

Zhao Liang's aesthetic style is one of unflinching exposure, however, which shares little in common with the theatricality of state power and mystification of sovereign violence. The gorgeous cinematography of *Behemoth* creates a new perceptual field of planetary destruction in a way that is unavailable to the prose of scientific description and political argument. As the poet Rainer Maria Rilke famously wrote in his *Duino Elegies*, 'For beauty is nothing but the beginning of terror, which we are still just able to endure, and we are so awed because it serenely disdains to destroy us. Every angel is terrifying' (Rilke 2009, 3). We follow the prophetic guide into the Inferno, but we do not come out the same.

The narrative of *Behemoth* follows what Zhao Liang describes as a 'supply chain' (*chanyelian*) of urban construction.[1] The film opens with a long-shot of an open-pit coal mine in Inner Mongolia, explosions are heard in the distance, coal ash rains from the sky into the frame, accompanied by the rasping of traditional Mongolian throat-singing. The camera descends into coal mines, swelters in the heat of iron smelting furnaces, dispassionately gazes on coal miners in their dormitories and hospital beds, and finally sojourns in the utopian 'ghost city of Ordos' where the film ends.

For those who are unfamiliar with the context, Ordos is a Prefecture-Level Municipality located in the Gobi Desert in Inner Mongolia. After a natural resource boom beginning in 2004, the Ordos government decided to invest its windfall revenue in the construction of a new administrative capital named Kangbashi in an area that was mostly desolate wasteland. Despite its modern architecture and urban trappings, Kangbashi has failed to attract residents, earning it the reputation of China's most infamous 'ghost city' (*gui chengshi*) (Sorace and Hurst 2016). For some China watchers, it is a portent of the inevitable bursting of China's real estate bubble inflated by political incentives and speculative land development. In *Behemoth*, Kangbashi is described as the 'paradise of our dreams'—a perfect, clean, and empty city.

The Other Side of Urbanisation

Urbanisation and the extraction of coal, natural gas, and rare earth minerals contribute to the desertification of China's grasslands, which has triggered massive sandstorms that have blown into Beijing and Tianjin. In *Behemoth*, we witness the scars of urban modernity: craters from open-pit coal mines, vegetation desiccated due to the consumption of surface water by mining operations, billowy clouds of pollution. According to Zhao Liang, filming 'the shattered mountains and rivers and last gasps of life' (*posui de shanhe, canchuan de shengming*) were the scenes that 'pierced' (*citong*) him the most.

Part of *Behemoth*'s visual power is its formal treatment of human bodies and natural landscapes as the same damaged matter. The bodies of coal miners belong to the landscape. The camera glides across their creased faces, blistered hands, and bodies covered in the 'inky make-up' soot and sweat. In one scene, we hear the laboured breathing of a coal miner suffering from pneumoconiosis, hooked up to a respiratory apparatus, lying in bed. He is indifferent to the camera's presence. Later, we see a woman holding up a funerary portrait of a man who may or may not have been him.

Even though *Behemoth* is ostensibly a documentary, none of the miners are given a voice in the film. To some, this may appear as an additional layer of exploitation. For me, however, the decision to exclude biographical details and life trajectories from the film's narrative content allows a different kind of speech to occur.

The silent bodies and gazes of the miners speak of their expendability. A miner's individual life, dreams, and medical records matter little to the coal mining boss, Party secretary, financial speculator, and middle class home-owner. From the standpoint of those who benefit from the urbanisation process, the miner's life is valued as long as he is healthy enough to show up for work. When he can no longer work, he will be replaced. The decision not to give the miners a voice amplifies the singularity of each physical presence in the face of its precarity and serial interchangeability.

Behemoth is about more than 'the human and environmental costs of coal mining and consumption in China' (Qin 2015) because the word 'cost' remains within a political economy of commensurability. A miner's health is not the 'cost' of his need to survive. The destruction of the planet is not some unfortunate 'price' of modernisation but its suicidal involution. The Anthropocene has moved us beyond the calculation of cost-benefit equivalences into a

A shot from Zhao Liang's *Behemoth*

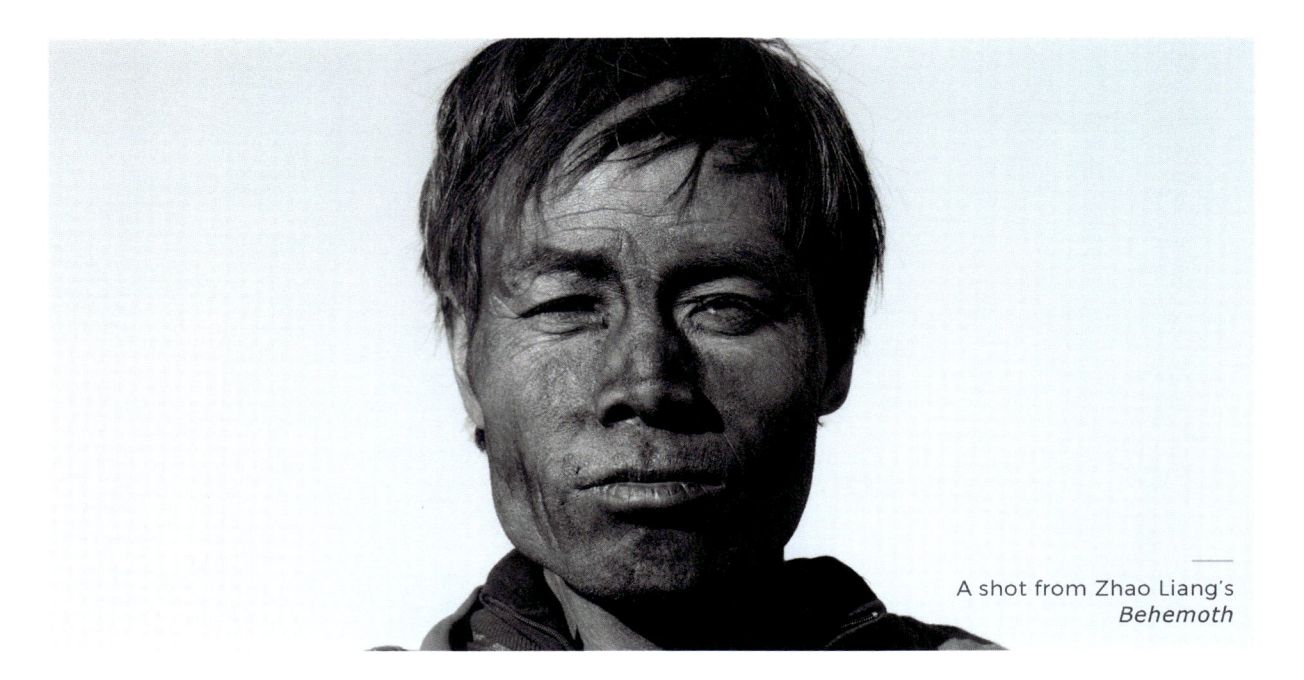

world where new values, systems, and myths are needed (Burke et al. 2016).

As the philosopher Jean-Luc Nancy put it, 'Yet we can oppose nothing to "growth" unless we can conceive of another civilization, a new sense of existence not enslaved to production but freed for itself. Which implies that this "for itself" finds its own meaning, the meaning of its "own" fact of being' (Nancy 2014, 47). The end of capitalism will only be the beginning of a life we have not yet imagined.

After the Promise of Communism

It is significant that Zhao Liang's dystopian vision of reality takes place in post-socialist China. Twentieth century communism promised an end to exploitation, the emancipation of all human beings, and the liberation of our creative faculties. Instead of achieving these goals, it generated its own forms of lethal oppression and, in doing so, destroyed our ability to dream of a political solution to the inequalities of capitalism.[2]

In a conversation that I had with him at his workshop in Beijing this past June, Zhao Liang referred to 'humanity as a cancer of the earth' (*renlei shi diqiu de aizheng*). When I asked him why he thought we are 'incurable' (*meijiu*), his answer was 'original sin' (*yuanzui*) which he defined as 'the defect of boundless desire' (*yuwang de wuxianxing de quexian*). He is also increasingly skeptical of the transformative power of art. In an interview from March 2016 with *Slant Magazine*, the artist recalls feeling 'compelled by social responsibility' when he first started making documentaries but 'no longer' sees his 'work as a catalyst for creating social benefit' (Suber 2016). When I asked what precipitated his abandonment of political optimism, his response was the 'cruelty of the real world' and 'powerlessness' to change it (*xianshi shijie de cankuxing he wuligan*).

Although such arrant nihilism is modish in China's art scene, it is not without historical basis. Zhao Liang's pessimistic view of human nature raises important, unresolved, and unfashionable questions about the failure of China's twentieth century communist project. To put it somewhat coarsely, for all of the Communist Party's laudable as well as violent attempts to 'change the human being in what is most profound', they were unable to eradicate the venality, cruelty, and boundless desire of human nature (Badiou 2005, 482).

Art in the Anthropocene

As McKenzie Wark points out, 'The unspeakable secret about climate change is that nobody really wants to think about it for too long. It's just too depressing' (Wark 2015, 25). It is also cognitively impossible to grasp the totality of climate change's complex non-linear temporalities and uneven geographies. Instead, as Jodi Dean argues, it is much easier to circulate platitudes that generate enjoyment in moral outrage and self-exoneration (Dean 2016). For these reasons, I suggest that art in the age of the Anthropocene has the power to convey scientific and political truths in images and sensory environments in ways that disturb our complacency, enjoyment, and ignorance.

In China, several contemporary artists have been grappling with the problems posed by the Anthropocene, inventing new aesthetic forms, and creatively working with damaged materialities. In the series of photographs called *New Landscapes*, Yao Lu re-creates traditional Chinese landscapes of mountains and rivers using trash and debris from landfills (Phaidon 2013). He Xiangyu's *Cola Project* required boiling thousands of litres of cola, which hardened into a coal-like substance that could be ground into ink and used for Song Dynasty-style landscape paintings (White Cube 2014). Cai Guo-Qiang's 2014 exhibit *The Ninth Wave* included the manufacture of a contemporary Noah's Ark 'carrying 99 fabricated animals in various states of decline' which 'sailed along the Huangpu River' before docking at the Power Station of Art in Shanghai (Davis 2014; e-flux 2014). Cai's ship of tattered stuffed animals followed the same course as 16,000 dead pigs, which mysteriously floated down the river a year earlier in March 2013 (Davison 2013). In these works, the mimetic relationship between art and nature becomes recursive as we are no longer able to discern human artifacts from natural processes.

Dreaming from the Ruins

With unforgettable cinematography and soundscapes, *Behemoth* reveals the devastation of the Inner Mongolian grasslands due to fossil fuel extraction. The mobility of the camera enables it to traverse, and record, different scales and topographies of damaged matter. It brings into view a dystopian reality that we would otherwise be unable to visualise.

This is not to suggest that art can save us from extinction. Perhaps Zhao Liang's pessimism is correct and humanity is a 'cancer' that will metastasise until we have killed our host. I am not convinced. For me, *Behemoth* prophesises that it is time to dream of a new paradise that can mobilise the political energy and will to build a world in common from the ruins of the one we have destroyed. It may fail, but it is our only hope.

---

[1] This description is from an advertisement on WeChat for a private screening of Behemoth in Beijing. The advertisement was 'harmonised', i.e., deleted, from WeChat and the screening was cancelled.

[2] Today, the Chinese Communist Party officially promises to engineer a 'moderately prosperous society' (*xiaokang shehui*), and the 'China dream' (*Zhongguo meng*) is deployed in the service of 'social stability' (*weihu shehui wending*), capitalist accumulation, and exploitation. They are a far cry from the dreams of universal emancipation and working class power.

Christian Sorace

Christian Sorace is a Postdoctoral Fellow at the Australian Centre on China in the World, the Australian National University. He is the author of *Shaken Authority: China's Communist Party and the 2008 Sichuan Earthquake,* scheduled for publication with Cornell University Press in Spring 2017. He is currently conducting research on the urbanisation of the grasslands in Inner Mongolia, China and ger districts in Ulaanbaatar, Mongolia.

The Cow and the Goat Descend the Mountain: Fighting Modernity with Poems

Ivan Franceschini

A few years ago—it must have been towards the end of 2010—a big crowd had gathered in a loft in the Centre of Contemporary Arts in Shenzhen to enjoy the music of blind folk singer Zhou Yunpeng, an artist famous for his socially committed songs on issues such as child abuse, unemployment, sky-rocketing housing costs, and much more. Halfway through the concert, Zhou announced: 'Contemporaneity is helpless, antiquity will now make its entrance.' Then time seemed to stop, while a flow of words from poets of different ages and places started chasing each other, softly accompanied by the music of Zhou's guitar. Voices from the Tang era engaged in a lively conversation with bards from the Song and Qing ages. People who lived centuries apart borrowed Zhou's voice to express exactly the same feeling: an acute longing for their families and their hometowns.

Zhou was performing songs from his then recently released album, *The Cow and the Goat Descend the Mountain* (*niuyang xiashan*), a collection of ancient Chinese poetry set to music which appeals to a dimension of human life that transcends time and space. Listening to the lines of Du Fu (712–770) 'it is almost as hard for friends to meet as for the morning and evening stars' (*ren sheng bu xiang jian, dong ru shen yu shang*), or to Meng Jiao (751–814) lyrically describing how 'the thread in the hands of a fond-hearted mother makes clothes for the body of her wayward boy; carefully she sews and thoroughly she mends, dreading the delays that will keep him late from home' (*ci mu shou zhong xian,*

Zhou Yunpeng
PC: Tommaso Bonaventura

you zi shen shang yi; lin xing mi mi feng, yi kong chi chi gui), it is easy to forget that such words were written centuries ago. The same happens with Li Bai (701–762) and his poem 'The Moon over the Fortified Pass' (*guanshanyue*), which recounts how soldiers marching through the Jade Gate under the moonlight 'turn round, looking toward the border, and think of home, with wistful eyes and of those tonight in the upper chambers who toss and sigh and cannot rest' (*shu ke wang bian se, si gui duo ku yan; lou dang ci ye, tan xi wei ying xian*), or with the soldier in a poem by Nalan Xingde's (1655–1685), who dreams of his peaceful home while encamped on a river bank during a snowstorm.

Two Faces of Nostalgia

The recurrence of these feelings of detachment and homesickness all through *Niuyang xiashan* is unsurprising, since nostalgia is everywhere to be found in Chinese traditional poetry. As James Liu explained in *The Art of Chinese Poetry*, Chinese poets seem to be perpetually bewailing their exile and longing to return home, a feature that he attributes to

> the vastness of China, the difficulties of communication that existed, the sharp contrast between the highly cultured life in the main cities and the harsh conditions in the remoter regions of the country, and the importance of the family in traditional Chinese society with the consequent deep attachment to the ancestral home. Moreover, being an agricultural people and a nation of landlubbers, the Chinese as a whole are noticeably lacking in *Wanderlust*. (Liu 1962, 55)

But why sing these poems today, when distances in China, as elsewhere, have been dramatically shortened by improved communications? The simple answer is that this nostalgia is now more present than ever in the life of the Chinese people. Today's China is still a country of people on the move. Farmers leave the countryside to look for jobs in urban areas, students move to bigger cities to gain access to a better education, merchants travel from town to town to pursue their businesses. Families often have no other choice than to split up: rural mothers leave their children behind in the villages—husbands, wives and sons live and work in completely different places. Most of them meet no more than once a year, during the Spring Festival. Once they were soldiers and exiled poets, now they are migrant workers, students, and businessmen. Their existence may appear less poetic, but the underlying feelings do not seem to have changed.

Chinese language has two different words to express the concept of 'nostalgia': on the one hand, *huaijiu*, literally 'embracing the old'; on the other, *sixiang*, 'homesickness'. Yet, as Niuyang xiashan clearly demonstrates, these expressions are both sides of the same coin. Singing those ancient poems, Zhou Yunpeng recounts stories of a long lost bucolic idyll mixed with melancholic feelings of nostalgia for a distant hometown. The title of the album itself is an allusion that exudes sadness and nostalgia—'the cow and the goat descend the mountain' paraphrases a verse from 'The Gentleman Serves in the Army' (*junzi yuyi*), a poem in the *Classic of Poetry* (*shijing*) about the wailing wife of a soldier far away from home. In the evening, the family's chickens are back in the henhouse, a yellow dog is sitting on the doorstep, even the cow and goat have come down from the mountain where they were grazing, only the husband is nowhere to be seen.

Reminiscences from a Golden Age

Ancient poetry is very much alive in today's China. As Bill Porter writes in *Finding Them Gone*, a recent book about his pilgrimages to the graves of the greatest poets of Chinese antiquity:

> The graves of the poets I'd been visiting were so different. Some were simple, some palatial, some had been plowed under by farmers, and others had been reduced to trash pits. Their poems, though, had survived. They were still fresh in the minds of cigar-smoking farmers who most likely never attended high school. The same couldn't be said for the pronouncements of the high and mighty. Poetry is transcendent. We carry it in our hearts and find it there when we have forgotten everything else. (Porter 2016)

This holds particularly true for the selection of poetry included in *Niuyang xiashan*. All the poems performed by Zhou on this album belong to the collective memory of the Chinese people, and they therefore strike a chord with a Chinese audience from all walks of life. In an interview that I had with him in April 2012, Zhou explained that all those verses are reminiscences from his own childhood in the 1970s, when he had to learn them by heart at school: 'These poems are among the most popular in China, they are like a souvenir in your backpack, an old photo. I have been in many places, I have lost many books, but these poems are always with me. When I am on the road or I am waiting for a car or a flight, I just go over them in my head. It is like a spiritual massage and in doing so my spirit becomes peaceful. I did not choose those poems, they just popped up in my mind, it was so natural.'

Zhou lost his sight when he was nine years old. In the following decades, in spite of all the hardships he was forced to endure, he became a tireless traveller and an insatiable reader. During our interview, he repeatedly used the verb 'to look' (*kan*) to describe his experiences on the road. Still, this 'looking' seems to go well beyond the realm of the sight he had lost, being more like an act of 'contemplation' (*guanzhao*). In Zhou's own words: 'Contemplating is more than looking, it means experiencing something with all your body and mind, with the optic nerve of your soul.' Zhou believes that poetry has a fundamental role in this kind of contemplation: 'Ancient poems are very visual. Every single poem has a lot of images of mountains, rivers, flowers, smokes, trees, and skies and this is very good for blind people. These verses give us another reality, a reality that can be seen through the eyes of people from other ages. Those are the skies and the water of the Tang Dynasty and through poetry we can experience that world.'

An Escape from Modernity?

After many years of producing music that dealt critically with the plights of contemporaneity, one cannot but wonder whether *Niuyang xiashan* represent Zhou's escape from the many hardships of contemporary society. However, this does not seem to be the case. According to Zhou, this album is not just a return to the past, since those ancient poems bear extraordinary resemblances to today's social issues. As examples, during our interview he quoted two series of poems by Du Fu: 'Three Functionaries' (*san li*) and 'Three Separations' (*san bie*). In the first series, Du Fu writes about local cadres who press-gang all the able-bodied men into the army until only an old lady remains at home, and then also force this woman to join the army as a cook (Fu 2015, vol. 2, 82-97). According to Zhou, this story recalls today's forced relocations. 'Three Separations' instead tells the stories of elderly people without any kind of social security, and therefore with nothing to lose. From Zhou's point of view, the similarity to the situation of many old people today is obvious.

Neither 'Three Functionaries' nor 'Three Separations' are included in *Niuyang xiashan*, but contemporaneity still makes a few explicit appearances in this album. The first one is in the middle of 'A Song of Spring' (*chunge*), a composition that contains lines from three different poems by Wumen Shenshi (1183–1260) and Liu Yuxi (772–842). After sketching a series of bucolic images, Zhou starts telling the story of Li Bai, who reportedly one day saved his friend Wang Lun from drowning in a river. All of a sudden, in the middle of the song, Zhou Yunpeng directly addresses Li Bai: 'Comrade Li Bai, being an old Communist Party member from the Tang dynasty, what were you thinking when you dived into the water to save Wang Lun?' And Li Bai answers with nonchalance, mixing plain language with pompous lines from one of his most famous poems: 'Ah, purple mists rose from the Incense Peak in the sun, that day it was very hot; cascading from atop three thousand feet adown, I went to the river to bathe. While I was in the water I picked up Wang Lun.' With this joke, originally inspired by a child he once met, Zhou candidly mocks the Party propaganda about Lei Feng and other 'miraculous' model workers.

The second appearance of the modern age occurs in the last song, 'Love Without Speaking' (*bu hui shuo hua de aiqing*). This song, the only one on the album entirely written by Zhou Yunpeng, opens with a couple of verses of ancient flavour—'You are tired of doing your embroidery, even the cow and the goat have come down from the mountain' (*xiu hua xiu de lei le ba, niu yang ye xia shang lo*)—then plunges into a love story full of hatred and regret. Zhou is particularly proud of this song, which he deems the best work he has ever done:

> 'Love Without Speaking' is not a kind of pastoral sadness; it is a story of urban anxiety, that kind of anxiety, struggle, and hate that prominently feature in the life of people today, in a world dominated by material desires. I think that a love without hate would be incomplete. This is not only a love song, it is more a song about life in general. For instance, you can, at the same time, love and hate Beijing: your relationship with a place, a person, a time always has this kind of mixture of love and hate.

Ancient Poetry as Resistance

And love and hate are what Zhou Yunpeng feels toward this age, with all its progress in the field of communications, which have weakened the bond between people and their homes; with the rapid expansion of the Internet, which has destroyed the pleasure of writing letters and appreciating the relationships with far away friends; and with the systematic destruction of significant parts of China's cultural heritage. In the face of all this, the choice to recover these fragments of ancient poetry and give them new life through music seems to be more an act of resistance than an escape. As Zhou puts it: 'In the contemporary world, nostalgia, distance, and homesickness are all luxuries which belong to a utopia. We can only experience them through the bodies of the people from ancient times. Their way of life has become an ideal, something that we can only find by accident but not seek out on purpose. That is the reason I love the people in Niuyang xiashan: they still can experience those feelings.'

The translations of the verses of Li Bai, Meng Jiao, and Du Fu quoted in the text are by Witter Bynner.

Ivan Franceschini

Ivan Franceschini is a Marie Curie Fellow at Ca' Foscari University of Venice and at the Australian Centre on China in the World working on a project on Chinese labour in a global perspective. From 2006 to 2015, he lived in China, where he worked as a journalist and as a consultant in the field of development cooperation. His research interests focus on Chinese labour and civil society.

Chinese Dreams of Happiness: What Are the Chances?

Gerda Wielander

Statue of a sleeping Buddha in Bali. PC: Sculpture Design

The happiness of the Chinese people is one of the declared aims of the Chinese dream. An educational volume on social governance and welfare published by the official Red Flag Press titled *Building a Happy China* sums it up like this: 'The process of the reinvigoration of the Chinese nation equates to the building of a happy China; without people's affluence, development cannot be considered successful; without people's happiness, the reinvigoration will not be complete' (Shu 2013, I). The happiness of the Chinese people is not just an aim, but has also become a measure for the realisation of the Chinese dream. Put differently, being happy is the required spiritual state of the Chinese people in this new project of the Party-state. But what methods are available to the Chinese people to achieve happiness? In the following essay, I will briefly look at three different options from the field of psychology and psychotherapy—psychodynamic therapies, positive psychology, and Morita therapy—to discuss the chances for fulfilment of China's dream of happiness.

A Process of Collective Transformation

Moving from a state of unhappiness to happiness requires a transformation at the individual level, which—provided that enough individuals go through the same process—then becomes a collective transformation. This is an evolutionary process guided by people's ability to adapt their strategies to maximise happiness depending on needs and opportunities. When needs shift for many people at the same time (due to massive changes in their socio-political environment, for example), then similar adaptation strategies will be adopted. These, in turn, accumulate into collective trends, which have the potential to lead to social change (Welzel and Inglehart 2010).

The marketisation of most, if not all, aspects of the Chinese economy and the liberalisation of society have brought into existence a wide range of potential role models and 'happiness maximisation strategies' for the Chinese individual to choose from. In a radically changed economic and social environment, people's readiness to choose and try out new strategies to maximise happiness has increased considerably. At the same time, today the government's attempts at re-affirming normative expectations of behaviour and the 'correct spirit' around the values of socialism compete with alternative value systems derived from religions and different schools of thoughts that have been circulating among the population. Various schools of psychology also play a role in this.

The Limits of Freudian Psychoanalysis

Western culture in the twentieth century has grown up on the pervasive influence of Freudian concepts of the unconscious and tends to focus on the importance of individual transformation in isolation from the social. Only very few psychoanalytical schools offer perspectives on transformation that go beyond the individual. Otto Gross (1877–1920), an Austrian psychoanalyst, could not conceive of transforming the self without the transformation of the socio-political context; to him factors outside the individual's history needed to be taken into account in an individual's unhappiness (Heuer 2003). More recently, the British Jungian analyst Andrew Samuels has argued that the inner world of emotion and fantasy about survival and status builds up in a ceaseless feedback loop with the outer world; and outer world problems in society gain emotional and fantasy elements within the individual (Samuels 2014). Hence—according to him—the economic (and political) and the psychological mutually irradiate.

Freudian ideas of the unconscious—introduced to China in the 1920s—with their focus on sexual trauma never really suited Chinese culture, and interest in its application to the Chinese mind was limited, despite a brief 'Freud fever' in the 1980s. But, although the soul or the unconscious have never played a significant role in the Chinese concept of psychological transformation, China's transformation into a 'happy and prosperous socialist society'—a slogan used in the 1950s—always required the transformation of both the individual and the external circumstances. The overthrow of the existing social order or the redistribution of means of production alone were never considered enough to achieve happiness even in socialist China.

Psychodynamic therapies have developed from Freudian and Jungian ideas, and in essence are based on an engagement with one's individual past and on working through trauma through verbal exchanges, often over a long period of time. It is an individualistic, non-directive, backward-looking process, which is painful, costly, and while often successful, results don't appear quickly. It requires a willingness to critically engage and often break with one's past before being able to move forward. Considering how important the tight control of all interpretations of China's past is for the legitimacy of the ruling power and promoter of the Chinese dream, the chances or even possibility of gaining closure, and hence happiness, by working through past traumas are nil.

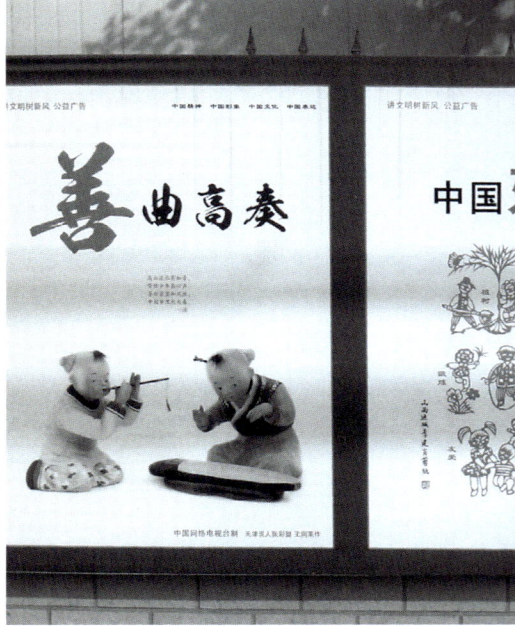

The Communist Party's Love Affair with Positive Psychology

The Chinese Communist Party (CCP) is, however, very much enamoured with positive psychology, a field of psychology that developed out of the behaviourist school, which focuses on 'flourishing', that is psychological functioning at its best. The central premise is that too much of psychology has been focusing on negativity, complexes, depression, and other shortcomings, while the needs of 'normal people' (not usually put in quotation marks in the Chinese literature) and the myriads of beautiful and positive things in the world have been neglected.

Positive psychology has developed out of humanistic psychology, which, in turn, responded to the limitations of psychodynamic approaches built on Freudian psychoanalysis. The philosophical foundations of humanistic psychology lie in existential philosophy, with its concern for human freedom, choice and responsibility, and search for meaning. However, despite this shared philosophical tradition there are fundamental differences between humanistic and positive psychology in relation to freedom, will, agency, personal responsibility, and determinism on the one hand, and the nature of phenomenological experience on the other. Existentialist philosophy holds that there are no absolute standards or criteria that can be used when making life decisions. Existentialists view experience as something inherently individual and thus inter-subjectivity is a problem that can be only partially resolved. Existential philosophy—and humanistic psychology—consider communication, by necessity, unreliable. No existentialist philosopher—and no humanistic psychologist—will tell an individual what to do (Waterman 2013).

Positive psychology, on the other hand,

Recent propaganda posters in China. The slogans read (from left to right): 'China: move forward!'; 'Good words provide a good inspiration'; 'The good children of China'; 'The Chinese dream, the spirit of a bull'; 'Loving China dearly'; 'Bless the Fatherland'.

places great emphasis on science, which in turn is founded on determinist assumptions and defined standards or criteria. As a consequence, positive psychology excludes certain things from scientific consideration. 'Uncaused causes'—that is matters without scientific explanation (like transcendence and the existence of God, for example)—are not taken into consideration by positive psychology. In contrast to the long-term, in-depth dialogue between the patient and the therapist with a focus on the unique history and context of each individual humanistic and psychodynamic psychology, positive psychology lends itself to 'techniques' and short-term optimisation of one's psychological potential (Waterman 2013).

The basis for positive psychology's popularity in China lies in the way it complements the socialist concept of *jingshen* or 'spirit', which in turn was shaped by an amalgamation of Chinese culture's belief in self-improvement and the influx of psychological theories in the early twentieth century (Larson 2009). This socialist concept of *jingshen* encapsulates a rejection of the unconscious, an emphasis on human agency, and the belief in the individual's ability for self-transformation. Positive psychology's philosophical foundations in relation to ontology and epistemology are far more compatible with the Chinese socialist state project. Furthermore, the techniques of positive psychology are not dissimilar to traditional Chinese 'self-reflection' and the more coerced forms of 'thought work', which form part of the institutionally embedded management of *jingshen*, both of which put the onus on the individual to uncover and resolve internal struggles (Yang 2013).

Positive psychology makes very specific ontological assumptions about what constitutes human nature, the nature of the world humans inhabit, and how individuals experience the world and others. Positive psychology's assumptions and associated methods not only suit the Chinese concept of *jingshen* with its emphasis on conscious individual effort and expectations of a 'can do' mentality, but also conforms to the 'scientific outlook on development' (*kexue fazhan guan*), which is a key aspect of contemporary Chinese socialist ideology. In terms of efficacy, positive psychology, like many other forms of cognitive behavioural therapy, can have great results in the short term, but do not tend to have a long-lasting effect. As such, China may be able to hit its happiness targets in the short run, but should expect a magnified wave of unhappiness to return in the mid-term (Burkeman 2016).

Beyond Mind Control: Morita Shoma and Acceptance

One of the main reasons why positive psychology does not help in the long run is that it does not provide any answers to the profound existential questions about the meaning of life, moral value, and the question of transcendence, which so many Chinese individuals are now contemplating as their livelihoods have been improved and middle-class anxieties are growing. Nor is positive psychology interested in individual (hi) stories or journeys and in-depth dialogue or engagement with individuals in the way psychodynamic or humanistic therapies and some religious practices are.

Xi Jinping pays great lip service to the importance of China's indigenous religions when it comes to looking after the spiritual needs of the Chinese people. He may therefore be open to the approach taken by Morita therapy, which was developed in the first half of the twentieth century by a man called Morita Shoma. Building on Western psychiatric medicine without the influence of Freudian psychoanalytic concepts, and drawing on the concepts and practices of Zen Buddhism, Morita therapy is not concerned with technique or procedure, but with the enhancement of a philosophical view that is strongly rooted in the Buddhist and Daoist views of life, and of the relationship between mankind and nature (Kenji 2005).

Morita therapy focuses on present circumstance and does not believe in the value of digging into the past. Morita Shoma saw no therapeutic meaning in searching and bringing to consciousness certain traumatic incidents. On the contrary, in his view, the source of unhappiness lies in the nature of one's disposition and in an excessively acute awareness of the reactions of one's own mind and body—something that is of course encouraged, almost celebrated, in psychodynamic approaches. But Morita therapy also contradicts positive psychology or any other attempts to control and use our minds to relieve anxiety. Positive psychology shuns negative emotions and focuses the individual's energy to change or avoid them, but in Morita therapy negative emotions are simply part of nature and not problematic; it is the decision to view them as negative and undesirable which creates the problem. By deciding that a certain emotional state is somehow negative in the context of one's life, too much focus is placed on the reaction to the negative emotion, which in turn intensifies the emotional reaction, attracting the person's attention to it even more. A destructive circle of obsession is thus created.

A photo portrait of Morita Shoma in old age.
PC: Wikipedia.

The aim of Morita therapy is not to identify the cause of unhappiness, but the destruction of this vicious circle, which creates this obsession with negative emotion. Morita therapy strives for harmony between nature and ideas—where nature includes all emotions, desires and bodily feelings, and ideas are all theories substantiated by means of language. According to Morita therapy it is counter-productive to try to control one's emotions. The starting point in the healing process is acceptance of suffering, its goal an awareness of the causes—always multiple—of suffering, without seeking to control the suffering.

The ideal state of mind in Morita therapy is that of *arugamama*, which is the ability to accept things as they are:

> When we can accept reality, then we become more obedient. In reality, there is no such thing as making great strides. To think that one suddenly becomes enlightened and becomes a better person is not based on object reality. It is an assessment based on moods. One becomes great by taking one step at a time. One should not take it for granted that one has become great. (Kenji 2005, 179)

Pursuing Utopian Dreams

Aspirational, utopian dreams rarely improve people's lives, including their psychological lives. The German Chancellor Helmut Schmidt (1918–2015) famously advised: 'Anyone who has visions should go to the doctor.' Angela Merkel—who lived through thirty years of socialist utopia—and her Northern European counterparts are all famously down to earth and pragmatic, and yet their countries lead the world's happiness rankings. So, to paraphrase Morita, and to return to the development targets of the Chinese dream, one should not take it for granted that one will become happy. The first obstacle on the road to China's happiness is the articulation of the Chinese dream itself. Giving up the obsession with the dream will be the first step towards its fulfilment.

Gerda Wielander

Gerda Wielander is Associate Professor in Chinese and Head of Modern Languages and Cultures at the University of Westminster, London. Her main research interest lies in the link of the personal and spiritual to wider social and political developments in modern and contemporary China. She is the author of *Christian Values in Communist China* (Routledge 2013) as well as several book chapters and articles in leading peer-reviewed journals. She is currently working on an edited volume called *Perspectives on Chinese Happiness*, which is part of her wider research on happiness targets and education in China's political project.

Bibliography

Kojo S. Amanor, 'Expanding Agri-business: China and Brazil in Ghanaian Agriculture', *IDS Bulletin*, vol.44, no.4 (July 2013): 80–90.

Kojo S. Amanor, 'Rising Powers and Rice in Ghana: China, Brazil and African Agricultural Development', Future Agriculture Working Paper n.123, July 2015, online at: **https://opendocs.ids.ac.uk/opendocs/bitstream/handle/123456789/7091/FAC_Working_Paper_123.pdf**

Kojo S. Amanor and Sérgio Chichav, 'South–South Cooperation, Agribusiness, and African Agricultural Development: Brazil and China in Ghana and Mozambique', *World Development*, vol.81 (May 2016): 13–23.

Auditor General (Zambia), 'Report of the Auditor General on the Management of Occupational Safety and Health', June 2015, online at: **http://www.ago.gov.zm/reports/Special/2015/AUDITOR%20GENERAL%20MANAGEMENT%20OF%20OCCUPATION%20SAFTEY.pdf**

Alain Badiou, 'The Cultural Revolution: The Last Revolution?', *Positions: East Asia Cultures Critique*, vol.13, no.3 (2005): 481–515.

Steef Baeten, Tom van Ourti, and Eddy van Doorslaer, 'Rising Inequalities in Income and Health in China: Who is Left Behind?', Discussion Paper No. 12-091/V, 13 June 2012, Rotterdam: Tinbergen Institute, online at: **https://papers.ssrn.com/sol3/papers.cfm?abstract_id=2144244**

Milford Bateman, *Why Doesn't Microfinance Work? The Destructive Rise of Local Neoliberalism*, London: Zed Books, 2010.

BBC, 'Dozens Killed in Zambia Explosion', *BBC News*, 21 April 2005, online at: **http://news.bbc.co.uk/2/hi/africa/4466321.stm**

Bill Birtles, 'Wukan: What a police crackdown in the so-called 'democracy village' says about Xi Jinping's China', *ABC*, 15 September 2016, online at: **http://www.abc.net.au/news/2016-09-15/wukan-what-a-police-crackdown-says-about-xi-jinping's-china/7845752**

David Blair, 'Zambian Poll Unleashes Anger at Chinese', *The Age*, 4 October 2006, online at: **http://www.theage.com.au/news/world/zambian-poll-unleashes-anger-at-chinese/2006/10/03/1159641326318.html**

Ben Bland, 'China Plans Shake-Up of State-Owned Enterprises to Boost Growth', *Financial Times*, 13 September 2015, online at: **https://www.ft.com/content/aff90924-5a01-11e5-9846-de406ccb37f2**

Andrew Browne, 'The Danger of China's Victim Mentality', *The Wall Street Journal*, 14 June 2016, online at: **http://www.wsj.com/articles/the-danger-of-chinas-victim-mentality-1465880577**

Chris Buckley, 'Official Admits He Gave Misleading Account of Chinese Miners' Plight', *The New York Times*, 13 March 2016, online at: **http://www.nytimes.com/2016/03/14/world/asia/china-heilongjiang-governor-mine-protest.html**

Chris Buckley and Javier Hernandez, 'China Seeks to Avoid Mass Layoffs While Cutting Production', *The New York Times*, 16 March 2016, online at: **http://www.nytimes.com/2016/03/17/world/asia/china-premier-li-keqiang-economy.html**

Anthony Burke, Stefanie Fishel, Audra Mitchell, Simon Dalby, and Daniel J. Levine, 'Planet Politics: A Manifesto from the end of IR', *Millennium: Journal of International Studies*, vol.44, no.3 (June 2016): 499–523.

Oliver Burkeman, 'Therapy Wars: The Revenge of Freud', *The Guardian*, 7 January 2016, online at: **http://www.theguardian.com/science/2016/jan/07/therapy-wars-revenge-of-freud-cognitive-behavioural-therapy**

Fang Cai, 'Hukou System Reform and Unification of Rural-Urban Social Welfare', *China & the World Economy*, vol.19, no.3 (2011): 33-48.

José Casanova, *Public Religions in the Modern World*, Chicago: University of Chicago Press, 1994.

CCTV, 'Shebao: Jiaofei jiangdi, baozhang bu bian' (Social Security: Payment Reduction, Protection Unchanged), *CCTV*, 27 April 2016, online at: **http://tv.cctv.com/2016/04/27/VIDEztPK1LEFvnsVhAGAMLZV160427.shtml**

Central Committee of the CCP, 'The Basic Viewpoint and Policy on the Religious Question During Our Country's Socialist Period (1982)', translated in Donald MacInnis, *Religion in China Today: Policy and Practice*, New York: Orbis Books, 1989, pp. 8-26, online at: **https://www.purdue.edu/crcs/wp-content/uploads/2014/08/Document_no._19_1982.pdf**

Anita Chan, 'Organising Wal-Mart: The Chinese Trade Union at a Crossroads', *The Asia-Pacific Journal: Japan Focus*, vol.4, no.9 (2006), online at **http://apjjf.org/-Anita-Chan/2217/article.html**

Anita Chan, 'Did Unionization Make a Difference? Work Conditions and Trade Union Activities at Chinese Walmart Stores', in Anita Chan ed, *Walmart in China*, Ithaca: ILR/Cornell University Press, 2011, pp.217-238.

Anita Chan, 'Trade Union Elections at Foreign-Owned Chinese Factories', *China: An International Journal*, vol.13, no.3 (2015): 94-113.

Chris King-Chi Chan and Ngai Pun, 'The Making of a New Working Class? A Study of Collective Actions of Migrant Workers in South China', *The China Quarterly*, no.197 (2009): 287-303.

Chris King-Chi Chan, Ngai Pun, and Jenny Chan, 'The Role of the State, Labour Policy and Migrant Workers' Struggles in Globalized China', in Paul Bowles and John Harriss eds, *Globalization and Labour in China and India: Impacts and Responses*, London: Palgrave Macmillan, 2010, pp. 45-63.

Kai Chang and Fang Lee Cooke, 'Legislating the Right to Strike in China: Historical Developments and Prospects', *Journal of Industrial Relations*, vol.57, no. 3 (2015): 440-455.

Jay Chen, 'Zhongguo weiquan zhengti xia de jiti kangyi: taizichang dabagong de anlifenxi' (Protest Mobilisation in an Authoritarian Regime: A Wildcat Strike in Southern China), *Taiwan Shehuixue*, no.30 (2015): 1-53.

China Labor News Translations, 'Promising Wal-Mart Trade Union Chair Resigns over Collective Contract Negotiations', *China Labor News Translation*, 22 September 2008, online at: **http://www.clntranslations.org/article/34/promising-wal-mart-trade-union-chair-resigns-over-collective-contract-negotiations**

China Labor News Translation, 'Chinese Labour NGOs and Free Legal Services Always in a Precarious Situation', *China Labor News Translation*, 26 January 2010, online at: **http://www.clntranslations.org/article/51/citizen-agents**

China Labour Bulletin, 'The Lide Shoe Factory Workers' Campaign for Relocation Compensation', *China Labour Bulletin*, 22 June 2015, online at: **http://www.clb.org.hk/en/content/trying-hit-moving-target-lide-shoe-factory-workers%C3%A2%E2%82%AC%E2%84%A2-campaign-relocation-compensation**

China Labour Bulletin, 'China's Social Security System', *China Labour Bulletin*, 2016, online at: **http://www.clb.org.hk/content/china%E2%80%99s-social-security-system**

China Labour Watch, 'Study Casts Doubts on Apple's Ethical Standards', *China Labour Watch*, 24 February 2016, online at: **http://www.chinalaborwatch.org/report/113**

China Law Translate, '2016 PRC Law on the Management of Foreign Non-Governmental Organizations' Activities within Mainland China', *China Law Translate*, 28 April 2016, online at: **http://www.chinalawtranslate.com/2016-foreign-ngo-law/?lang=en**

Joanna Chiu, 'Charity Overhaul in China, but Only with Government Approval', *IRIN*, 21 September 2016, online at: https://www.irinnews.org/analysis/2016/09/21/charity-overhaul-china-only-government-approval

Jennifer Jihye Chun, 'Public Dramas and the Politics of Justice: Comparison of Janitors' Unions Struggles in South Korea and the United States', *Work and Occupations*, vol.32, no.4 (2005): 486–503.

Seth Cook, Jixia Lu, Henry Tugendhat and Dawit Alemu, 'Chinese Migrants in Africa: Facts and Fictions from the Agrifood Sector in Ethiopia and Ghana', *World Development*, vol.81 (May 2016): 61–70.

Gordon Crawford, Coleman Agyeyomah, Gabriel Botchway, and Atinga Mba, 'The Impact of Chinese Involvement in Small-scale Gold Mining in Ghana', International Growth Centre, Policy Brief no.33110, May 2016, online at: http://www.theigc.org/wp-content/uploads/2016/08/Crawford-et-al-2016-Policy-brief.pdf

Gordon Crawford and Gabriel Botchway, 'Conflict, Collusion and Corruption in Small-scale Gold Mining in Ghana: Chinese Miners and the State', *Global Governance/Politics, Climate Justice & Agrarian/Social Justice: Linkages and Challenges: An International Colloquium*, International Institute of Social Studies, no.48 (4–5 February 2016), online at: https://www.iss.nl/fileadmin/ASSETS/iss/Research_and_projects/Research_networks/ICAS/48-ICAS_CP_Crawford_and_Botchwey.pdf

Becky Davis, 'Q. and A.: Cai Guo-Qiang on Art, the Death of Nature and China's Modern Reality', *The New York Times*, 3 September 2014, online at: http://sinosphere.blogs.nytimes.com/2014/09/03/q-and-a-cai-guo-qiang-on-art-the-death-of-nature-and-chinas-modern-reality

Nicola Davison, 'Rivers of Blood: The Dead Pigs Rotting in China's Water Supply', *The Guardian*, 30 March 2013, online at: https://www.theguardian.com/world/2013/mar/29/dead-pigs-china-water-supply

Jodi Dean, 'The Anamorphic Politics of Climate Change', *e-flux*, no.69 (2016), online at: http://www.e-flux.com/journal/69/60586/the-anamorphic-politics-of-climate-change/

Dominique Decherf, 'French Views of Religious Freedom', Brookings Institution, 1 July 2001, online at: https://www.brookings.edu/articles/french-views-of-religious-freedom

Simon Denyer, 'Strikes and Workers' Protests Multiply in China, Testying Party Authority', *The Washington Post*, 25 February 2016(a), online at: https://www.washingtonpost.com/world/asia_pacific/strikes-and-workers-protests-multiply-in-china-testing-party-authority/2016/02/24/caba321c-b3c8-11e5-8abc-d09392edc612_story.html

Simon Denyer, 'As China Slashes Coal Jobs, Miners Protest in Party's Revolutionary Base', *The Washington Post*, 1 March 2016(b), online at: https://www.washingtonpost.com/world/as-china-slashes-coal-jobs-miners-protest-in-partys-revolutionary-base/2016/03/01/e59535e1-8f7c-46ca-9d85-602eccc42fb7_story.html

Chull Shin Doh, 'How East Asians Understand Democracy. From a Comparative Perspective', paper presented at the Asian Barometer Conference on 'Democracy in East Asia and Taiwan in Global Perspective', 24–25 August 2011, Taipei, online at: http://www.asianbarometer.org/publications/5f13c361a1b4edcc4b3cd33ae67412c0.pdf

Fu Du (translated and edited by Stephen Owen), *The Poetry of Du Fu*, Boston and Berlin: De Gruyter, 2015, online at: https://www.degruyter.com/viewbooktoc/product/246946

Yi Duan, 'Gongyunxing laogong NGO de qianjing yu tiaozhan' (Prospects and Challenges for Labour NGOs of the Labour Movement Type), *Xin Gongmin Yundong*, 20 May 2015, online at: http://www.chengbiancun.com/2015/0805/45866.html

Thomas David DuBois, *Religion and the Making of Modern East Asia*, Cambridge: Cambridge University Press, 2011.

Thomas David DuBois, 'Before the NGO: Chinese Charities in Historical Perspective', *Asian Studies Review*, vol.39, no.4 (2015): 541–553.

Thomas David DuBois, 'Religious Services Law (China), 2005 vs. 2016', 2016, online at: **https://www.academia.edu/28414977/Chinas_Religion_Law_2005_vs._2016**

Thomas David DuBois, *Empire and the Meaning of Religion in Northeast Asia: Manchuria 1900–1945*, Cambridge: Cambridge University Press, 2017.

E-Flux, 'Cai Guo-Qiang: 'The Ninth Wave', *e-flux*, 25 August 2014, online at: **http://www.e-flux.com/announcements/cai-guo-qiang-the-ninth-wave**

Joseph V. Femia, *Gramsci's Political Thought: Hegemony, Consciousness, and the Revolutionary Process*, Oxford: Clarendon Press, 1987.

Steve Finch, 'China's Not so Secret War on Religion', *The Diplomat*, 16 June 2014, online at: **http://thediplomat.com/2014/06/chinas-not-so-secret-war-on-religion**

Michael Forsythe, 'Q. and A.: Tony Saich on What Chinese Want from their Leaders', *The New York Times*, 11 September 2015, online at: **http://sinosphere.blogs.nytimes.com/2015/09/11/anthony-saich-china-communist-party/**

Ivan Franceschini, 'Labour NGOs in China: A Real Force for Political Change?', *The China Quarterly*, no.218 (2014): 474–492.

Mark Frazier, 'State Schemes or Safety Nets? China's Push for Universal Coverage', *Daedalus*, vol.143, no.2 (2014): 69–80.

Mark Frazier and Yimin Li, 'Stemming the Tide of Demographic Transformation through Social Inclusion: Can Universal Pension Rights Help Finance an Ageing Population?', in Beatriz Carrillo, Johanna Hood, and Paul Kadetz eds, *Handbook of Welfare in China*, Cheltenham: Edward Elgar Publishers, 2017.

Eli Friedman, *Insurgency Trap: Labor Politics in Postsocialist China*, Ithaca: Cornell University Press, 2014.

Chloé Froissart, 'The Rise of Social Movements among Migrant Workers: Uncertain Strivings for Autonomy', *China Perspectives*, no.61 (2005): 30–40.

Mary Gallagher and Baohua Dong, 'Legislating Harmony: Labor Law Reform in Contemporary China', in Sarosh Kuruvilla, Ching Kwan Lee, and M. Gallagher eds, *From Iron Rice Bowl to Informalization: Market, Workers and the State in a Changing China*, Ithaca: Cornell University Press, 2011, pp. 36–60.

Mary Gallagher, John Giles, Albert Park, and Meiyan Wang, 'China's 2008 Labor Contract Law: Implementation and Implications for China's Workers', *Human Relations*, vol.68, no.2 (2015): 197–235.

Mary Gallagher and Yuhua Wang, 'Users and Non-Users: Legal Experience and its Effect on Legal Consciousness', in Margaret Woo and Mary Gallagher eds, *Chinese Justice: Civil Dispute Resolution in Contemporary China*, Cambridge: Cambridge University Press, 2011, pp. 204–233.

Emilio Gentile, *Politics as Religion*, Princeton and Oxford: Princeton University Press, 2006.

Xuezeng Gong, 'A Survey of Marxist Perspectives on Religion in New China', in Daji Lü and Xuezeng Gong eds, *Marxism and Religion*, New York and Leiden: Brill, 2014, pp. 292–320.

Antonio Gramsci (translated and edited by Quentin Hoare and Geoffrey Nowell Smith), *Selections from the Prison Notebooks*, New York: International Publishers, 1971.

Gary Gutting, 'How Religion Can Lead to Violence', The New York Times, 1 August 2016, online at: **http://www.nytimes.com/2016/08/01/opinion/how-religion-can-lead-to-violence.html**

Dan Haglund, 'Regulating FDI in Weak African States: A Case Study of Chinese Copper Mining in Zambia', *The Journal of Modern African Studies*, vol.46, no.4 (December 2008): 547–575.

Aaron Halegua, 'Who Will Represent China's Workers? Lawyers, Legal Aid, and the Enforcement of Labor Rights', U.S.–Asia Law Institute, 2016, online at: https://usali.org/chinasworkers

Huifeng He, 'Quest for Gold in African Mud', *South China Morning Post*, 6 June 2013, online at: http://www.scmp.com/news/china/article/1254333/quest-gold-african-mud

Gottfried Heuer, 'The Devil Underneath the Couch. The Secret Story of Jung's Twin Brother', *Harvest*, vol.49, no.2 (2003): 130–145.

Afua Hirsch, 'Influx of Chinese Goldminers Sparks Tensions in Ghana', *The Guardian*, 24 April 2013, online at: https://www.theguardian.com/global-development/2013/apr/23/influx-chinese-goldminers-tensions-ghana

Jude Howell, 'Shall We Dance? Welfarist Incorporation and the Politics of State-Labour NGO Relation', *The China Quarterly*, no.223 (2015): 702–723.

HRW, ' "You'll Be Fired if You Refuse" Labor Abuses in Zambia's Chinese State-owned Copper Mines', 4 November 2011, online at: https://www.hrw.org/report/2011/11/04/youll-be-fired-if-you-refuse/labor-abuses-zambias-chinese-state-owned-copper-mines

Chang-Tai Hsieh and Zheng Song, 'Grasp the Large, Let Go of the Small: The Transformation of the State Sector in China', Brookings Institution, Spring 2015, online at: https://www.brookings.edu/wp-content/uploads/2015/03/2015a_hsieh.pdf

Philip C. C. Huang, 'Misleading Chinese Legal and Statistical Categories: Labor, Individual Entities, and Private Enterprises', Modern China, vol.39, no.4 (2013): 347–379.

Yinglai Huang, 'Guangdongsheng zonggonghui: fandui woerma quanyuan shishi zonghe gongshi zhi' (Guangdong Province Federation of Trade Unions: Opposing the Implementation of the Comprehensive Working Hour System for All Walmart Employees), Nanfang Ribao, 3 August 2016, online at http://news.xinhuanet.com/fortune/2016-08/03/c_129201104.htm

William Hurst, *The Chinese Worker after Socialism*, Cambridge: Cambridge University Press, 2009.

William Hurst, 'Chinese Labor Divided', *Dissent Magazine*, (Spring 2015): 127–135, online at: https://www.dissentmagazine.org/article/chinese-labor-divided

International Labour Organization, 'Zambia', July 2009, online at: http://www.ilo.org/labadmin/info/WCMS_112936/lang--en/index.htm

Jonathan Kaiman and Afua Hirsch, 'Ghana Arrests 168 Chinese Nationals in Illegal Mining Crackdown', *The Guardian*, 7 June 2013, online at: https://www.theguardian.com/world/2013/jun/06/ghana-arrests-chinese-illegal-miners

Benjamin Kang Lim, Matthew Miller, and David Stanway, 'China to Lay Off Five to Six Million Workers, Earmarks at Least $23 Billion', Reuters, 3 March 2016, online at: http://www.reuters.com/article/us-china-economy-layoffs-exclusive-idUSKCN0W33DS

Kitanishi Kenji, 'The Philosophical Background of Morita Therapy: Its Application to Therapy', in Wen-Shing Tseng, Suk Choo Chang, and Masahisa Nishizono eds, *Asian Culture and Psychotherapy: Implications for East and West*, Honolulu: University of Hawaii Press, 2005, pp. 169–185.

Joseph Kitagawa, 'One of the Many Faces of China: Maoism as a Quasi-Religion', *Japanese Journal of Religious Studies*, vol.1, no.2/3 (1974): 125–141.

KPMG, 'Employer Social Security Tax Rates', 2016, online at: https://home.kpmg.com/xx/en/home/services/tax/tax-tools-and-resources/tax-rates-online/social-security-employer-tax-rates-table.html

Wendy Larson, *From Ah Q to Lei Feng: Freud and Revolutionary Spirit in 20th Century China*, Stanford: Stanford University Press, 2009.

Ching Kwan Lee, 'From the Specter of Mao to the Spirit of the Law: Labor Insurgency in China', *Theory and Society*, vol.31, no.2 (2002): 189–228.

Ching Kwan Lee, *Against the Law: Labor Protests in China's Rustbelt and Sunbelt*, Berkeley: University of California Press, 2007.

Ching Kwan Lee, 'The Spectre of Global China', *New Left Review*, vol.89 (September–October 2014): 29–65.

Ching Kwan Lee, 'Precarization or Empowerment? Reflections on Recent Labor Unrest in China', *The Journal of Asian Studies*, vol.75, no.2 (2016): 317–333.

Ching Kwan Lee and Yuan Shen, 'The Anti-Solidarity Machine? Labor Nongovernmental Organizations in China', in Sarosh Kuruvilla, Ching Kwan Lee, and Mary E. Gallagher eds, *From Iron Rice Bowl to Informalization*, Ithaca and London: Cornell University Press, 2011, pp. 173–187.

Lynn Lee and James Leong, 'Wukan: After the Uprising', Al Jazeera, 26 June 2013, online at: www.aljazeera.com/programmes/specialseries/2013/06/2013626153044866869.html

Kevin Lin, 'Contesting State Ownership', *The China Story Journal*, 22 July 2013, online at: https://www.thechinastory.org/2013/07/contesting-state-ownership/

James J. Y. Liu, *The Art of Chinese Poetry*, Chicago: Chicago University Press, 1962.

Jixia Lu and Anna Lora-Wainwright, 'Historicizing Sustainable Livelihoods: A Pathways Approach to Lead Mining in Rural Central China', *World Development*, vol.62 (October 2014): 189–200.

Ministry of Finance, 'Guanyu jieduanxing jiangdi shehui baoxian feilü de tongzhi' (Notice on the Interim Reduction of Social Insurance Contribution Rates), 14 April 2016, online at: http://www.mof.gov.cn/zhengwuxinxi/zhengcefabu/201604/t20160421_1959347.htm

Ministry of Human Resources and Social Security, 'Guanyu zai huajie gangtie meitan hangye guosheng channeng shixian tuokun fazhan guocheng zhong zuohao zhiye anzhi gongzuo de yijian' (Opinion on Resolving Production Overcapacity in the Steel and Coal Industries and Successfully Reallocate Workers), 7 April 2016, online at: http://www.mohrss.gov.cn/gkml/xxgk/201604/t20160413_238000.html

Modern Ghana, '2 Chinese Miners Shot Dead', *Modern Ghana*, 4 January 2013, online at: https://www.modernghana.com/news/438139/1/2-chinese-miners-shot-dead.html

Giles Mohan, May Tan-Mullins, Ben Lampert, and Daphine Chang, *Chinese Migrants and Africa's Development : New Imperialists or Agents of Change?*, London: Zed Books, 2014.

Jin Mou, Jinquan Cheng, Dan Zhang, Hanping Jiang, Liangqiang Lin, and Sian M. Griffiths, 'Health Care Utilisation amongst Shenzhen Migrant Workers: Does Being Insured Make a Difference?', *BMC Health Services Research*, vol.9, no.214 (2009): 1–9.

Jean-Luc Nancy (translated by Charlotte Mandell), *After Fukushima: The Equivalence of Catastrophes*, New York: Fordham University Press, 2014.

National Assembly of Zambia, 'Daily Parliamentary Debates for the First Session of the Tenth Assembly', 11 July 2007, online at: http://www.parliament.gov.zm/node/1858

National Bureau of Statistics, 'Guojia tongjiju fabu 2015 nian nongmingong jiance diaocha baogao (Quanwen)' (The National Bureau of Statistics Releases the Report of the Survey on Migrant Workers in 2015), *Xinhua*, 28 April 2016, online at: http://news.xinhuanet.com/politics/2016-04/28/c_128940738.htm

Larry Ong and Dongyan Xie, 'Xi Jinping Hints at Shifting Regime Stance Toward Falun Gong', *The Epoch Times*, 6 May 2016, online at: http://www.theepochtimes.com/n3/2058843-xi-jinping-hints-at-shifting-regime-stance-towards-falun-gong

People's Bank of China, 'Xiagang shiye renyuan xiao'e danbao daikuan guanli banfa de tongzhi' (Notice on the Management of Microcredit for Laid-off workers), 24 December 2002, online at: http://www.gov.cn/gongbao/content/2003/content_62594.htm

Elizabeth Perry, 'Studying Chinese Politics: Farewell to Revolution?', *The China Journal*, no. 57 (2007): 1–22.

Phaidon, 'The New Landscapes of Yao Lu', *Phaidon*, 8 March 2013, online at: http://au.phaidon.com/agenda/photography/articles/2013/march/08/the-new-landscapes-of-yao-lu

Stephen Philion, *Workers' Democracy in China's Transition from State Socialism*, New York: Routledge, 2009.

Melanie Pichler, Cornelia Staritz, Karin Küblböck, Christina Plank, Werner Raza, and Fernando Ruiz Peyré eds, *Fairness and Justice in Natural Resource Politics*, London and New York: Routledge, 2016.

Karl Polanyi, *The Great Transformation: The Political and Economic Origins of Our Time*, Boston: Beacon Press, 1944.

Bill Porter, *Finding Them Gone: Visiting China's Poets of the Past*, Port Townsend: Copper Canyon Press, 2016.

Alejandro Portes, Manuel Castells, and Lauren A. Benton eds, *The Informal Economy: Studies in Advanced and Less Developed Countries*, Baltimore and London: Johns Hopkins University, 1989.

Ngai Pun and Huilin Lu, 'Unfinished Proletarianization: Self, Anger, and Class Action among the Second Generation of Peasant-Workers in Present-Day China', *Modern China*, vol.36, no.5 (2010): 493–519.

Ngai Pun and Yi Xu, 'Legal Activism or Class Action? The Political Economy of the "No Boss" and "No Labour Relationship" in China's Construction Industry', *China Perspectives*, no.2 (2011): 9–17.

Amy Qin, 'As China Hungers for Coal, "Behemoth" Studies the Ravages at the Source', *The New York Times*, 8 December 2015, online at: http://www.nytimes.com/2015/12/29/world/asia/china-film-zhao-liang-inner-mongolia-coal-behemoth.html

Kwei Quartey, 'Ghana's Chinese Gold Rush', *Foreign Policy in Focus*, 11 October 2013, online at: http://fpif.org/ghanas-chinese-gold-rush/

Rainer Maria Rilke (translated by Stephen Mitchell), *Duino Elegies & The Sonnets to Orpheus: A Dual-Language Edition*, New York: Vintage International, 2009.

Andrew Samuels, 'Economics, Psychotherapy and Politics', *International Review of Sociology*, vol.24, no.1 (2014): 77–90.

Flora Sapio, 'From Rogue Tiger to Global Player: China's Foreign NGO Management Law', *T.note*, no. 12, (May 2016), online at: http://twai.it/upload/pdf/t.note12.pdf

Sally Sargeson, 'Violence as Development: Land Expropriation and China's Urbanization', *The Journal of Peasant Studies*, vol.40, no.6 (2013): 1063–1085.

Barry Sautman and Hairong Yan, 'Bashing "the Chinese": Contextualizing Zambia's Collum Coal Mine Shooting', *Journal of Contemporary China*, vol.23, no.90 (2014): 1073–1092.

Stefan Schmalz, Brandon Sommer, and Hui Xu (2016), 'The Yue Yuen Strike: Industrial Transformation and Labour Unrest in the Pearl River Delta', *Globalizations*, 5 August 2016, online at: **http://www.tandfonline.com/doi/abs/10.1080/14747731.2016.1203188**

Winfried Georg Sebald (translated by Michael Hulse), *The Rings of Saturn*, New York: Vintage, 2011.

Amartya Sen, 'Human Rights and Asian Values', New York: Carnegie Council on International Affairs, 1997, online at: **https://www.carnegiecouncil.org/publications/archive/morgenthau/254.html/_res/id=sa_File1/254_sen.pdf**

Elizabeth Shakman Hurd, *The Politics of Secularism in International Relations*, Princeton: Princeton University Press, 2008.

Elizabeth Shakman Hurd, *Beyond Religious Freedom: The New Global Politics of Religion*, Princeton: Princeton University Press, 2015.

Shih-Jiunn Shi, 'Towards Inclusive Citizenship? Rethinking China's Social Security in the Trend towards Urban-Rural Harmonisation', *Journal of Social Policy*, vol.41, no.4 (2012): 789–810.

Shawn Shieh, 'Overseas NGO Law FAQs', *NGOs in China*, 1 May 2016, online at: **http://ngochina.blogspot.com.au/2016/05/overseas-ngo-law-faqs.html**

Tiange Shu ed, *Jianshe xingfu zhongguo* (Building a Happy China), Beijing: Hongqi Chubanshe, 2013.

Sophie Song, 'A Modern Day Gold Rush: How People of One County in China are Making Millions in Ghana', *International Business Times*, 15 May 2013, online at: **http://www.ibtimes.com/modern-day-gold-rush-how-people-one-county-china-are-making-millions-ghana-1260801**

Christian Sorace and William Hurst, 'China's Phantom Urbanisation and the Pathology of Ghost Cities', *Journal of Contemporary Asia*, vol.46, no.2 (2016): 304–322

Alex Suber, 'Interview: Zhao Liang Talks Behemoth and Censorship', *Slant Magazine*, 16 March 2016, online at: **http://www.slantmagazine.com/features/article/interview-zhao-liang-talks-behemoth-and-censorship**

Winnifred Fallers Sullivan, *The Impossibility of Religious Freedom*, Princeton: Princeton University Press, 2005.

Didi Tang, 'China's 168 Million Migrant Workers are Discovering their Labor Rights', Associated Press, 6 April 2015, online at: **http://www.businessinsider.com/chinas-168-million-migrant-workers-are-discovering-their-labor-rights-2015-4**

Wenfang Tang, *Populist Authoritarianism: Chinese Political Culture and Regime Sustainability*, Oxford and New York: Oxford University Press, 2016.

The Economist, 'The March of the Zombies', *The Economist*, 25 February 2016, online at: **http://www.economist.com/news/business/21693573-chinas-excess-industrial-capacity-harms-its-economy-and-riles-its-trading-partners-march**

The World Bank, 'Making Mining Work for Zambia', *Zambia Economic Brief*, June 2015, no.5, online at: **http://documents.worldbank.org/curated/en/305141468189249424/pdf/97390-Zambia-Economic-Brief-5-web-version.pdf**

Charles Tilly, 'Mechanisms in Political Processes', *Annual Review of Political Science*, vol.4 (2001): 21–41.

Luigi Tomba, 'A New Land Reform?', in Geremie R. Barmé and Jeremy Goldkorn eds, *China Story Yearbook 2013: Civilising China*, Canberra, Australian Centre on China in the World, 2014, pp.235–241, online at: **https://www.thechinastory.org/yearbooks/yearbook-2013/forum-land-law-and-protest/a-new-land-reform/**

United Nations General Assembly, 'Universal Declaration of Human Rights',1948, online at: **http://www.un.org/en/universal-declaration-human-rights/**

U.S. Department of State, 'International Religious Freedom Act of 1998', 1998, online at: **http://www.state.gov/documents/organization/2297.pdf**

Harro Von Senger, 'Recent Developments in the Relations between State and Party Norms in the People's Republic of China', in Stuart R. Schram ed, *The Scope of State Power in China*, New York: St. Martin's Press, 1989, pp. 171–207.

WCWA, 'Woerma zhongguo yuangong lianming zhixin zhonghua quanguo zonggonghui de qingyuanshu' (The Employees of Walmart in China Jointly Sign a Petition to the All-China Federation of Trade Unions), *WCWA Blog*, 27 May 2016, online at: **http://blog.tianya.cn/post-7269517-116547277-1.shtml**

McKenzie Wark, *Molecular Red: Theory for the Anthropocene*, London: Verso Books, 2015.

Alan Waterman, 'The Humanistic Psychology–Positive Psychology Divide: Contrasts in Philosophical Foundations', *American Psychologist*, vol.68, no.3 (2013): 124–133.

Andrew Watson, 'Social Security for China's Migrant Workers: Providing for Old Age', *Journal of Current Chinese Affairs*, vol.38, no.4 (2009): 85–115.

Lingling Wei, 'China Unveils Overhaul of Bloated State Sector', *The Wall Street Journal*, 13 September 2015, online at: **http://www.wsj.com/articles/china-to-allow-state-owned-enterprises-to-sell-shares-to-public-1442138335**

Christian Welzel and Ronald Inglehart, 'Agency, Values, and Well-Being: A Human Development Model', *Social Indicators Research*, vol.97, no.1 (2010): 43–63.

Ya Wen and Jill Hanley, 'Enhancing Social Support for Migrant Families: A Case Study of Community Services in a Shanghai Urban Village and Implications for Intervention', *Asian Social Work and Policy Review*, vol.10, no.1 (2016): 76–89.

White Cube, 'He Xiangyu', *White Cube*, 2014, online at: **http://whitecube.com/exhibitions/he_xiangyu_inside_the_white_cube_2014/**

Gabriel Wildau, 'China's State-Owned Zombie Economy', *Financial Times*, 29 February 2016, online at: **https://www.ft.com/content/253d7eb0-ca6c-11e5-84df-70594b99fc47**

Cal Wong, 'China's Wukan Democracy Experiment Comes to a Violent End', *The Diplomat*, 21 September 2016, online at: **http://thediplomat.com/2016/09/chinas-wukan-democracy-experiment-comes-to-a-violent-end**

Chun Han Wong, 'Chinese Machinery Workers Protest Proposed Layoffs', *The Wall Street Journal*, 13 May 2015, online at: **http://www.wsj.com/articles/chinese-machinery-workers-protest-against-proposed-layoffs-1431534642?tesla=y**

Zengyi Xie, *Labor Law in China: Progress and Challenges*, Heidelberg and New York: Springer, 2015.

Feng Xu, 'The Emergence of Temporary Staffing Agencies in China', *Comparative Labor Law & Policy Journal*, vol.30, no.2 (2008–2009): 431–461.

Jieying Xu, 'Shengzong fawen mingque: lingshou hangye quanyuan shishi zonghe gongshi zhi bu fu guiding' (The Provincial Union Clarifies That in the Retail Industry Applying the Comprehensive Working Hour System to All Employees Is Against the Rules), *Nanfang Gongbao*, 14 June 2016, online at: **http://www.gdftu.org.cn/xw/yw/201606/t20160614_775432.htm**

Jiao Yang, 'Guest Post: Chinese Illegal Gold Miners in Ghana', *The China Africa Research Initiative Blog*, 21 June 2013, online at: **http://www.chinaafricarealstory.com/2013/06/guest-post-chinese-illegal-gold-miners.html**

Jie Yang, ' "Fake Happiness": Counselling, Potentiality, and Psycho-Politics in China', *Ethos*, vol.41, no.3 (2013): 292–312.

Lin Yang, 'Quangguo zonggonghui dangzu shuji: jingwai didui shili tongguo 'weiquan' yu gonghui zhengduo zhigong' (The Secretary of the Party Group of the ACFTU: Hostile Foreign Forces Contend Workers from the Trade Union through 'Rights Protection'), *Liaowang Zhoukan*, 28 February 2015, online at: **http://www.guancha.cn/society/2015_02_28_310576_1.shtml**

Ernest Young, *Ecclesiastical Colony: China's Catholic Church and the French Religious Protectorate*, New York: Oxford University Press, 2013.

Muhammad Yunus and Alan Jolis, *Banker to the Poor: The Autobiography of Muhammad Yunus, Founder of the Grameen Bank*, Oxford: Oxford University Press, 2001.

Jan Zalasiewicz, Mark Williams, Will Steffen, and Paul Crutzen, 'The New World of the Anthropocene', *Environmental Science and Technology Viewpoint*, vol.44, no.7 (2010): 2228–2231.

Moran Zhang, 'China State-Owned Enterprises Lead in Market Capitalization Loss in 2013: Bad Year for Banking, Coal and Beverage', *International Business Times*, 31 December 2013, online at: **http://www.ibtimes.com/china-state-owned-enterprises-soes-lead-market-capitalization-loss-2013-bad-year-1522698**

Xinping Zhuo, 'Religion and Rule of Law in China Today', International Center for Law and Religion Studies, 2008, online at: **http://www.iclrs.org/content/iclrs/symposium/2008/english/documents/China,%20Zhuo%2020081007.%20CH.pdf**

Wei Zou, 'Guangdong jingfang dadiao weiquan zuzhi ju 7 ren, zhufan bei cheng "gongyun zhi xing" ' (The Police in Guangdong Takes Down a Weiquan Organisation and Detains Seven People: The Main Culprit Was "Star of the Labour Movement"), Xinhua, 22 December 2015, online at: **http://m.thepaper.cn/newsDetail_forward_1412138**

'Constitution of the People's Republic of China', 20 September 1954, online at: **http://e-chaupak.net/database/chicon/1954/1954bilingual.htm**

MADE IN CHINA
2016

Yearbook 2016: Disturbances in Heaven

AUSTRALIAN CENTRE ON CHINA IN THE WORLD

CHINOIRESIE
mismatched shards of China

Australian National University

PRESS